PRAISE FOR *UNSTICKING DEALS*

"If you are like 99.9% of professional sales executives, you deal with the dreaded "stuck deal" and we all know a stuck deal always leads to the delay or even worse, the death of the sale. This book, and the techniques in it, will provide you with the tools to avoid the traps so many fall into. Having worked directly with James for over 2 decades, I have personally seen these methods used and succeed, more times than I can count. Do yourself a favor and make your life easier. Sharpen your saw and use what is taught here. It will have a massive impact on your business." —Kelly Skeen, Well Health, Director of Enterprise Sales

"James Muir's latest masterpiece, *Unsticking Deals*, is a sales game-changer! Like his book, *The Perfect Close*, he doesn't just offer a formula; he unveils the simple secrets to increased contracts. Picture this: unstuck opportunities and prospects who don't stick in the first place. The result – sales momentum. With genius insights and a whole host of 'Big Ideas' that are pure gold - Muir's approach is nothing short of brilliance. I especially love his strategy for mutual prospect action plans. Get ready to advance without interruption." —Lisa D. Magnuson, author of The TOP Sales Leader Playbook: How to Win 5X Deals *Repeatedly* and *The Top Seller Advantage: Powerful Strategies to Build Long-Term Executive Relationships*

"If you've been in sales a minute, you've experienced that big opportunity that got hung up, and you're not exactly sure what to do. The truth is, "stuck" deals can make a sales person's life miserable! Well, no more! This follow-up to The Perfect Close fills a huge void in the sales genre, and is cover-to-cover PACKED with strategies and tactics designed to 1) unstick your current deals, and, more importantly, 2) prevent stuck deals in the future! Well-written and presented in an easy-to-follow format, this book is sure to be one that you reference over and over!" —Kelly Riggs - Founder & Chief Sales Officer Business LockerRoom, Inc.

"No one outshines James Muir when it comes to deconstructing complexity. This book simplifies every action required to advance sales and avoid stallouts in sales. It's a practical guide packed with powerful strategies to make more sales!" —Deb Calvert, Founder and President of People First Productivity Solutions and Author of DISCOVER Questions

"Virtually every sales opportunity gets 'stuck.' We see data around lengthening buying/selling cycles and increases in No Decision Made. Customers struggle with buying and in those struggles they get stuck. Sometimes, it's the result of sellers not paying attention and helping the customer move forward. Stuck deals have become the norm. James Muir's "Unsticking Deals" is a pragmatic guide to identifying how deals get stuck, and what sellers can do to unstick them. It's not high level theory, it's practical guidance about how we and the customer get unstuck and move forward. It's a tremendous guide to help you and your customers achieve more." — David A. Brock, Author "Sales Manager Survival Guide," CEO at Partners In EXCELLENCE, Ruthless Pragmatist

"Stuck deals are an Achilles heel for every sales professional. James Muir provides an in-depth approach of how to recognize their symptoms and then mitigate them. This book will accelerate your win rate!" —Thomas J. Williams Chairman & Founder Strategic Dynamics Inc.

"Customers today are overwhelmed with options and therefore lack the confidence to make a buying decision when they perceive the stakes are high This book outlines different strategies to reduce indecision and increase your close rate, faster!" —Victor Antonio Founder, Sales Velocity Academy

"Unsticking Deals is a fresh and innovative approach on how to move deals forward. Deals often stop because of unknown information on the part of the salesperson or because of new issues affecting the customer. You worked so hard on this deal for it to fall through. You owe it to yourself to read James Muir Unsticking Deals to learn exactly what you can do when the deal gets stuck in the mud. Highly recommend it." —Ron Karr, Author The Velocity Mindset

"This is a book that very much needed to be written. Find me a sal the feeling of "stuckness"; good luck with that. The book begins that are rock solid, and follows with a series of outstanding "Unsti the concepts are brilliant, and the applications are clear. A perfec Close." —Jeff Shore Shore Consulting

D1551228

"Every sales professional knows what a stuck deal is and how frustrating they can be. James Muir's book, "Unsticking Deals," provides valuable insights into the reasons behind stalled and offers effective sales strategies to unstick them and prevent future complications. With Muir's guidance, sales professionals can enhance their skills to ensure deals never get stuck in the first instance. It is a unique book among sales books and I highly recommend it!"   —Mario Martinez Jr. - CEO & Keynote Speaker, FlyMSG.io

"In the intricate dance of deal-making, mastery isn't found in the steps of selling, but in the art of navigating the dance floor. This book is not a mere guide to the sales process; it's a strategist's map for deal breakthroughs. Where sales training ends, deal management training takes over—turning potential into performance and prospects into partnerships. It's not about winning someday, but today, with the deal at hand. James' book Unsticking Deals is one of a few books that accomplishes this. If you want to move past theory, and get to real, practical ways to win the deal you are working on right now, read this book." —David Weiss, CRO The Sales Collective

"Ghosted? Gone dark? The frustration of seeing a sizzling opportunity seemingly disappear before our eyes is what we dread in sales. All the work, the resources gathered, numerous meetings and all we have in return is asking "What happened?". We send emails and get crickets in return. Too many voicemails have been left. Doing more of the same is not the answer. What do we do? Thankfully, we now can get out the guidebook, Unsticking Deals masterfully written by James Muir, author of the brilliant book, The Perfect Close. Learn how to "Unstick" the stuck and do as much as you can to prevent this discouraging experience in the first place. I am betting you will revisit this "textbook" regularly so keep it handy." —Harry Spaight Author of Selling With Dignity

"The basics never go out of style. It's not about the stuck deals, it's what you did (did not) do earlier that needs to be addressed. Unsticking Deals gives you real life tools (Chap 11 is a good one!) that you can use earlier in a sale, so you don't end up having stuck deals 2 days before quarter end!" Skip MIller, Founder and President of M3 Learning and Author —ProActive Selling, Selling Above and Below the Line

"James Muir has done it again. I am a huge fan of his work because it works and now, more than ever, sellers need ideas that work. That stick! I am already re-reading this book because of the practical concepts, the visuals that help me process them and the motivating style that ensures I use them. Well done – such a timely piece of art!" —Bernadette McClelland, CEO, Sales Leaders Global LLC - Speaker and Bestselling author of Shift and Disrupt!

"James Muir does it again! In his classic, elegant style Muir continues to inspire simplicity and honesty in the business of sales. The ability to leverage one's critical thinking is an often-underdeveloped skill and Unsticking Deals elegantly coaches sales professionals through efficiency processes like a pocket personal trainer." —Nicole Holland, Personal Advisor To Visionary Leaders

"Not only does James speak to the realities of getting stuck in the selling process, he provides tactical, actionable steps anyone can take to overcome the challenges. I found myself nodding often, especially when I read Prevention Strategy #2 – Anticipate and Throttle Information and then again with Prevention Strategy #5 - Review Proposals with Clients Personally. It gets better from there! This is the kind of book I highlight, flag, and revisit to put the ideas into practice." —Diane Helbig, Chief Improvement Catalyzer – Helbig Enterprises

"Losing enterprise opportunities to indecision incurs significant costs for the company. To mitigate this risk, James presents various strategies to maintain an ideal opportunity cadence and safeguard sellers' time, energy, and focus. Authored by a practicing sales leader, "Unsticking Deals" offers genuine insights into expediting pipeline and enhancing win rates." —Lee Bartlett, Managing Partner Bartlett Schenk & Company

"Even the best of the best encounter stuck deals. Unsticking Deals is a uncommon book among sales books. Inside James Muir untangles the root causes of stalled opportunities and delivers short, practical plays for unsticking them. Even better, Muir hands over the key strategies to prevent deals from ever sticking in the first place. Tremendous insight here. Two thumbs up!" —Scott Ingram, Founder & CEO, Sales Success Media

UNSTICKING DEALS

WHY DEALS STALL,
HOW TO UNSTICK THEM, AND
HOW TO PREVENT THEM
FROM STICKING IN THE FIRST PLACE

JAMES MUIR
BEST PRACTICE INTERNATIONAL

Unsticking Deals
© Jan 2024
By James Muir

Best Practice International
14267 Bailey Hill Way
Herriman, UT 84096
http://www.bestpracticeinternational.com/

Ordering Information:
Quantity sales. Special discounts are available on quantity purchases by corporations, associations, and others. For details, contact the publisher at the address above.

For information visit http://PureMuir.com

Book Cover design by Ivan Terzic
Interior Design by Olivier Darbonville

Publisher Best Practice International

ISBN 979-8891700031
BISAC: Business & Economics / Sales & Selling / General
1. Business & Economics 2. Sales & Selling 3. General
First Edition: Jan 2024

Victor,
Thank you so much
for your leadership and
example. You are an inspiration
to me. #Gratitude
Happy Selling Always!

DEDICATION

To Leland J Muir, Jr. for being the tremendous
teacher, example, and father that you are.

CONTENTS

FORWARD

I N THE THIRD DECADE OF THE 21ST CENTURY, everything is getting better, while at the same time, much is getting worse. If you were ill, our medical treatments would be better and safer than what was available in the past. If you were to fly from New York to San Diego, you would have a trip that was much safer than earlier times. Your automobile is much safer and more comfortable.

Everything is getting better, except B2B buying and B2B selling. Every KPI is pointing downward, including win rates and quota attainment, two of the most important metrics. At the same time, the number of phone calls and emails begging prospective clients for a first meeting increases. In a recent Gartner survey, 75% of buyers said they prefer a "salesperson-free buying experience." That same survey also suggested 68% of the participants already bought without a salesperson.

Over the last two decades, B2B sales have been regressing to transactional approaches they believe will speed up the acquisition of a client. If one wished to alienate a prospective client, a legacy approach would do the trick. Trying to speed up the sales conversation will also repel your client, yet this is what most sales organizations pursue.

If you think selling is challenging, wait until you try to buy. First, you have to initiate a significant change, find the budget, acquire a senior sponsor, and build consensus within your organization. If you want to know why deals get stuck, some of it stems from the difficulty of buying.

Misguided Sales Management Strategies

Sales leaders and sales managers seem to have no real interest in increasing their team's sales effectiveness, something we can measure by win rates. Instead, their first commandment is to have the coverage that will ensure they reach their sales goals. In doing so, the salesperson is conflicted about whether to qualify the client or to log the opportunity in their CRM, even though they have had only one meeting. Most pipelines now look like a junk drawer of non-opportunities.

What is equally harmful is turning to technology to improve sales results. Under the guise of efficiency, sales stacks grow ever larger and more expensive. Those members of the cult of Efficiency would do better to join the cult of Effectiveness. I was able to grow my family's business from 3M to 7.8M in a year with a stack of index cards, a phone book, and a telephone.

It's Not A Closing Problem

James and I share something in common. We have both written a book on closing. My book is about facilitating the buyer's journey through ten conversations. James' Perfect Close is an exceptionally effective approach to move deals forward. But James is right about stuck deals. This isn't a closing problem. If it was a closing problem, you wouldn't need this book.

The truth about stuck deals is that buying isn't easy and there are always conflicts about priorities, budgets, and who gets credit. But there is another factor that is ever present in the 21st century, which is an environment of accelerating, constant disruptive change. One reason buyers fail to pursue their initiatives is because they are uncertain and lack the confidence to change without knowing what the future holds.

You can trust James to provide you the strategies you need to grease the skids and move your deals forward. You will learn if a deal is stuck, the proactive tactic will prevent getting stuck, how to leverage commitment, mutual action plans, and one of my favorites: Review proposals with clients face-to-face.

Were I to offer you advice on how to read this book, I would tell you to read each chapter slowly and work on one strategy at a time. This is a tactical and practical guide, which means you need to focus on the behavioral changes that will have you at the top of your stack ranking.

You are in good hands as this book is as good as it gets when it comes to solving the sales and buyer challenges that now plague us.

Do Good Work!
Anthony Iannarino
Author of Leading Growth, Elite Sales Strategies and Eat Their Lunch

Free Additional Resources

It was impossible to include everything in this book and still keep it to a manageable size. So I've created a place for you where you can download free resources that will help you diagnose and unstick your sales opportunities.

You can download these resources at **http://unstickingdeals.com**. There you will find illustrations, diagnostics tools, CRM reports, sample letters, mutual action plan templates and more.

I will continue to add to these resources as time goes on. I hope you find them valuable as you continue to expand your skills and knowledge.

WHY I WROTE THIS BOOK

EVER SINCE PUBLISHING MY BESTSELLING BOOK *The Perfect Close*, I have enjoyed the privilege of serving organizations of all kinds and helping them improve their close ratios - the ability to close.

Ironically, after some discovery, what often starts out as a conversation about how to more successfully get commitments, the conversation often turns into a discussion about targeting, messaging, prospecting, motivation and other possible reasons that they are not closing as much as they would like. I suppose this is natural. After all, the most obvious thing that is happening (or not happening) is that sales are not coming in. Opportunities are not getting closed. So that must be a closing problem, right?

After thousands of conversations, in almost half of these situations, the root cause of closing challenges is not about how to ask for the commitment - the next step. Rather, the root cause of the problem falls into one of three simple categories.

And after all those engagements, I discovered a surprising pattern. Almost all organizations have large, bloated pipelines. They all have huge numbers of stuck opportunities.

There are just three things that cause stuck deals. And once you discover the root cause of why your deal is stuck, there are very straightforward strategies you can employ to unstick them. And, as it turns out, you can employ these same strategies to prevent deals from ever sticking in the first place.

I am a voracious reader, and I often refer clients to the best resources for learning on a given topic. I will be doing the same for you here. However, in seeking to find resources to help my clients with their bloated pipelines I could not find a single, good, all-encompassing resource for addressing this topic. No one is sharing these details. So I wrote it myself.

I wrote this book for all those entrepreneurs, business leaders and sales professionals that want to close those bloated pipelines and prevent deals from getting stuck in the first place.

Reading this book will teach you how to unstick deals, shorten your sales cycle and prevent deals from sticking to begin with.

No deal should remain stuck. That would mean that the customer is missing an opportunity. The good news is, there is some very interesting science behind why deals get stuck. (It's fun to read) And the solutions for unsticking them are universal. They apply to all types of sales - big or small.

That means that whether you are in real-estate, professional services, or complex technology sales, the answer to how to unstick your deals and prevent sticking in the first place is now within your hands.

If you take the short amount of time it takes to understand these principles, you will dramatically improve your sales results and make all your interactions profoundly more enjoyable.

It is my hope that you will achieve the same level of success applying these principles as it has for me.

INTRODUCTION

S TUCK DEALS ARE THE BANE OF OUR SALES EXISTENCE.
Stuck deals are arguably the biggest problem in sales. Depending on the industry, between 40-60% of all sales are lost to no-decision. [1-5] No-decision, is in fact, every organization's largest competitor.

The implications of this fact are staggering. The fact that 40-60% of all sales are lost to "no-decision" means that the problem of "no-decision" effectively doubles the cost of every sale while simultaneously wasting somewhere around half of every sales professional's time.

It is a very big problem.

It is not uncommon for more than 60% of an organization's pipeline to consist of stalled opportunities.

40%–60% of all sales are lost to no–decision.

Figure I-1: 40-60% of all sales are lost to no-decision.

The good news is that if we can unstick our deals (or even better, prevent them from sticking in the first place) we can effectively double our sales, dramatically shorten our sales cycles, and double our commissions.

The even better news is that this book contains everything you need to unstick your current opportunities and prevent them from ever sticking in the first place going forward. It contains the science behind why deals get stuck, as well as the practical actions you can take to unstick them. If you have a stuck deal right now, this book will give you multiple actionable "plays" or "tactics" you can do right now to unstick it. In fact, if this is your situation, go to Chapter 8 right now to review the five key plays.

Understanding WHY your deal got stuck in the first place is helpful in selecting the best strategy. However, time is of the essence. If you are currently experiencing a stuck deal, you should act now and read Chapter 8 before reading the rest of this book.

Quick Reference Guide

This book is designed to be a quick reference guide. Each chapter has been designed to be brief and concise with actionable steps you can take right now to unstick your deal. Once you've identified why your deal is stuck you can jump right to that chapter for solutions. These short chapters are arranged into six logical parts:

- Part 1 – Preventing Deals From Sticking
- Part 2 – Unsticking Plays
- Part 3 – What Causes Stuck Deals
- Part 4 – Strategies for Unsticking Deals Caused by Sales Issues
- Part 5 – Strategies for Unsticking Deals Caused by Client Indecision
- Part 6 – Strategies for Unsticking Deals Caused by Business Case Issues

Intentionally Concise

A book of this nature has the potential to become a thousand-page monstrosity that covers every aspect of selling. I have intentionally avoided that. The goal here is to make the complex simple. Topics have been intentionally simplified to allow the reader to get through them quickly and benefit from the information right away.

Intentionally keeping things concise means that this is not a comprehensive book on the overall sales process. I have endeavored to look at the issue of stalled deals holistically and in such a way that it will apply to any type of sale and any type of sales process you might be using.

The Benefit

Today I see professionals working way too hard. In fact, when you survey professionals about how they plan to address their top sales challenges the top answer is always that they plan to do more. More contacts, more calls, more emails, more everything. Ratcheting up activity is the top strategy.

Here's the truth – effort does not equal paychecks. Rather than continually pouring more and more effort into deals, professionals would be better served investing some time in sharpening the saw. Effort doesn't equal paychecks. <u>Effective</u> equals paychecks.

Effort ≠ Paychecks. Effective = Paychecks

The good news is that minor changes in our sales approach can make a huge difference in terms of effectiveness. Minor changes make a big difference.

You'll discover what those minor changes are in the chapters ahead. And those small differences in approach bear great fruit. They will:

- Unstick your stalled deals.
- Speed up your sales cycles.
- Close more deals.
- Generate greater revenue and higher paychecks.
- Allow you to find more satisfaction and joy in selling.

Unsticking Deals

The longer a deal is stalled the less likely it is that it's going to happen. In the six parts of Unsticking Deals, we will address the root causes, plays, and strategies for unsticking deals and how to proactively keep them from sticking in the first place. We start in Part 1 by discussing five overlooked strategies for preventing your deals from sticking.

There are five key plays for unsticking your deal regardless of the strategy you are using. In Part 2 we explore these plays in-depth. Flexible enough to be employed in infinite ways, they are immediately usable and come complete with examples and templates. This may be the reason you purchased this book.

Surprisingly, stalled deals are caused by just three things and in Part 3 we explore those three reasons and the Universal Root Cause Maxim. It's important we address the right problem with our efforts, because solving the wrong problem (even if done perfectly) not only doesn't help, but sometimes can make things worse.

The very way we are selling often causes our deals to stick. In Part 4 we explore the top five sales issues that cause deals to stall along with simple strategies for unsticking them and preventing them from sticking in the first place.

In Part 5 we explore the challenge of client indecision, why it happens and how to address it. You will discover new insights. There are three reasons clients suffer from indecision. There is also a paradoxical pivot that professionals must make (but very often miss) in order to overcome client indecision. You will learn the strategies to overcome all three reasons and how to proactively prevent clients from getting stuck because of indecision.

In Part 6 you will discover how to unstick deals that are stalled because of business case issues. You will learn exactly how to ask, using special language, if business case is the issue. I will share a powerful technique called "Deal-In-Hand" that will get your management to approve 99% of the deals you bring to them even when they have special concessions. We'll discuss the formula for business case and discuss three ways you can improve your return without touching your price. You'll learn what you can do and how you can still win even when you don't have the best return.

We conclude by pulling it all together into one simple summary and a 3-step formula you can follow every time you're dealing with a stuck opportunity.

There is bonus material in Appendix 1 where you will find brief instructions on how to go about identifying your ideal customer. And in Appendix 2 you will find valuable material about mapping out your informational needs.

The Recommended Reading section contains some of my most highly recommended books for achieving sales success, many of which are mentioned in this book.

Together these tools and techniques will unstick your deals, shorten your sales cycles, increase your commissions and make selling far more enjoyable. Let's get started!

CHAPTER 1

WHAT IS A STUCK DEAL?

"The longer a deal is stalled, the less likely it's going to happen."
—DAVID BROCK

The Big Ideas:

- Stuck deals are opportunities that have achieved some level of progress but have stopped progressing.
- Know the leading and lagging indicators of stalled deals.

The word "stall" is from the Old English word "stalle" which is a fixed standing place for animals. Later it became used to describe when a horse pulling a wagon got stuck in the mud. In that sense, the horse was stuck in a fixed standing place and "stalled". That language has now become common in business to describe sales opportunities that are "stuck in the mud".

A stuck deal is a deal that has stopped progressing. Whether our sales cycle is short or long, the moment a prospective client stops advancing towards closure - it's stuck.

Stuck deals are not just deals that haven't closed yet. They are deals that have achieved some level of progress but are now no longer advancing. They're opportunities that you and the client have already invested time and energy in. Someone not responding to your prospecting effort is not a stuck deal because you haven't achieved any progress. In that scenario, you don't have a stuck deal - you don't have anything (yet).

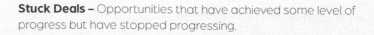

Stuck Deals – Opportunities that have achieved some level of progress but have stopped progressing.

Three of the biggest problems professionals have are:
1. Recognizing when a deal is stuck.
2. Identifying why it got stuck.
3. Knowing what to do next to unstick it.

This book answers all three of those questions.

Is My Deal Really Stuck?

In surveys of sales professionals (both managers and individual contributors), when you ask how they know when a deal is stuck you will predominately get two answers.

1. The client has gone silent. ("radio silent", "gone dark", "ghosting", etc.)
2. The deal has spent too much time in a particular stage.

These can be important indicators.

Years ago, I was conducting a <u>pipeline audit</u> for a client and ran across a stage called "Stalled". What is this, I asked? "That's where we put deals that might close someday but are currently stalled out. We don't want to lose track of them."

What the heck?

Newsflash – <u>"Stalled" is not a stage in the sales cycle</u>.

Open communication should be happening throughout the entire sales process. So extended periods of no communication are always a bad sign. And measuring stage conversion is important because it helps us identify where we might need to improve our skills. You can download how to calculate your stage conversion rate and create a "stuck deals" report for free at: **http://unstickingdeals.com.**

As important as these indicators are, we are not going to cover them here. Because, as it turns out, both are lagging indicators.

Lagging indicators are signs of an event after it has already happened. That is, the sign trails **after** the event.

Leading indicators are signs that predict an event before it occurs. It **leads**, the event.

While lagging indicators like radio silence and stalled pipeline are useful, the best of the best look toward leading indicators to identify issues and prevent deals from sticking in the first place.

Leading Indicator – Signs that predict an event before it occurs.

Lagging Indicator – Signs of an event after it has already happened.

Leading Indicators

Here are the early warning signs that your deal is at risk of getting stuck:

- Slow Responses
- Noncommittal Responses
- Behavior Incongruent with Stated Goals
- Preference for Indirect Communication (as opposed to direct conversations)
- Sudden Change in Communication Style
- Vague or Weak Responses
- Not Meeting Promised Timelines two or More Times
- Not Answering Calls
- Not Responding to Voice Mails
- Not Opening/Responding to Emails
- Not Responding to Texts
- Withholding Information
- Suddenly Dealing with a New Stakeholder
- Incongruent Body Language & Paralanguage
- No Access to Stakeholders (single point of contact)
- No Path to Closure - (client doesn't have a buying process or strategy)
- No Activity on Your Part - (if you are not engaging don't expect responses)
- No Decision When Client has Everything They Seem to Need - (the client hasn't said "no" but hasn't said "yes" either)
- The Force - (you feel something is wrong)

Leading Indicators	Lagging Indicators
• Slow Responses	• The client has gone silent. ("radio silent", "gone dark", "ghosting", etc.)
• Noncommittal Responses	• The deal has spent too much time in particular stage.
• Behavior Incongruent with Stated Goals	
• Preference for Indirect Communication (as opposed to direct conversations)	
• Sudden Change in Communication Style	
• Vague or Weak Responses	
• Not Meeting Promised Timelines 2 or More Times	
• Not Answering Calls	
• Not Responding to Voice Mails, Email or Texts	
• Withholding Information	
• Suddenly Dealing with a New Stakeholder	
• Incongruent Body Language & Paralanguage	
• No Access to Stakeholders (single point of contact)	
• No Path to Closure - (client doesn't have a buying process or strategy)	
• No Activity on Your Part - (if you are not engaging don't expect responses)	
• No Decision When Client has Everything They Seem to Need - (the client hasn't said "No" but hasn't said "Yes" either)	
• The Force - (you feel something is off)	

Figure 1-1: Leading and Lagging Indicators of Stuck Deals

These are all signs that your deal may be at risk of getting stuck and that you should consider some possible interventions before that happens.

What to Do

Consider possible interventions the moment you sense that your deal may be at risk of getting stuck. Be proactive about it. It is much easier to prevent deals from sticking than to unstick them once they are stalled.

This book covers strategies to unstick your stuck opportunities as well as how to prevent your deals from ever sticking in the first place. Taken together these strategies will shorten your sales cycles and increase your win rate.

We begin with proactive strategies for preventing deals from sticking in Part 1.

PART 01

Preventing Deals From Sticking

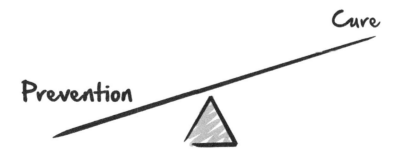

Figure P1–1: Part 1 – Preventing Deals From Sticking

CHAPTER 2

THE TWO APPROACHES TO UNSTICKING DEALS

"An ounce of prevention is worth a pound of cure."
— BENJAMIN FRANKLIN

> *"Every minute you spend in planning saves 10 minutes in execution."*
> - BRIAN TRACY

The Big Idea: Prevention is better than cure. It is better to prevent deals from sticking than to unstick them after the fact.

Research across various industries suggests that for every hour or dollar spent in prevention, approximately ten are saved in execution. [1, 2]

There are two fundamental approaches when it comes to unsticking deals:

1. We can unstick deals when they happen, or
2. We can prevent them from happening in the first place.

Figure 2-1: Prevention is better than cure.

Prevention is More Valuable Than the Cure

In all cases it is better to inoculate than to overcome.

When a deal becomes stuck, we've already invested a ton of time, money, and energy in it. Unsticking strategies require even more time and energy and only offer us a chance to undo or overcome whatever is causing our deal to stall. There is no guarantee they will restart our deal.

> When it comes to unsticking deals, an ounce of prevention is worth a pound of cure.

It is far better to prevent our deals from sticking in the first place.

Good execution of your sales process is the best way to prevent deals from sticking. And as it turns out, the strategies for unsticking deals, when used proactively, will also prevent your deals from getting stuck.

As we proceed, you'll notice that there is overlap in the strategies we use to prevent deals from sticking and the strategies we use once they're stuck. That is because many of the root causes are the same and interrelated.

In the remainder of Part 1 we explore five simple, but often overlooked strategies you can employ to prevent your deals from ever sticking in the first place.

Five Overlooked Strategies for Preventing Deals from Sticking

The five key prevention strategies are:

1. Secure Executive Sponsorship
2. Anticipate and Throttle Information
3. Leverage The Perfect Close
4. Create a Mutual Action Plan
5. Review Proposals with Clients

These strategies apply to all types of sales, the first and the last apply far more to complex sales than simple sales. If your type of sale has just one or two stakeholders and can be completed in one or two meetings, you are welcome to skip prevention strategies one and four.

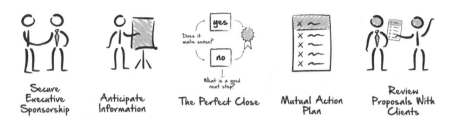

Figure 2-2: The Five Key Prevention Strategies

✓ The first, and one of the best prevention strategies, is to Secure Executive Sponsorship. This strategy will allow you to go back to your Executive Sponsor any time your deal gets stuck, or you are having trouble.

✓ The second strategy is Anticipating and Throttling Information. That is, we make sure we are introducing exactly the right information to the right person at the right time.

✓ The third prevention strategy is to use The Perfect Close to advance your opportunities. By using small Advances to leverage the enormous power of commitment consistency and endowed progress, we create continuous momentum until closure.

✓ Fourth, we have Mutual Action Plans. Mutual Action Plans are shared plans between client and seller that outline the critical steps to achieve the client's goal. They are very effective.

✓ And finally, we have Reviewing Proposals with Clients. This is time spent face to face with the client discussing the proposal.

To be fair, there are more prevention strategies than this, but the goal here is to make the complex simple. These are the top five.

The key principle here is: A stitch in time saves nine.

By preventing your deals from sticking in the first place you will shorten your sales cycle, save massive amounts of time and energy, and accelerate your commissions.

In the next chapter, you'll discover a simple yet powerful prevention strategy that will give you the power to unstick deals at-will – obtaining executive sponsorship.

PREVENTION STRATEGY #1 – HOW TO SECURE EXECUTIVE SPONSORSHIP

"Executive sponsorship is key. It will dramatically improve the probability of your sale closing and dramatically shorten your sales cycle."
- MICHAEL HALPER

The Big Idea: Securing executive sponsorship will allow you to unstick deals at–will.

Secure Executive Sponsorship

Figure 3-1: Secure Executive Sponsorship

Prevention Strategy #1 – How to Secure Executive Sponsorship

Our first prevention strategy is to secure Executive Sponsorship. This is an amazingly effective strategy. If you have never used this approach, you are in for a treat.

An executive sponsor is a C-level executive who has a vested interest in seeing a project through to completion. Ideally, the executive sponsor should be the highest-ranking manager possible, relative to the size of the project.

Executive Sponsor – a C-level executive who has a vested interest in seeing a project through to completion.

In my opinion, it is easiest to start your engagement at the highest level possible and get delegated down to other parties. And in that process, we turn our initial contact into an executive sponsor. I have some major strategies in

Chapter 11 on how to get to this person even if you didn't initially start at the top. But starting at the top is my preference.

Once you have gotten to this person, you're going to invite them to be your Executive Sponsor. The context for this is so they can achieve the results you know they have an interest in. That is, it's in their best interest.

In that context you are going to ask something like this:

"Moving forward with a partner requires the work of a number of people and we know that without senior executive sponsorship, the work of the day, and competing priorities often keep organizations from moving initiatives like this along. Would you be willing to be our executive sponsor through the process? Let me tell you what that means."

Then you are going to hand them your executive sponsor letter and explain it. (We'll review the letter in just a moment.)

When you say, "Let me tell you what that means." and then go over the letter, it immediately elevates your stature ten times. They absolutely love it. They immediately realize they're working with a professional.

I once had an Executive Director who I asked to be an executive sponsor take the letter from me and sign it immediately with a pen in his pocket. He then asked me, "Do you have another copy of that letter?" To which I replied, "yes" and pulled it out of my folio. "Great!" He said. "Let's give it to Don." He then walked me over to his Director of Operations and with a smile on his face he said, "Don, I just signed this, and I think you should too."

Executive sponsors are all about getting things done.

Tips for Success

Before we review the letter let me give you some tips.

First, it is absolutely paramount that the executive understands that **you are not asking them to agree to do business with you**. And you can even say it just that way. All you are doing is ensuring that they are engaged in the process and are willing to provide the necessary resources to do good work.

Now, what if they say no? Good. That tells us that we haven't generated enough interest for them to provide the basic professional courtesies outlined in the letter or they were looking for free consulting. Go back and generate more interest or leave happily knowing that you were not going to get the deal anyway.

Does it have to be in writing? No. It doesn't. The whole thing can be done completely verbally. But using the letter is much more effective. Sometimes your executive meeting happens spontaneously, and you don't have a letter handy. No problem. You can do the whole thing verbally.

That said, try it. Use the letter when you can. I always have one in my binder. It's generic, you can use it with anyone. You'll be stunned how effective it is and you'll love how you feel every time you use it.

The Executive Sponsor Letter

Here's the letter:

"We know that moving forward with a partner requires the work of a number of people. We also know that without senior executive sponsorship, the work of the day, and competing priorities keep organizations from moving initiatives like this along.

We are not asking you to agree to do business with us at this point. It's too early. We are asking for you to be our executive sponsor through the process.

For us this simply means:

- **Access**. Your assistance in connecting to the right people is very important.

- **Priority**. Setting the appropriate level of attention for your organization so that the process is supported.

- **Interest**. We will be communicating with you throughout the process on what is happening. Let's stay connected back and forth on the progress.

- **Logjams**. If the process bogs down, we need to be able to come to you and be able to count on your assistance.

- **Clarity**. There are times when we will need to better understand your company and its unique culture. If we are confused, we ask you to provide clarity.

That's it. In being our Executive Sponsor, you are only ensuring that the process of determining our best fit with your company is fully executed."

generic logo
company

(999-999-9999
✉ name@company.com
◉ www.company.com

We know that moving forward with a partner requires the work of a number of people. We also know that without senior executive sponsorship, the work of the day, and competing priorities keep organizations from moving initiatives like this along.

We are not asking you to agree to do business with us at this point. It's too early. We are asking for you to be our executive sponsor through the process.

For us this simply means:

- **Access.** Your assistance on connecting to the right people is very important.
- **Priority.** Setting the appropriate level of attention for your organization so that the process is supported.
- **Interest.** We will be communicating with you throughout the process on what is happening. Let's stay connected back and forth on the progress.
- **Logjams.** If the process bogs down, we need to be able to come to you and be able to count on your assistance.
- **Clarity.** There are times when we will need to better understand your company and its unique culture. If we are confused, we ask you to provide clarity.

That's it. In being our Executive Sponsor, you are only ensuring that the process of determining our best fit with your company is fully executed.

Signed By Executive Sponsor:

_____

Figure 3-2: Example Executive Sponsor Letter

What does this strategy get us? It gives us the ability to unstick deals at-will because we've pre-programmed our Executive Sponsor to address all the various issues that tend to cause deals to stick right from the start.

It's very effective and I highly recommend it.

Now, I have had executive stakeholders come and confess bad news with me about the death of an initiative. But that is far better than radio silence. Securing an executive sponsor does not mean you will win every opportunity, but it does mean that you won't get left in the dark.

One final thought on leveraging executive sponsors - only the best of the best do this. Your competition is probably not doing it. So, when you have executive sponsorship and your competition doesn't, you have a major competitive advantage and are much more likely to win your deal.

Bonus Play - Executive Alignment Play

A related and complimentary strategy comes from David Weiss. He calls it the Executive Alignment Play.

> One of the top reasons deals get stuck is due to lack of executive sponsorship. The functional stakeholders want a solution but can't get the executive support they need. Part of an executive's job is to say no to new toys, and business disruption. They want everyone to stay focused on the work. Executives get approached so often to buy things both internally that they get buying fatigue. And like a parent who is tired of seeing all the toys the kids want go unplayed with, so too are executives with all the toys their employees want. We need to help executives see that this isn't just another toy, but a real solution to a real business problem.

> One of the ways to do this is with the Executive Alignment Play. A common trap sellers run into is that they don't get to executives early enough in the sales process. Waiting until the end can appear desperate and signal that you are just trying to get a deal done. You also lose out on all the value of a relationship developed early on. It is seen as a pure negotiation play when you wait until the last minute because that is the typical outcome. But if you start this play earlier, it is viewed differently, and you can set yourself up for a much better outcome later in the deal.

> To execute this play, identify the executives involved in the decision, then craft a note like the one below for your executives to send to their peers inside your target company.

> > "Hi [First Name], I am [Name], the CxO of [Company]. [Colleague's Name] on my team has been working with [Prospect's Name] and [Prospect's Name]. It sounds like there is interest in solving [Problem]. As a fellow CxO, I enjoy networking and want to understand your priorities and the projects you're working on. I find it helpful to create early alignment and understand your priorities to ensure my team is in lockstep with your

goals during the evaluation. Can we carve out some time to connect in the spirit of building a relationship and networking?"

Doing this early has a few strategic outcomes. First, it validates the support for the project. Second, if the meeting takes place, it allows you to align to validated executive priorities, and socialize early business cases for change. Third, it opens up lines of future communication in the event of changes or issues. Fourth, it sets you apart from competitors that haven't run this play. Lastly, if you keep the two executives communicating, it is way more natural and doesn't reek of desperation when the time for negotiation comes.

From David Weiss' Sales Tactician's Playbook.

In the next chapter, you'll learn the second prevention strategy which is anticipating and throttling information and getting the right information to the right person at the right time.

CHAPTER 4

PREVENTION STRATEGY #2 – ANTICIPATE AND THROTTLE INFORMATION

"When we move too fast, we actually slow down the sale."

- James Muir

The Big Ideas:

- Too much information too soon stalls deals.
- Customers follow a predictable process when making decisions.
- The right information to the right person at the right time prevents stalls.

Anticipate Information

Figure 4-1: Anticipate Information

Prevention Strategy #2 – How to Anticipate and Throttle Information to Prevent Stalls

When we say anticipate and throttle information, we mean <u>preventing</u> client indecision by introducing the right information to the right person at the right time.

The best approach is one that paces at the rate the other person is ready for.

As you guide clients through each step of the sales process, you will be giving them more of what they expect—while at the same time improving their perception of your solution. This is because by pacing at a rate they are ready for, the client can see the entire picture, the import-

Introduce the right information, to the right person, at the right time.

ant major and minor milestones, and outcomes that happen before, during, and after the sale.

Salespeople often present their solutions at a speed far in excess of the client's ability to absorb it—feeding them from the proverbial fire hose. This happens because they think (erroneously) that delivering more information sooner is speeding up the sales cycle.

It isn't.

It's quite the opposite. Clients can't absorb information, and make sense of it, at the same rate you can deliver it. Too much information too soon unnecessarily creates the perception of complexity and triggers feelings of risk and uncertainty. It stalls deals.

> It is important to throttle information at a rate clients can receive and digest.

It is important to throttle information at a rate they can receive and digest. We need to deliver the right information, to the right person at the right time.

Talk 150–300 WPM
Process 800→ WPM

What is the "Right" Information?

That begs the question, "What is the right information then?"

Information is delivered in many ways. It may be delivered verbally, via website, email, brochures, whitepapers, videos, and many other ways.

How to develop effective sales messaging is a large topic that I will be covering in a future work and beyond the scope of this book. We will also drill-down on this subject in more detail in Parts 3 and 5. For now, here is a brief primer on messaging that will give us a framework to work from.

A Predictable Process

Customers follow a predictable process when making decisions. It has come to be known as "The Buyer's Journey." This is tremendously useful to us when it comes to identifying the "right information" and "the right time".

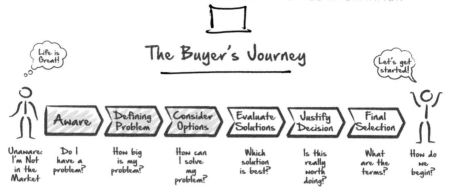

Figure 4-2: The Buyer's Journey

Here you see a model of the buyer's journey.

- Initially they're unaware and not in the market.
- In the next phase they become aware that they might have an issue and so they ask themselves "Do I really have a problem?"
- Once they're convinced they have a problem, they ask themselves if it's really big enough to do something about.
- Once they decide that it's big enough to do something about, they start looking for possible ways they can solve it. That might include your type of solution, or it might not. Everything is fair game at this stage.
- Once they've decided that a particular kind of solution is the best way to solve the problem, they start looking at which specific solution in that category is best for them.
- Once they think they've figured out which solution is best, they begin to justify the decision to move forward and ask themselves, "Is this really worth doing?"
- If they get past that, they start thinking "What's the best possible deal I can get?"
- And then of course, once they've made the final decision, they're all excited and want to get started yesterday.

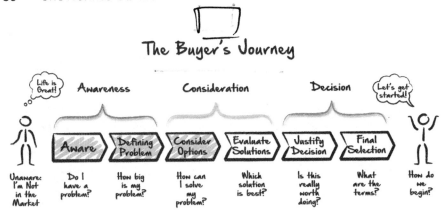

Figure 4–3: The 3 Basic Stages of the Buyer's Journey

Now inside this model there are three basic stages.

1. Awareness
2. Consideration
3. Decision

The Most Common Mistake in Messaging

When it comes to delivering information, the most common mistake I see is the salesperson trying to have a conversation with a customer in one stage when they are actually in another.

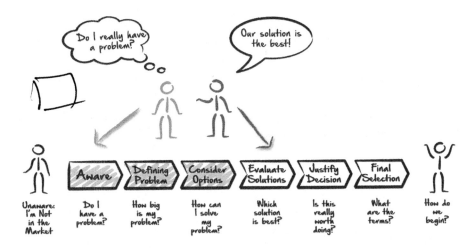

Figure 4–4: TThe most common mistake in messaging – trying to have a conversation in one stage when the customer is in another.

Here we see the salesperson speaking to the Evaluate Solutions stage by talking about how great their solution is, while the customer is still in the Awareness Stage and wondering if they really have a problem.

> **The Golden Rule of Sales Engagement: Meet the customer where they are.**
>
> *How much Research have you done?*

When a salesperson speaks to a stage farther along the buyer's journey than where the customer actually is, the customer becomes frustrated, and the salesperson comes off as being pushy - even when it's unintentional. It triggers feelings of risk and uncertainty and damages rapport. This is bad. We want to avoid this.

The Golden Rule of Sales Engagement is: Meet the customer where they are. Not where you are. Not where you want them to be. But where they ARE.

That means it's very important to know what stage of their journey your customer is in.

Where is my Customer on their Buyer's Journey?

So how do we know? How do we know what stage our customer is in?

The easiest solution is to simply ask. There are lots of ways. Here are some possible examples:

- "So where are you at in your buyer's journey right now?"
- "Tell me a little bit about where you are in your process?"
- "Where are you at in your evaluation process?"
- "What stage is your project in right now?"
- "Would you say you are still sizing up the problem right now or are you farther along than that?"

There are infinite ways to ask. Just create something that matches your style. <u>That</u> you ask is more important than <u>how</u> you ask.

If the client tells you they're not even sure they need to really do something, then they are in the Awareness stage.

If the client tells you they're still sizing up the challenge, then they are in the Defining Problem stage.

If the client tells you they're exploring different ways of addressing things, they are in the Consider Options stage.

And so on. You get the idea.

An Informational Shortcut

Once you know what stage of the buyer's journey your client is in, there is a shortcut you can use to know what information to deliver.

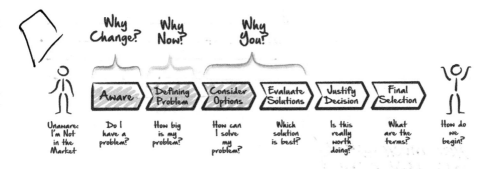

Figure 4-5: The Buyer's Journey and the 3 Whys.

Initially, you can simplify things down to three basic questions:

- Why Change?
- Why Now?
- Why You?

It's not perfect, but these three simple questions can help you identify what the "right information" is for this stakeholder.

If our client is in the Awareness stage, then the information they seek is answered by the question: Why Change?

If our client is in the Defining Problem Stage, then the information they seek is about urgency and answered by the question: Why Now?

And if our client is in the Consider Options or Evaluate Solutions stage then the information they are seeking is about differentiation and answered by the question: Why You?

Answering these three questions will take you a long way towards identifying the right information to deliver.

Mapping Informational Needs

You can now see how we can leverage the Buyer's Journey to anticipate the information our customers will need during their evaluation process. The questions Why Change, Why Now, and Why You are a great place to start when it comes to defining the information you will need during your sales cycle. It's

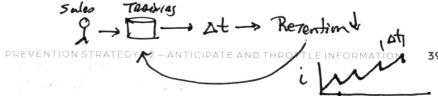

best to do this proactively. That is, anticipate the information you are going to need, and have it prepared before you need it. That's what makes this a prevention strategy.

Now, the three questions model starts to break down towards the end of the buyer's journey when clients start asking questions about justification and financial terms. So to speed up your learning, I have outlined the Buyer's Journey for you complete with some suggested informational assets and strategies you will likely need to pull the client into the next stage in Appendix 2.

This concept is sometimes referred to as "Exit Criteria". These are the things that the client needs to see, hear, feel, understand, and believe before moving to the next stage of their Buyer's Journey. Mike Kunkle has described this masterfully in his book **The Building Blocks of Sales Enablement** which I recommend. You'll soon discover that the concept of exit criteria permeates the entire sales process, which makes his book valuable for salespeople and marketers alike.

The Strategy for Introducing Information

With this framework you are now ready for the strategy which you already know as: Introduce the right information to the right person at the right time. There are three easy steps for accomplishing that.

1. Identify the Information Needed
2. Deliver It
3. Get Feedback

That's it.

Identifying the "Right" Information

Every stakeholder travels the Buyer's Journey independently. One stakeholder may be in the Awareness stage while another may be in the Evaluate Options stage. So their information needs are different.

So how do we know what information to deliver?

Once again, the best way to identify what information to deliver is simply to ask. I have found the following to be very effective:

"I don't want to bury you with information. What type of information would help you most?"

Then just listen. Their reply will tell you where they are at in their buyer's journey.

Locate them on the spectrum w/ Qs

> "I don't want to bury you with information. What type of information would help you most?"

"I don't want to bury you with information. What type of information would help you most?"

If they ask for return-on-investment calculations, then you know they are in the Defining Problem or Justify Decision stage.

If they ask you how your technology compares to outsourcing or some other alternate solution, then they haven't settled on a type of solution yet and they are in the Consider Options stage.

If they ask you for a comparison between you and one of your competitors, then you know they are in the Evaluate Solutions stage.

Once you know the stage of the Buyer's Journey they are in, you'll be able to add value by suggesting additional possible options.

Examples:

For example, I asked this exact question to a prospective client. I said, "I don't want to bury you with information. What type of information would help you most?"

They responded by asking me how our solution compared to our competition.

I said, "Well, I'm totally biased. I love my company. But do you know what I think would help? Blackbook Research just came out with their annual report that compares us to them, along with the top six vendors in the space. I think I can get you a copy of it. Would that be helpful?" Of course, they were ecstatic.

After they had time to digest the report, I asked them if it was in-line with what they were looking for and they said that it was something they had been searching for and that I had just saved them a lot of time.

How does this prevent stalls?

First, we can easily tell that this stakeholder is in the Evaluate Solutions stage. And we know they are going to do their due diligence evaluating all the options. My deal will slow down or stall by the amount of time it takes them to accomplish that due diligence.

So, by providing an objective 3rd party industry comparison that included all my possible competitors, I shortened my sales cycle by speeding up the client's buying cycle. By knowing their buying stage, I suggested information that was even better than they had requested and got them to *their goal faster*.

See how this follows the Right Information strategy?

Here's another example:

I told a client "I don't want to bury you with information. What type of information would help you most?"

"We're just trying to figure out if you guys do rebadging or not. We're still not sure the direction we want to go yet."

"Yes, we can." I said and gave them some details about it.

"Did that answer your question?"

"Yes. That's perfect. That really narrows the field down. Thank you so much."

See how this works? This second example took no more than 90 seconds.

How does this prevent stalls?

This client clearly hasn't decided which approach to solving the problem they want to pursue, so they are clearly in the Consider Options stage. If I hadn't asked them directly, they might have tried to get their answer somewhere else which might have stalled my deal or at least lengthened my sales cycle.

I didn't oversell it. An affirmative answer and a few details were all that was needed. I gave them the *minimum amount* of information necessary.

Then I got feedback to confirm that I had provided what they needed.

See how this follows the strategy?

Who Gets the Information?

In terms of who we are delivering information to, it is important to consider the dynamics involved. The wrong person with the right information can trigger fear, uncertainty, and risk. If a particular stakeholder gets the impression from your information that their workload is going to increase or even that their very existence is threatened, you have created a new problem for yourself.

There is no need to introduce information to certain stakeholders until it is necessary. This can get tricky when presenting to groups. Any sufficiently influential stakeholder can cause a deal to stick. We will discuss stakeholder management more in Chapter 11, but it's important to remember that each stakeholder travels the Buyer's Journey independently and that the information that helps one stakeholder is not necessarily helpful to another.

Conclusion

Introducing new information is a primary sales skill and doing it well will prevent your deals from sticking.

In this chapter we introduced a framework to help you identify what information to introduce, and when to introduce it. We then provided a simple 3-step strategy for identifying and delivering information. We will extend your understanding of both in upcoming chapters.

You will learn more about **how** to introduce information in Chapter 8 – The 5 Key Plays for Unsticking Deals. And we will dive deeper into the specific information strategies in Chapter 18 – Unsticking Deals Caused by Lack of Information Issues.

Introducing the right information to the right person at the right time prevents deals from sticking. The benefit of doing so is higher win rates and faster sales cycles.

In the next chapter you will discover a strategy that amounts to a Jedi mind trick (that you promise to only use for good) to prevent deals from sticking and advance your deals to closure.

CHAPTER 5

PREVENTION STRATEGY #3 – HOW TO USE THE PERFECT CLOSE TO GARNER COMMITMENTS

"Closing is the act of obtaining commitments, including all of the decisions that advance the sale."
— ANTHONY IANNARINO

The Big Idea: Use The Perfect Close and the power of commitment/consistency and endowed progress to accelerate deals and keep them from sticking.

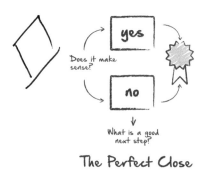

The Perfect Close

Figure 5–1: The Perfect Close

Prevention Strategy #3 – How to Use The Perfect Close to Garner Commitments

Our third prevention strategy is to use The Perfect Close to garner commitments. The strategy here is to use small Advances to leverage the amazing power of **commitment consistency** and **endowed progress** to create momentum.

The Perfect Close allows us to set appropriate **call objectives** (an Ideal Advance and a couple of back-up Advances) for each meeting or encounter. And that allows us to Advance the sale on every single encounter, so we achieve an unbroken chain of successful Advances that ultimately leads to closing the sale.

The Perfect Close

You can read more details about The Perfect Close in my bestselling book convincingly called: The Perfect Close. Here it is in a nutshell.

Before you go into any sales encounter you should have a couple of outcomes in mind. By that, I mean, what do you want to happen as a result of this interaction? What you should have, is an Ideal Advance and a couple of Alternative Advances.

Just in case the term "Advance" is new to you let me explain what an Advance is. The simple definition is: Moving the sale forward in a little way.

An Advance - Moving the sale forward in a little way.

A great man named Neil Rackham coined the term "an Advance" in relation to a sale. Neil Rackham conducted the largest sales study ever conducted. It involved over 35,000 face-to-face sales interactions. And we learned a lot about selling from his research.

The reason that Neil Rackham had to invent this new term is because in all that research, he discovered that 9 out of 10 sales interactions don't end with a close or a no-sale. (That's not what happens.) What happens in 9 out of 10 sales interactions, is we get an Advance (where the sale moves forward in a little way) or we get what he called a Continuation - which Rackham defined as a condition where the sale will continue but no progress is made.

Before going into any sales interaction, we want to have an Ideal Advance, as well as a couple of Alternative Advances just in case our ideal advance proves unrealistic. It's like having a backup plan. With that, you're ready to execute The Perfect Close.

There are two basic questions to the perfect close.

And the first question is this: "Does it make sense for us to X?" Where X is your ideal advance.

For example, "Does it make sense for us to schedule an assessment to see what the best options are?" In that example, the assessment is our Ideal Advance.

Now, there's only two things they can respond with: Yes or No. If they say yes, then Boom! - you got your Ideal Advance and you're off to the races. If they say no, then we just ask the second question.

And that question is some variation of: "Ok. Well, what do you think is a good next step then?" And in 90% of cases the client will simply suggest an

Advance that is appropriate for where they're at right now in their buying process. And that's important for several reasons we go into in The Perfect Close book.

And if this seems too simple, just know that Gong.io, who specializes in call analytics for companies that do outbound sales calling, analyzed over a million calls looking for the answer to this question: "What is the best closing approach there is?" And after analyzing over a million sales calls, they determined that The Perfect Close is hands-down the best closing approach there is. And, that top performers are using it about three times per hour on average. [1]

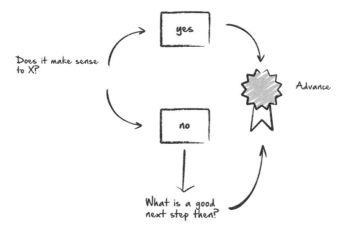

Figure 5-2: The Perfect Close Basic Model

There are some nuances, but basically, this is the model. So, what we end up with is either an Advance or a close every time we use it. If you do nothing more than leverage this simple model, you'll end up with a close or an advance 90% of the time.

As it turns out there are actually five variations of The Perfect Close and this is the kindergarten version. The other variations will help you make it even more effective.

The Perfect Close allows us to successfully use small Advances to leverage the power of **commitment consistency** and **endowed progress** to create an unbroken chain of successful Advances that ultimately leads to closing the sale.

How to Leverage Commitment Consistency and Endowed Progress to Close Deals

There are two scientific concepts that reveal why it is that getting sales Advances is so effective. And they are:

- Commitment/Consistency
- Endowed Progress

These are both principles in "behavioral economics" which is a fancy way of saying measured human behavior. Understanding how these principles work almost amounts to a Jedi mind trick. So, I commission you now that you are only allowed to use these forces for good.

Commitment Consistency

The first principle is Commitment/Consistency and here's how it works. This applies to all humans.

The first element of Commitment Consistency is that once we have committed to an idea or goal, we are strongly compelled to honor that commitment. So, for example, once you say you are a Green Bay Packers fan, you are strongly compelled to act like a Green Bay Packers fan. Or, if you say you support teaching children critical thinking, you are strongly compelled to be consistent with that statement.

This is why when you set a goal, all the gurus tell you to share your goal with others. Because this creates a strong compulsion to maintain consistency between your statement and your achievement of that goal.

The second element of Commitment Consistency is that once we accept small commitments, we become more willing to commit even further. For example, if you're willing to march in a parade or demonstrate for a certain cause, you are much more likely to be willing to donate money to that cause to remain consistent. This is a very powerful dynamic and people are willing to do very surprising things to remain consistent. Persuasion psychology expert Robert Cialdini has devoted an entire chapter to this topic in his excellent book **Influence: Science and Practice**.

So how do we apply this to selling?

> Once we accept small commitments, we become more willing to commit even further.

We ask clients to take a little step. An Advance. Once a client agrees to take a small step forward, there is a strong compulsion to remain consistent with the process & take additional and bigger steps. Each advance creates further momentum and further increases the likelihood that our client will take additional steps, and so on. And that chain of Advances ultimately leads to the culmination of the sale. [2]

The key is to define the little steps. These are the Advances you just learned about.

Endowed Progress

The next principle is called Endowed Progress. You can think of this concept simply as closure. It has two parts. Here's how it works:

1. Once we feel like we've made progress towards a given goal, we become even <u>more committed</u> to achieving that goal.
2. Once we set out to attain something (say the acquisition of a new solution or service, for example) the closer we get to completion, the more our efforts to do so <u>accelerate</u>.

Once we feel like we've made progress towards a given goal, we become even more committed and accelerate our efforts to achieve that goal.

You can easily see how this applies to sales Advances and unsticking deals. Once a client has made progress toward getting our solution, they become more and more committed. And the closer they get to the end, the more and more they accelerate their efforts.

Again, the key here is to get them to take a small step to start the process.

You may have noticed that in the first principle I used the word "feel". "... once we FEEL like we've made progress..." There is an interesting dynamic to this element. It turns out that the **perception** of progress is just as effective as **actual** progress in getting people to accelerate their efforts.

In order to test this principle, scientists staged a frequent buyer program at a car wash. I'm sure you've seen these programs where there's a card and every time you make a purchase, they punch the card and then after some number of punches you get something – like a discount, or a free meal or whatever.

Here's what the scientists did. They created two sets of cards for the carwash. One set had 8 punches, and after 8 punches customers got a free car wash. The other set of cards had 10 punches on it, but they instructed the people issuing the card to immediately punch two of the spots. So the amount of effort was exactly the same between the two cards – it was 8 punches.

The crazy result is that the 10-punch card with two already punched performed 44% better than the card with just 8 punches to begin with. The **perception** of progress accelerates effort.

So how do we apply this to unsticking deals?

There are a lot of things you can do to increase the client's perception of just how far along they are. Even simple statements like, "Oh, you're much farther along than I thought" or "than other clients at this stage" change that perception. As they make any sort of progress you can call it out and let them know they're getting closer and closer. In revenue cycle, after having completed an analysis, we'd let them know, "Man, you've already done all the hard work. Now all we need to do is apply it." There's lots of things you can do as your clients plan and go through the process to give them a greater perception of progress.

> The perception of progress is as effective as actual progress in getting clients to accelerate their efforts.

The key takeaway here is that: The perception of progress is as effective as actual progress in getting clients to accelerate their efforts. Making a client aware that they are closer toward their goal than they may have realized, and communicating to them how much progress they are making toward their goal, accelerates their efforts and makes them want to continue.

These two things – Commitment/Consistency and Endowed Progress, are the primary reasons why utilizing Sales Advances is so effective at accelerating momentum and keeping deals from getting stuck in the first place. They feed into each other. Done correctly, these two principles create a virtuous cycle where each one synergistically aids the other in ultimately closing the sale. [2]

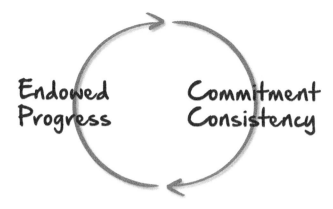

Figure 5-3: Commitment/Consistency and Endowed Progress create a virtuous cycle that brings deals to closure.

Conclusion

The Perfect Close is a tremendous selling skill. It's just two questions, zero pressure and 95% effective. It will prevent your deals from sticking by continually advancing your sales in an authentic and facilitative way. You can download copies of all of The Perfect Close models for free at PureMuir.com.

In the next chapter you will learn an amazingly effective and wildly underused strategy that maintains progress and momentum of even the most complex sales and keeps them from sticking.

PREVENTION STRATEGY #4 – HOW TO USE MUTUAL ACTION PLANS TO PREVENT STALLED DEALS

"Buyers buy into that which they help create."

– CHAD RAWLINGS

The Big Idea: Use Mutual Action Plans to prevent stalled deals.

Mutual Action Plan

Figure 6-1: Mutual Action Plan

Prevention Strategy #4 – How to Use Mutual Action Plans to Prevent   Stalled Deals

Mutual Action Plans are shared plans between client and seller that outline the critical steps to achieve the client's goal. It's a project plan. And in this case, the project is for the client to achieve some kind of result. And you are the project manager.

The strategy in using Mutual Action Plans is to help define and facilitate the steps the client needs to take for them to achieve their goal.

There are four primary reasons why Mutual Action Plans work so well:

1. They are a reminder to the client of the goal they are working to achieve.
✔2. They garner consensus with the client on what steps will be followed to achieve that goal.
✔3. They trigger Commitment Consistency which we just learned about.
4. They identify who is responsible for each of the steps in the plan.

The clarity that you're delivering when leveraging Mutual Action Plans is inherently valuable to the client. It elevates your relationship with the client to that of a valuable consultant and trusted advisor.

How to Create and Leverage Mutual Action Plans

So how do we create a Mutual Action Plan and leverage it to speed up the sales cycle and prevent stalls?

> **What are the steps you and your team are going to take as you go through your process?"**

The first thing we need to do is create it. I have tested several approaches over the years and found that the easiest way is simply to do this: After you've established what their goal is, simply ask something like: "What are the steps you and your team are going to take as you go through your process?"

This is a great question to ask a group. Don't be surprised if they hesitate a bit before they answer because it's very likely that you are the first person to ask this question. What will happen next is they will start to outline all the steps they're going to take, and you are going to write each one of these down.

Next, you'll help them flesh out all the details. Make sure to include:

- **The overall goal of the project.** Remember, the project is not to acquire an XYZ solution. Rather it's the results that their XYZ solution is going to deliver. This is an extremely important distinction. It is a common and classic mistake to treat the Mutual Action Plan like a plan to purchase your solution. The result your client is seeking may come long after that. If the client detects that your goal is simply to sell your solution, they will not follow the plan and your Mutual Action Plan will not work.

- **A buyer-centric completion.** Completion is not "sign the contract". That is seller-centric. Completion is the results they'll achieve after everything is fully implemented. Just ask them how they'll know when their project is completed, and when they will have achieved their goal. That will give you the metrics you need to be watching.

- **The correct sequence for each milestone.** Some folks get ambitious and place dates on each milestone. If there are key dates or deadlines where something has to happen, absolutely add those. But I recommend just sequencing the milestones because once they fall behind on the dates (which they always do) it tends to invalidate the plan, which we don't want. It's your call.

- **Identification of who will be responsible for each milestone.** What will we do? What will they do? Specifically, which individual will do what?
- **The outcome or deliverable for each milestone.** There's usually an outcome or deliverable to each milestone. Help them identify each one. For example, if they need to know our IT requirements, then that's our responsibility and our specifications document is the deliverable. If they're having a meeting where they are discussing goals, budget, and criteria, then that's their responsibility and the deliverable is the goals, budget and criteria decided on in the meeting.

After they've run out of gas describing their process, recommend any milestones and criteria you feel they have missed or will benefit them. This is a cool trick. You can literally insert your criteria and the things that benefit you right into their plan. (Again, just like the earlier Jedi mind trick, you are only allowed to use this for good.) Let's say you have rock star references, and your competition doesn't. Not checking references could be a major misstep in their process that could cost them dearly. If they have forgotten to include checking references in their milestones, you can suggest it and improve the client's outcome as well as your competitive position.

An example of this might sound like: "Most clients we work with like to check three separate references before moving on to X just to be certain the results are there, and to ask about potential pitfalls. Is that something you'd like to add?" They will always say yes.

What I'm about to say may sound counterintuitive. If they say they are going to evaluate the competition, then put the steps for evaluating the competition into the plan. Because if you don't, your deal is going to stall at that point. They will think it's awkward to mention the competition and try to do it secretly or (even worse) they may never get around to evaluating the competition which will again, stall your deal. I've even gone as far as introducing my client to my competitors and arranging meetings to keep my sale moving. That's pretty extreme, but you get the point.

We want this plan to be THEIR PLAN. The one they are looking at to complete their project. So, stuff that doesn't have to do with you or even with selling is going to end up in there. Embrace this reality and make sure it gets in there.

Managing and Leveraging Mutual Action Plans

Create a professional-looking document that outlines the plan and continually update it. While this may sound like work, it is actually a gift, because we're always looking for ways to re-engage the prospect. So, any time progress is made on your or their part, update the document and resend it out with your summary. Remember Endowed Progress. The car wash. This creates endowed progress like nothing else. It is very powerful.

And now all we have to do is help them follow their own plan.

Again, remember why this works. It constantly reminds the client of their goal. It creates consensus. And it creates accountability.

If things start to slow down, just look at where they are on the Mutual Action Plan and help them achieve that next step whatever it is. If that makes it sound like you're a project manager – Good! You are. And your project is helping them achieve their goal. You're a facilitator. And as I mentioned, I've done some creative things to help them get to the next step even when it's someone else's responsibility. Don't be afraid to do that. They will love you for it. Everyone loves a coach.

You can find example mutual action plans and templates free for download at http://unstickingdeals.com.

Conclusion

Mutual action plans are probably the most useful, under-utilized strategy in sales today. They are easy to implement and tremendously effective at maintaining momentum and preventing deals from sticking.

In the next chapter, you will discover the single best practice that addresses and prevents the root cause of a huge number of stuck deals – how you deliver proposals.

CHAPTER 7

PREVENTION STRATEGY #5 – REVIEW PROPOSALS WITH CLIENTS PERSONALLY

"Look at proposals as another opportunity for you to get in front of new prospects and continue establishing trust and building the relationship."

- KENDRA LEE

The Big Idea: Review proposals with clients face to face.

Review Proposals With Clients

Figure 7-1: Review Proposals With Clients

A common complaint of salespeople is that after providing a proposal to their prospective client, all communication with the client mysteriously stops.

Most salespeople conclude that there is something wrong with the proposal or that the price is too high. Occasionally this is the case, but in my experience, it is not the primary cause. There are multiple factors that we address later in the book that can cause clients to go silent. However, after hundreds of deal reviews across multiple industries, I can tell you that this particular stall can be primarily attributed to just one thing.

Emailing proposals.

In most cases the salesperson has simply emailed the proposal at the client's request without any sort of collaboration or review.

Indiscriminately emailing proposals is an error in selling that has reached epidemic proportions. It is manifestly apparent across all industries and all positions. It seems that no organization is immune to this universally bad practice.

Have you ever just emailed a proposal to a client without reviewing it together with them? Be honest.

> Indiscriminately emailing proposals is an error in selling that has reached epidemic proportions.

Well, you're in good company. I'm embarrassed to say that I've done it too.

The implications are staggering. So many deals have become stalled due to this one bad practice.

The good news is that this one challenge is easy to fix. Simply review proposals with clients before you send them.

The Peril of the Easy Path

The allure of just emailing your proposal is very seductive. It's easy to get sucked into it. Clients will request it and it's so easy to do.

You must resist it. Because the ramifications are colossal. At best you will miss an opportunity to deepen your relationship with the client and it will lengthen your sales cycle. At worst you will lose your opportunity altogether.

Here's why:

✓ **You will have lost control of the conversation.** In a live review presentation, you get to see your client's visceral and immediate reactions and you can adapt and respond in real time. Clients always have questions. Always. When you email proposals, this is irrevocably lost.

You also won't know whether your proposal was on-target or missed the mark. You'll be in the dark. And you won't get an opportunity to correct or even enhance the proposal for greater value. That opportunity will have been squandered.

✓ **Clients will miss the value you deliver**. I have used several proposal analytics tools over the years and in virtually all cases clients jump directly to the pricing and spend 90% of their time there without reading much of anything else. So even if you are thoughtful enough to include all the important elements in your proposal, when you just email it to clients, **they skip it**. This leaves the client without the critical value context of the initiative.

For example, when you email a proposal, you will miss the opportunity to review the challenges and goals the client is hoping to address with your solution. This is an important frame that gets lost without a live review.

Also, the total value of your business case will not be presented or understood. There is much more to your business case than just the price. (See Part 6) There will be soft value and intangibles that are not typically reflected in the investment pages. The opportunity to highlight this value is completely wasted when we simply email proposals.

Without the appropriate context in which to view the offer, clients are likely to make poor decisions. Because the overall business case is not presented appropriately, we inadvertently turn what should be a thoughtful comparison into a price-driven decision. And that shouldn't be the case. Done properly, the investment price is simply a detail.

You will miss the chance to build trust with an additional touch-point. More touches are better. We discuss this in Chapter 13. Building trust and credibility is a process and every interaction with clients has great value potential. These touchpoints create opportunities to invoke positive emotions and identify stakeholder Win-Results. (See Chapter 11) We lose these valuable opportunities when we email proposals and risk becoming seen as distant and transactional.

Clients take no ownership in the crafted solution. Clients buy into that which they help create. Discussing possible approaches and collaborating with clients makes us partners and infuses their creative thinking into the proposed solution. They become vested. When we define and propose solutions in a vacuum, customers are not engaged, and they feel no ownership.

Important details of the proposal will be missed. To set proper expectations, important details need to be discussed with clients. This includes things like timing, constraints, trade-offs, responsibilities and more. Two-thirds of what clients are most worried about is them – not you. (See Chapter19) When we fail to discuss these things with clients, they feel uncertainty and risk – and this stalls deals. Simply emailing a proposal squanders these valuable opportunities as well as the opportunity to allay their fears by painting a picture of a wonderful future.

Opportunities to leverage stories and testimonials will be lost. Most proposals include testimonials. But because clients jump right to pricing in emailed proposals they are never leveraged properly. In live reviews, however, we can invoke the tremendous power of storytelling which is far more memorable than facts and figures.

A higher level of qualification is lost. Unfortunately, asking for a proposal is often a way for clients to politely avoid telling you they don't want to work with you. Requesting to collaborate and review the proposal with the client creates a valuable hurdle that reveals the quality of the opportunity. Without it, time and energy poured into proposal creation is wasted.

You lose the ability to train your client. Proposals are tools for selling to stakeholders that cannot be present. Live proposal reviews are coaching and rehearsal for when those in attendance are presenting to others. We are literally training them on how to deliver the proposal. Failing to do so by emailing our proposal, completely destroys this opportunity and lowers the quality of internal selling that takes place without us.

All these compromises and the stalls that accompany them can be eliminated simply by doing live proposal reviews with clients.

Implementing the Proposal Review Strategy

Implementing this strategy is simple. It consists of just one main step: The moment the client requests a proposal, schedule a time to review it with them right then.

That's it.

> The moment the client requests a proposal, schedule a time to review it with them right then.

Setting the Expectation

Clients will try and get you to email the proposal. That's because this bad practice is so commonplace. Expect that they will ask, but don't do it. Clients don't realize that they are hurting themselves by receiving proposals without a review. It fosters bad decision-making.

Next time you are asked to email a proposal I want you to say something along the lines of:

"Sure. I'll definitely email it to you. But before I do that, I'd like to review it together first to make sure everything is accurate, that we're both on the same page, and that we're meeting your expectations. When would be a good time to schedule that?"

Then schedule it.

95% of the time you'll get agreement with no pushback whatsoever.

One in twenty times, however, the client will ask you to email the proposal in advance of the meeting. Don't do it. Instead say something like this:

"I'll send the proposal as soon as we've vetted it together and made sure it's exactly what you want. This isn't a presentation. I just want to review it together to make sure we've gotten everything right."

So you've made it clear that they're not getting the proposal until after a review.

It's very uncommon, but one in a hundred times you'll still get someone who still pushes back.

On the rare occasion you encounter this, be prepared to say something along these lines:

"I've had a couple of very costly experiences where a misunderstanding in the proposal created a major problem. So I don't offer proposals without a review. It's better for everyone, and that way no one ends up getting surprised or disappointed."

Just remember, you have all the cards. They want to see your solution and the investment for it. Your requirement is that you do a review together before sending it. You will elevate your credibility and their respect for you when you describe this approach. It will immediately set you apart from the competition.

After all this, if the client does not agree, then you don't have a real opportunity. They just want your proposal as leverage against some other vendor they prefer over you. Walk away knowing you just saved a bunch of time creating a proposal.

The Type of Meeting You Schedule

When it comes to the type of meeting you schedule, as with all things in life, there is good, better, and best.

The best option is a face-to-face meeting with the client where you are sitting side by side with the client reviewing all the elements of the proposal.

The next best option is a video call of some sort where you can see their faces and share your screen.

And the bare minimum is a phone call where you can verbally review all the details of the proposal.

Seeing the client's reactions in real time is very powerful. Video and in-person meetings greatly strengthen your relationship. They generate more feedback and make them like you more which increases trust and eliminates out-come uncertainty. (More details in Chapter 19) Leverage it at every possible opportunity.

What to Cover on The Call

Make no mistake, this is a presentation. It's just not a formal presentation. It is very casual and in the context of simply vetting the quality and accuracy of the proposal. Parts of your proposal can be wrong at this point, and it will not hurt you because that's the purpose of the meeting. In fact, it's actually better if the proposal is not perfect at this stage. More on that below.

You are going to cover the entire proposal in your meeting. But you are going to do it in a very summarized manner. This will give you the opportunity to cover the important elements that are beyond pricing. Elements that they would normally miss. Do not read the proposal. You are summarizing elements and highlighting *only*.

The specific elements that need to be in your proposal vary depending on your industry. The best book written on this continues to be Tom Sant's **Persuasive Business Proposals: Writing to Win More Customers, Clients, and Contracts** which I highly recommend.

At a minimum you're going to need at least four elements:
1. Executive Summary
2. Client Challenges & Goals ✔ *Reminder*
3. Solution
4. Investment and Business Case

Executive Summary

This briefly summarizes the entire proposal. Usually, two pages or less.

Client Challenges & Goals

This reminds the client why they are engaging you. It should communicate that you understand their challenges and goals. It should also include financial impacts if appropriate.

Solution

This is the solution you are recommending based on your understanding of the client. The goal of this section is to get the client vested in the solution. During the review stage I recommend you include many different options. There should be more in the proposal than they need at this point. This will give you the opportunity to discuss and sell each one with the client. This turns your review into a creative session where the client tailors the solution to exactly what they want and gets them vested.

Investment and Business Case

This is the price along with the return on investment. Your business case should include the three universal elements of muchness, soonness and sureness that you will learn about in Part 6.

Discussion

Chat through the proposal with these questions in mind.

1. Is the approach and solution as crafted going to address the client's goals?
2. Does the business case make the solution worthwhile?
3. Will the proposal as designed be compelling to those who need to review it?
4. What changes need to be made?

Script Here is some sample dialogue you can adapt when launching a review:

"The goal here is just to make sure that we fully understand your goals and that what we're proposing is going to get you there. We want to make sure that we're creating enough value here to make this worth doing. And we want to make sure that the way we've laid everything out is going to be useful for everyone that needs to see it. So as we go through it, just let us know what changes need to be made and we'll do that."

Challenge and Goals

Briefly review the client's challenges and goals. Ask, "Did we get that right?" "Is there anything that you would add?" And take good notes.

The first and very important milestone is that the client feels understood. Your review of the client's challenges and goals communicates to the client that the successful outcome is the accomplishment of their objectives – not just the purchase of your solution. Surprisingly, when you can describe the client's challenges and goals accurately, clients will assume you can solve the problem – even without seeing your solution.

Solution

During the solution section you will review and micro-sell, line-by-line, every option that you are presenting. Most of the discussion happens here. You are going to explain what you're recommending and the

Key

trade-offs for each option. Get the client vested by having them make changes and tailor the solution. You **want** them to make changes.

Business Case

The business case is simply the price of the recommended options contrasted with the return. It must include the quantity of the return, how soon the return will be achieved, and the certainty of the return. If you have guarantees this is where you will discuss them. More on this in Chapter 21.

Not every solution produces a business return. If your solution does not directly affect a financial return this is where you describe the final benefits of ownership to your client. The elements of how soon they will receive those benefits and how certain they are to receive those benefits should still be there.

> More touchpoints are less efficient but more effective.

You are going to take all their feedback and then create a corrected, more perfect proposal. You can then schedule another review, or if the changes are minor and you feel comfortable with it, you can send the final proposal on.

Wait a minute, James! Shouldn't I have just gotten the proposal perfect the first time?

No. You shouldn't have gotten it perfect the first time. We want the client to make changes.

Isn't this adding steps to my sales process? Isn't this less efficient?

Yes. It's less efficient. But it's more **effective**.

These interactions are extremely valuable because it gets them vested. It increases trust and reduces outcome uncertainty which is a major cause of stalled deals. We discuss this at length in Chapter 19.

Not only do I recommend that you show options that you know the client will remove, but I also have occasionally inserted errors intentionally knowing that I will have to remove them and then review again with the client. This creates more touchpoints – which are good.

Live proposal reviews are informal. They are casual, enjoyable and greatly improve your relationships with clients. At some point you will want to offer to do a formal presentation of the same material to the appropriate audience. Avoid relying on stakeholders to sell for you internally.

Conclusion

Decide right now that you will never email a proposal without a review ever again. Schedule live proposal reviews instead. Proposal reviews:

- Allow you to see client responses in real time.
- Allow you to maintain control of the conversation.
- Allow you to get valuable feedback on your proposal.
- Increase trust and make clients feel understood.
- Get clients vested in your solution.
- Allow you to cover value that clients will miss otherwise.
- Help clients make better decisions by giving them full context.
- Avoid turning what should be a thoughtful decision into a price-driven decision.
- Allow you to leverage testimonials and stories that clients would normally miss.
- Ensure that the accounts you are investing time creating proposals for are qualified.
- Allow you to train and rehearse your client for selling to others internally.

And most importantly, it prevents stalls caused by the deadly post-proposal email silence.

Section Summary

These are your top five prevention strategies.

1. **Secure Executive Sponsorship** – Prevent sticking from happening by securing an Executive Sponsor.
2. **Anticipate and Throttle Information** – Introduce the right information to the right person, at the right time.
3. **Leverage The Perfect Close** – Use small Advances to leverage commitment consistency and endowed progress to create momentum.
4. **Create a Mutual Action Plan** – Facilitate the steps the client will take to achieve their goal.
5. **Review Proposals with Clients** – Schedule live proposal review with clients.

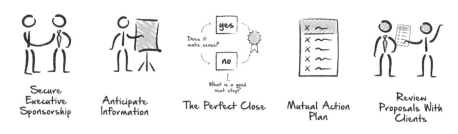

Figure 7-2: The Top 5 Prevention Strategies

A stitch in time saves nine. An ounce of prevention is worth a pound of cure. Leveraging these strategies will prevent 80% of your deals from sticking and make them vastly easier to unstick if they do get stuck. They are simple, straightforward elements you can easily add to your sales process right now. The reward for incorporating them is dramatically fewer stalls, faster sales cycles, and accelerated commissions.

In the next chapter we will unpack the five key plays you will use to unstick a deal that has already become stuck based on the root cause. This might be the reason you bought this book. It's showtime.

PART 02

Unsticking Plays

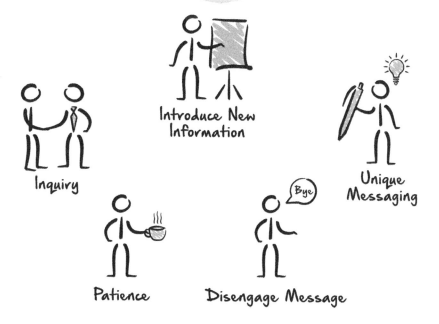

Figure P2-1: The 5 Key Plays for Unsticking Deals

CHAPTER 8

THE 5 KEY PLAYS FOR UNSTICKING DEALS

«Sales plays are essential for equipping the sales manager and sales
team with the best practices that can be learned and repeated."
- JACK DALY

The Big Idea: There are 5 key plays for unsticking deals: Inquiry, Introducing New Information, Unique Messaging, Patience, and Disengage Messages.

Despite our best efforts to prevent our opportunities from stalling, it is inevitable that some of our deals will get stuck. It is now time to discuss the plays and tactics for unsticking those deals. In this chapter we will discuss the five key interventions or "plays" that you will use to unstick stalled opportunities. And in the chapters that follow we will apply these plays to specific unsticking strategies.

The 5 Key Plays

If prevention is a strategy, then I think it's appropriate to refer to the interventions we use to unstick deals as "Plays". These are the 5 key plays for unsticking a deal that is stalled. (For the record, there are more plays than this, but these five are the most relevant. I have also included a number of bonus plays throughout the book for you, many of which are contributed by my good friend David Weiss from his book The Sales Tactician's Playbook which I recommend.)

These are meta-plays and there are a huge number of ways each of these plays can be employed. I share them with you here before going into specific methods so you can invent your own applications once you understand how they work.

1. **Inquiry** – If the client is still communicating with us, then the easiest and most straightforward approach is to engage, inquire, and diagnose the reason for the stall and then address it.

2. **Introduce New Information** – Often times clients stall because of an incorrect perception about our solution or company. They may have eliminated us, or perhaps are considering other options. When people have incorrect notions, we cannot simply tell them they are wrong. They do not respond well to that. Instead, if we want them to change, what the data shows is that rather than telling them they are wrong, we need to introduce new information that shifts the client's paradigm. That's what this play does.

3. **Unique Messaging** – This play leverages special messages to recapture the client's attention and gets them to respond.

4. **Patience** – This play is about waiting and preparing for trigger events or new information that will increase the priority of the initiative.

5. **Disengage Message** – This play is where we communicate our intention to disengage. This often causes the client to reengage.

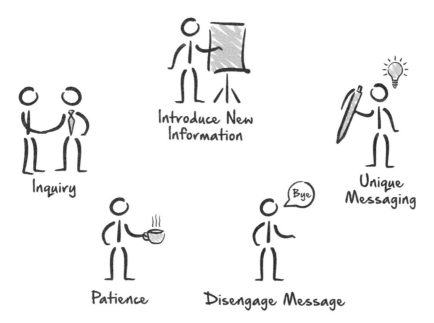

Figure 8-1: The 5 Key Plays for Unsticking Deals

These are meta-plays. There is quite a lot of variability in how these plays can be applied depending on the root cause of why our deal is stuck. We will first cover these at a high level and then explore very specific approaches you can use depending on the root causes of your stuck deal.

Inquiry

Figure 8-2: Inquiry

Unsticking Play #1 – Inquiry

Our first and best play is simply inquiry. If our client is still communicating with us, then we're just going to engage, inquire about it and diagnose the reason for the stall. Then with that information, we will choose the appropriate strategy to address and unstick our deal. When clients are still communicating with us, this is our first and best option.

Context: Can be used when clients are still communicating.

Play: Engage, diagnose the reason for the stall, then choose the appropriate strategy to unstick the deal.

Introduce New Information

Figure 8-3: Introduce New Information

Unsticking Play #2 – Introduce New Information

Our second play is Introducing New Information. There are infinite ways to introduce new information. It can be applied conversationally, via email, using marketing assets, 3rd party articles and more. This means we can use this play regardless of whether the client is still communicating with us or not. We very often use this play to get clients to re-start communicating with us.

In general, the play is this: We introduce new information that shifts the client's paradigm in some way. And that paradigm shift reengages the client.

Context: Can be used regardless of whether the client is still communicating or not.

Play: Introduce new information that shifts the client's paradigm.

Here's an example. While I was at NextGen Healthcare, we once had a client go silent on us after a competitor had parachuted in with some bat-phones (I'm not kidding, these phones were a direct connection to their celebrity CEO). This competitor was making big noise about the quality of their services including claim denial management which was particularly important to this client. Ironically, this particular competitor didn't really do post-denial management and follow-up. Rather, they would push that work back onto the client.

We knew this particular client would be unhappy about the post-denial follow-up being pushed back on to them, but we couldn't get them to respond. They had gone radio silent. We let them know via both email and voice mail but got no replies. They were too smitten by their celebrity CEO.

In a fit of desperation, we printed out the competitor's KLAS ranking (KLAS is like Consumer Reports for healthcare solutions) along with all the comments. It was like 80-90 pages. Then we created a special document from those comments that highlighted the negative comments about denial management. We sent that to nine different stakeholders. They all got it. Less than a week later they had called us back and our deal was back on the table. And we ultimately won the contract.

We are technically combining both plays 2 and 3 here. The point I want to accentuate now, is that this experience illustrates some important key principles about Introducing New Information.

The Dynamics of Introducing New Information

First, you can't tell the customer they are wrong. It doesn't work. In this experience, we knew that our competition was not going to manage claim denials in the way this client wanted. But they were so enamored with the competition and their celebrity CEO, they wouldn't listen. Telling the client directly that they were wrong about their understanding of our competition didn't work at all.

People don't like to be told they are wrong. It is too blunt, and too direct. Effective persuasion is much more subtle.

Paradigm Shifting and Effective Persuasion

Rather than trying to force the client to change by telling them they are wrong, it is much more effective to be subtle and have them change on their own.

Effective persuasion is like Judo. The word judo consists of two Japanese characters which you can see here: "ju", which means "gentle", and "do", which means "the way". So, Judo literally means the way of gentleness. And the most gentle and effective way to get someone to change is to get them to change on their own, by introducing new information. **INSIGHT**

When we introduce new information, it forces the other person to take it into consideration. And when that information is genuinely paradigm shifting, it shifts the other person's paradigm and they become open to change.

Figure 8-4: Judo - The way of gentleness.

handwritten note at top: ✱ yes, and I could add to that _____

This is what happened in my story. When we told them straight-out that they were wrong, they wouldn't change. But when we introduced new information from a reliable 3rd party, they changed on their own.

The Power of the Yes–And Formula

I want to introduce you to a concept called "Yes-And". "Yes-And" means that we first, acknowledge the other person's point of view, and then after they see that we've listened and understand their position, THEN we introduce new information.

It's called the "Yes-And" Formula.

For example: A prospect might say, "We don't like the experience we have when our vendors use offshore resources." To which we might say, "Yes. Exactly. That can be a major barrier to communication. That's why it's important that all interactions between companies be with on-shore, English-speaking personnel.

Or

A prospect might say, "Auditing every single chart would be a huge waste of resources." To which we might say, "Yes. And that's why it's so critical that we identify and know exactly the charts that need to be audited." That is "Yes-And."

You get the idea. There are infinite examples and possibilities.

Here's the irony. Changing people's minds in this way works, even when the "and" part of the message directly contradicts the message we are acknowledging.

For example: They might say, "It's a beautiful red." Other person, "Yes. And there's just a hint of green."

Amazingly, even though this "and" statement directly contradicts the first statement, people feel completely different about it. They do not **feel** they've been told they are wrong. It is an amazing phenomenon, and the studies are fascinating. What is happening here is that both parties are collectively trying to get closer to the actual truth. So even when our new information essentially contradicts their statement, it is not seen as hostile or condemning when we use the "Yes-And" formula.

Tips on Adding New Information

What researchers have discovered is that of all the elements that improve response - proof is the most important element. Focusing on proof improves response more than anything else. So when you are introducing new information, I encourage you to think of it in terms of proof. Your new information should be:

- **Paradigm Shifting** - It should be relevant and shift their paradigm in the direction we want.
- **Compelling** - The new information should be believable and impactful.

Introducing information that doesn't shift the paradigm in our direction is pointless. For example: If our client's perception is that our solution is slow, then introducing new information about how the solution *slowly* walks users through each step only reinforces that perception. Or introducing something unrelated like how great support is, doesn't address the perception. Rather, we might be better served by introducing information about how higher accuracy with the slower approach eliminates 95% of all errors and saves 50% more time overall. (i.e., slower is actually faster)

The new information you introduce should be believable, compelling, and impactful.

When it comes to making claims (like the error reduction and time-savings in the above example), research shows that clients are very skeptical. They know that anyone can make a promise or a claim. So, unless a claim is supported by proof, they slip off customer's backs like water off a duck. Research shows that the most effective forms of new information (i.e., proof) come from objective third parties. Clients know that information from objective 3rd parties is much harder to fabricate. So they weigh it more heavily. In the experience I shared above, we used a KLAS Research report to make our case because we knew it would be seen as unbiased and objective.

That said, there are many types of new information that come from you directly, that clients will have 100% confidence in. For example, when working with the neurosurgeons I mention in the Hail Mary, Circle of Influence Letter below, it was new information that there was another method to acquire their system but that it came with some legal baggage. Since you have complete control over things like terms, agreements, promotions, etc., clients will readily accept this type of new information from you.

There is tremendous potential here. You have a great deal of flexibility and creativity at your disposal when it comes to introducing new information. Introducing new information is an important sales play regardless of whether our deal is stuck or not. Introducing new information in the right way will enable you to shift paradigms, persuade others, and unstick deals. We will delve more deeply into specific ways you can introduce information coming up. But understanding the concept of how to introduce new information in a way where it can be received is extremely important. The "way of gentleness" must be used. This one concept, if fully understood and utilized, will open infinite ways you can apply it.

Unsticking Play #3 – Leverage Unique Messaging

The third unsticking play is to leverage unique messaging. This play, in all its variations, is typically employed once a deal has gone silent. The goal is to recapture the client's attention by using a unique message, format or medium. That essentially sums up the play - using special messaging to recapture the client's attention and get them to engage. There are an infinite number of ways you can do this. You may already have some of your own. I highlight a few possibilities here to illustrate.

Unique Messaging

Figure 8–5: Unique Messaging

Context: Mostly used when the client has gone silent.

Play: Use special messages to recapture the client's attention and get them to engage.

Unique Messaging Ideas

There are so many unique messaging possibilities that this one idea could be a book all unto itself. Covering each idea exhaustively would make this book overly complex and violate our goal of making the complex simple. I summarize some of my favorite ideas for you here.

The general idea is to send a message that is so unique, that it regains the client's attention, shocks them back to life, and gets them to respond. With very few exceptions, you will almost always combine this with Play #2 that you just learned - Introduce New Information. In most cases we need to do more than just get their attention, we also need to change something by supplying new information and give them a compelling reason to respond. These two represent a 1-2 punch that unsticks deals.

Video Email

Because it's easy to do, the first thing on my list is to simply send a video message instead of a regular email. During the holidays I had several clients that had promised to get me data for analysis. But these clients were procrastinating and extending the sales cycle. To jolt things loose, I put on my funny Santa cap, got me some jingle-bells, and made a video saying that Santa's elves were standing-by to help them pull their data if they wanted.

Figure 8-6: Video messages are easy ways to create noticeable, unique messaging.

It totally worked. They watched the video a bunch of times and I got my data. (and my elves didn't even need to help)

Simple One-Sentence Email that Brings Deals Back to Life

Chris Voss, in his excellent book **Never Split the Difference**, offers a very simple email for jump-starting communication that has worked for me many times. It is very simple and very low-cost.

Find the most recent email from your key stakeholder and reply to it with a one-sentence email that says: "Have you given up on this?" That's it. I get a reply back about 2/3 of the time.

Do not send this email to a group. You *can* send it to each stakeholder individually if you want. There is some cool psychology behind why this works, but I'll spare you that. If you are interested, you can find the details in Chris Voss' book. This is very simple and effective. Give it a shot.

Gift Baskets, Food and Flowers

My next favorite thing to do is to send a gift basket, food, or flowers. During the holiday videos I mentioned above, one of my Santa cap videos didn't get me a response even though I could see that they had watched it a few times. Fortunately, it turned out that this particular client was local. So, I donned my funny Santa cap and bought them an edible Christmas gift basket for their team and hand-delivered it with a smile on my face.

Their central business office had a very strong gatekeeper, so I couldn't hand it to my key stakeholder personally. (So much for my amazing charm.) I could tell this office really didn't get much walk-in traffic. So, me with my silly, but still professional look, I handed my gift basket over to my gatekeeper and wished her a Merry Christmas!

Right after I got into the car, I started getting notifications that my original Santa cap video was being watched. And by the time I got home, they had watched the video I had sent previously another 8 times. I know exactly what was happening. They were showing my gatekeeper the video of me and asking, "Is this the guy that brought the gift basket?"

Again, it totally worked. The next day I got a direct email from the CFO thanking me for the gift basket for his team along with a promise to send me the data.

The Consistency Message

I call this next one the "Consistency Message". This one combines copywriting with a Jedi mind trick. So, if that's not really your thing, use one of the other methods. What's good about this one is that it's really just an email. So, it's very inexpensive compared to some of the other methods.

The psychology here is the same as the Chris Voss email. You're basically going to remind them that they said this was important to them before. And as we learned earlier, Commitment Consistency is a powerful force. So, to remain consistent, they have to reply. If they don't, it creates what scientists call "cognitive dissonance" which is essentially a kind of mental pain.

I used this once with a nationally recognized client that had gone silent because we couldn't present on the exact date and time the CEO wanted. Because of that, he was going to eliminate us from the running. So, in an email, I reminded him how critical he told me this initiative was, I reviewed what the repercussions of getting it wrong might be and reminded him that especially because they were nationally recognized, not all patients that want to come to their clinic get to see the physician they want, on the day they want. Long story short – it worked. Not only did we get the date and time we wanted, but we also won a very large and noteworthy client. In fact, I ultimately became very good friends with that CEO. Landing that client changed the history of our company forever in a very positive way. It blows my mind now to think that it all hinged on that single email that I wrote.

The Hail Mary, Circle of Influence Letter

One of my all-time favorites for complex sales is the Hail Mary, Circle of Influence Letter. It has never not worked for me. I have also used this idea for prospecting. In fact, many of these ideas will also work with your prospecting. What makes this work is New Information (Play #2) and Social Pressure. It's time-consuming, but extremely effective. Here's how it works.

You're going to identify your main stakeholder. This is the person you want to reply to your effort. Then you will identify all the other relevant stakeholders in this initiative. If we have done our selling properly, you will have already identified these stakeholders before the client has gone silent. (if not, your root cause is likely a sales issue) But if you need to, go ahead and identify any additional stakeholders you need. Basically, what you're looking for is your key stakeholder's boss, a couple stakeholders that are peers, and a couple of subordinates. So, there might be six or so stakeholders involved.

Then what you're going to do is write a **physical letter** and send it to each one of them **individually**. And you're going to send this physical letter via FedEx in a flat envelope. So, in this example, you're sending out six separate FedEx envelopes.

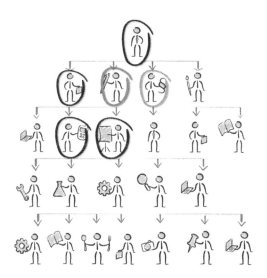

The letter is going to say you have new information that changes everything but because things have gone silent you don't know who to contact about the change. And for that reason, you sent this letter to all six (or whatever the number is) of your stakeholders. Then at the bottom of your letter you're going to show your CC

Figure 8-9: Identify your target stakeholder's circle of influence.

and list the name of all the other folks you sent letters to. This is extremely important.

Here's what will happen. They all open the letter immediately because it's FedEx. And they see all the other stakeholders that got the letter at the bottom. Then they all start thinking, "Holy smokes, what if Bob (or whoever they're worried about) thinks we need to do something about this." This will cause them to have a conversation about you. In fact, I guarantee 100% that they will talk about you. They all show the letter to each other and say, "All right, well, who's going to call this guy back?" And then one of them will call you back.

Now, that doesn't necessarily mean they're going to buy your stuff. But it will get you another conversation and another chance to swing at the plate.

There is some nuance to the letter. For unsticking purposes, you need to remind them of the original reason they got engaged with you. This is commitment consistency again. You need to very briefly remind them of the value you can bring. And then you're going to mention the new information that you have, but you're not going to reveal it entirely. (Or they won't need to call you back, right?)

Let me share a real-life experience to illustrate. I was working with a large group of neurosurgeons on an expensive healthcare IT system. After sharing and reviewing the proposal with them, the client went silent on me. After many failed attempts to rekindle the conversation, I began to fear that I might have lost to a competitor. So I used the Hail Mary, Circle of Influence Letter.

I sent the letter FedEx, as described above, to the eight surgeons that were all equity holders in the clinic. In my letter, I mentioned that I had discovered a new way for them to acquire the system at a greatly discounted rate but that it did come with some legal baggage that we need to discuss.

Notice how this works. There is a benefit there, and they can vaguely see the mechanism, but not enough so they don't have to call me. They need to engage to find out what it is.

And it worked! They called me back within 24 hours, and we won the business.

To satisfy your curiosity, what I did was instead of having them purchase the system directly from me, I had them acquire it through an agreement I had with a local IPA (Independent Physician Association). They ended up joining the IPA which made my IPA client very happy, and we won a deal we thought was lost.

Approach:
- Identify Key Stakeholders.
- Send a Separate FedEx Letter to Each Stakeholder.
- Letter MUST have a CC: at the bottom showing all the stakeholders who received the letter.

Letter Must Include:
- Reminder of the original reason you got engaged.
- Remind them of the value you bring.

▪ Disclose (vaguely) the new information that changes everything and the possible benefit.

NOTE: Do not try this with email. I've tried it, and it doesn't work. What happens every time, is one of the stakeholders does a reply-all that they are not interested and you're dead. There is a method similar to this that I have used for prospecting with decent success. Each email is sent to each stakeholder **separately** and the reference to the others receiving the email mentioned in the body of the email. It is reasonably effective but nowhere near as effective as sending physical letters. This might be an approach worth trying if the value of your opportunity doesn't warrant investing in the FedEx letters.

Leveraging Social Media

Another thing I have seen work is writing something nice and tagging the stakeholder on social media. I've also seen folks write recommendations on LinkedIn to reengage the client. In one case, not only did it wake up a silent client, but it also turned them into a close friend.

Call Them Out

The final one I want to share with you is to simply call them out. Here is an example script you can model and adapt to help you do that.

"It's been my experience with past opportunities that when the silence cycle goes past a few weeks, it is not a good sign. It usually means that you either have bad news for me, or the project has been significantly delayed. I can handle either piece of information, but I would appreciate a chance to hear it from you. If I am wrong, that's ok too, but I really need for us to connect so I know whether to move on, stay the course, or change our approach."

Here, the appeal is to professionalism and making it safe for them to tell you whatever the news is - good or bad. And in my experience, it usually works to break the silence.

Other Examples to Consider

There are really no end to the possibilities depending on how much time, effort, creativity, and expense you're willing to invest. I have seen folks send half of something cool, like an expensive radio-controlled car and then keep the remote for it and tell them they'll get the remote when you meet. And there are many similar concepts out there.

If you would like to see some exotic but extremely effective examples, pick up: **Get the Meeting!: An Illustrative Contact Marketing Playbook** by Stu Heinecke, and his other book, **How to Get a Meeting with Anyone: The Untapped Selling Power of Contact Marketing**. Fair warning, most of these methods are very expensive but they are off-the-charts effective. Like – 99% of the time they work. So, if you are involved in high-value sales these are worth looking at.

Patience

Figure 8-10: Patience

Unsticking Play #4 – Patience

Everybody wants a silver bullet that will jumpstart any stalled deal. And we've already discussed some great plays. But here's the truth. Sometimes deals get stuck and go silent for very legitimate reasons. There may be organizational changes, a financial crisis, or a slew of other things that have nothing to do with you that can make your deal stick. That doesn't mean that the fundamental value of our core business case has changed. Rather, it means that some other change has temporarily become a higher priority and stalled our opportunity. All the fundamentals are still there.

Just because a pandemic or a new stakeholder has taken over, doesn't change the fundamental reasons why the client needs to address their issue or problem. Those things don't just go away. In fact, they tend to just get worse. But temporarily, they end up becoming a lower priority, while the client works through the higher priority issues.

Sometimes deals get stuck and go silent for very legitimate reasons.

A Metaphorical Example

Let's say you have a serious basement flooding issue that is destroying your home from the bottom up. That's a high priority problem.

Now let's say while you're in the middle of working on your flooding problem, your house catches fire and starts burning down.

Are you going to fix the flooding problem first? Or are you going to address the fire now?

Fixing the flooding won't matter if the whole house burns down, right?

Despite both issues being important, the right thing to do here is first put out the fire and wait to address the flooding.

Clients sometimes have messed-up priorities. They might be addressing the wrong stuff. But in **their** minds, they are putting out the fire. And it's important to remember that.

As much as we don't want this to be true, sometimes the best strategy is just to be patient and wait for whatever is causing the stall to resolve, and then our issue will become higher on the priority list again.

When clients are openly communicating with you, these types of priority shifts are pretty easy to identify. It's a lot harder when they aren't.

We don't want to destroy our opportunity by becoming annoying or sending disengage messages when the root cause isn't really related to us. Look closely. See if you can identify any internal issues that might be causing the stall. Sometimes clients go silent because they are ashamed by the cause of the stall, and they don't want to suffer through the embarrassment. So they prefer silence over an uncomfortable conversation.

I had a client that was engaging us because they were trying to get their bad E&M coding under control. Then right in the middle of their evaluation they went silent. (For readers who are not in healthcare, E&M coding is how physicians indicate the difficulty of medical exams.) And when you're working with the government (like Medicare and Medicaid) there are laws one must follow. Not following these rules can cause you to have to pay fines and even go to jail.

Do you want to know what the cause of the silence was?

Right in the middle of our sales process the prospect got audited and fined by the government! So, as you can imagine, while they were going through all that with the government, they didn't want to talk. It was embarrassing. After that, however, because of that very uncomfortable experience, our sale was easy. It would have been a shame to walk away because we misinterpreted the signs.

In certain cases, the right play is just to be patient and wait.

Context: Typically used when a deal is stuck due to priority, political or other internal issues.

Play: Wait and prepare for a trigger event or new information that will increase the priority of the initiative.

Disengage Message

Figure 8-11: Disengage Message

Unsticking Play #5 – Disengage Messages

The last play we'll cover is to use some form of disengage message. I know you've seen these, so I'm not going to belabor them here.

Before you send any disengage messages, do a quick assessment. At each step in the sales process there was information you were exchanging. You were meeting and introducing stakeholders. In one or more of these steps, we missed something. So, just like looking for your keys when you've lost them, we retrace our steps, room by room, to figure out where we put our keys. This is the same thing. Something went wrong somewhere in the sales process - let's find out where.

- Who did we meet? Who did we introduce? How did they fit? And who did we miss?
- What information were we exchanging at each stage? What would have made it better?
- Were there any unforeseen issues or stakeholders that caused delays in the process? What was the reason?

You don't have to be a CSI investigator to figure it out, but these brief assessments are the key to growing and getting better.

After your assessment, if we can't make progress by engaging in some way, then our best option is to disengage to protect our precious time.

It is true that when we send disengage messages, many times clients suddenly reassess their priorities and come running back. It is unfortunate that this happens. But sometimes we have to take them right up to the point that they're going to lose something before they will reassess.

They might come back. They might not. Either one of these options is good. As professionals, all we have is our time. We convert time to money. So, it's important that we are investing our time in opportunities that can actually close. The worse scenario is wasting even more time chasing a bad deal.

How to Craft Disengage Messages

As you craft your disengage message here are some things to consider.

Decide if you are walking away permanently. If you are walking away permanently and this is not a gambit, then prepare to not look back.

I prefer to leave the door a little bit open. So when I respectfully decline, I suggest some possible way to re-connect sometime in the future. That creates an opportunity for either of us to reengage if things change.

My walk-away emails tend to be highly tailored, so I did my best to create a template of sorts for you. It has 10 components.

1. I've enjoyed working together with you and your team.
2. Report any progress you accomplished together.
3. Keep it positive by suggesting their challenges or initiatives are "exciting."
4. It's been a long time since we had any correspondence.
5. My experience - long silence means you have bad news or things have changed.
6. Sympathy for them being busy (this gives them an out if that is the issue)
7. For now, I'm going to close your file.
8. If you want help achieving your goals, I'm happy to help.
9. Tell them past progress can be leveraged.
10. Here are my contact details (usually in the email sig)

Here's an example with gaps where you can put your own information. You'll see how positive and open it is. To be candid, there is a fair amount of psychology going on in this email. I will spare you the analysis. All we're really doing here is letting them know we are walking away but leaving the door open just wide enough that they can walk through it and engage us when the time is right.

This template is intended for when you've already had some engagement. If you're looking for walk-away emails from prospecting that hasn't worked, that is not a stuck deal and the internet is littered with examples of those, so you can get those there. Here's a templated example you can adapt for your own use.

Hey [name],

I've enjoyed working with you and [team names go here] on [initiative and any progress to this point]. You guys have some exciting stuff going on.

It's been some time since we had any correspondence and it's been my experience that when the silence goes past a few weeks it usually means that you have bad news or that priorities have changed. I can handle either piece of information, that's just business, right?

At the same time, I've been in your shoes so I know how busy things can get. For now, I'm going to close your file. If you want to [achieve their original desired results] I'd be happy to help. Just reach out and we can leverage all the work that we've done to this point.

Keep fighting the good fight.

Disengage Message Tips

Let me just offer a couple of tips:

- First, I sometimes see walk-away emails that have an accusatory or disappointed tone — don't do that. We want them to reengage us. And you can't get there with guilt and blame – it doesn't work. Save your energy.
- Second, the email needs to be emotionally positive or neutral. This isn't a high school breakup; you're a professional. Don't express any blame, criticism, or disappointment. Rather, show empathy.

Context: Can be used to when we can't make progress by engaging.
Play: Send a disengage message that signals our intent to walk away.

Summary

In this chapter we discussed the five key interventions or "plays" that you will use to unstick stalled opportunities. The five key plays are: Inquiry, Introducing New Information, Unique Messaging, Patience, and Disengage Messages. These plays can be combined for maximum effectiveness. The most common combination is play #2 - Introduce New Information and #3 - Unique Messaging.

Each play has an optimal context and strategy. By assessing the root cause of your stuck deal, you will know which plays to use.

Unsticking Plays Summary

Unsticking Play	Context	Play
Play #1 - Inquiry	Can be used when clients are still communicating.	Engage, diagnose the reason for the stall, then choose the appropriate strategy to unstick the deal.
Play #2 - Introduce New Information	Can be used regardless of whether the client is still communicating or not.	Introduce new information that shifts the client's paradigm.
Play #3 - Leverage Unique Messaging	Mostly used when the client has gone silent.	Use special messages to recapture the client's attention and get them to engage.
Play #4 - Patience	Typically used when a deal is stuck due to priority, political or other internal issues.	Wait and prepare for a trigger event or new information that will increase the priority of the initiative.
Play #5 - Disengage Messages	Can be used to when we can't make progress by engaging.	Send a disengage message that signals our intent to walk away.

Figure 8-12: The 5 Key Plays for Unsticking Deals.

Armed with our five key plays for unsticking deals, we now turn our focus onto the three things that cause deals to get stuck.

PART 03

What Causes Stuck Deals?

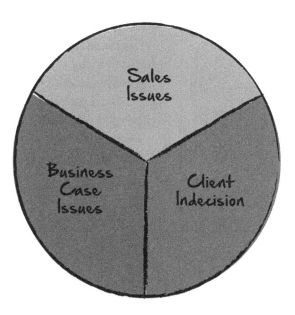

Figure P3–1: The 3 Causes of Stuck Deals

CHAPTER 9

WHAT CAUSES STUCK DEALS?

"Stuck deals are the seller's problem, not the customer's."
- COLLEEN FRANCIS

The Big Idea: Stalled deals are caused by three things - Sales Issues, Client Indecision and Business Case Issues.

What causes deals to get stuck?

After an exhaustive review with hundreds of clients, I can tell you definitively that there are just three things that cause stuck deals:

1. Sales Issues
2. Client Indecision, and
3. Business Case Issues

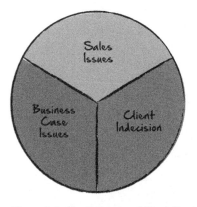

Figure 9-1: The 3 Causes of Stuck Deals

That's it.

All three of these are interrelated. Sales issues and business issues very often **cause** client indecision. And client indecision and business issues very often trigger or exasperate sales issues.

This can sometimes make it challenging to diagnose the actual root cause. So, it's helpful to have a guide. Misdiagnosis can lead to using the wrong strategy which, in some cases, makes the problem worse rather than better.

> The root causes of stalled deals are Sales Issues, Client Indecision and Business Case Issues. All three are interrelated. Issues in one area very often cause or exasperate issues in another.

For example, if we use a business case strategy that leverages the fear of not purchasing (or FOMO - fear of missing out) when the root cause of the stall is actually client indecision, the strategy will likely backfire and actually create even more client indecision.

So, knowing the root cause is important. More on that below.

The good news is, within each of these three areas, there are a surprisingly small number of things to account for. These few things in each area account for the vast majority of all stuck deals.

Sales Issues

Your sales process is the steps you and your client go through as you facilitate their purchase decision. Sales issues are things in the sales process itself that cause deals to stall. That is, the very way we are selling is causing our deal to stick. Assuming you have a solid sales process, this usually means a failure to properly execute some part of our sales process.

> **Sales Issues** - Things in the sales process itself that cause deals to stall.

After over 30 years in sales, I'd say that there are an infinite number of ways to mess up a deal. Just when you think you've got everything covered, some new thing you'd never thought of, catches you by surprise.

The good news is that there are just five Sales Issues that account for the majority of stuck deals.

1. Bad Targeting
2. Wrong or Incomplete Stakeholders
3. Champion Management
4. Relationship
5. Competition

These are in descending order of commonality. Most common are on top.

Bad Targeting – Bad targeting is by far the biggest issue. This is where the solution doesn't genuinely match the client we are selling to. Maybe we didn't know that going in, or maybe we turned a blind eye to it. Regardless, here we are, and now we have a stuck deal.

Wrong or Incomplete Stakeholders – This is selling to the wrong people or an insufficient number of people.

Weak Champion / Coach – As they say, No Champion, no sale.

Relationship – Relationship issues are simply some sort of personality mismatch between us and one or more of our stakeholders.

Competition – Competition is one of three things: 1. The status quo, 2. Alternative investments or 3. A competitor selling a similar type of solution to ours.

Client Indecision

Client indecision is when deals stall due to the customer's inability to decide. There is a strong correlation between win-rates and client indecision. When client indecision increases, win-rates plummet.

> **Client Indecision** – Indecision on the customer's behalf that causes deals to stall.]

There are three reasons why clients suffer from indecision:
1. Valuation/Comparison Problems
2. Lack of Information
3. Outcome Uncertainty

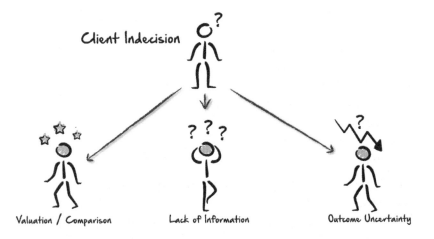

Figure 9-2: 3 Reasons Clients Suffer From Indecision

Valuation/Comparison Problems – Valuation/Comparison problems are where the client is worried about choosing the wrong option and/or is struggling with how to compare all options and the related trade-offs.

Lack of Information – Lack of information problems are where the client is worried, they haven't done sufficient homework to make an intelligent decision.

Outcome Uncertainty – Outcome uncertainty is about risk. This is where the client is worried, they won't get the outcome they're paying for and being promised.

We address each of these and the strategies you can use to address these issues in upcoming chapters.

Business Case

Business case issues are when deals stall due to the business case being offered to the client. At its core, Business Case is about just one thing – Priority.

That's it.

We will cover this in more detail ahead, but if you think about the business case in these terms, it will make creating your business case much easier and much more effective.

Our business case, helps the client answer this question: "Is solving this problem the best use of our time and money right now?" Clients have a lot of possible projects they can invest their time and money on. Our business case helps them compare all these different initiatives against each other.

The problem with all these different initiatives is that they are hard to compare. They're apples and oranges.

There is a way to compare wildly different initiatives using three criteria. And those criteria are:

- **Muchness** – Muchness is how much revenue will the project return.
- **Soonness** – Soonness is how soon that return will materialize.
- **Sureness** – Sureness is how certain they are to get the return being promised.

Muchness   Soonness   Sureness

Figure 9-3: The 3 Universal Business Criteria

We will dive more into this later, but by using these three criteria, clients can compare wildly different initiatives.

The Universal Root Cause Maxim

With this background we can now sum up what causes stuck deals in one sentence:

If your deal is stuck, you've made an error in your sales process, your business case isn't good enough to be a priority, or our customer is uncertain about something in the deal.

Believe it or not, that's it. That covers it all.

If our deal is stuck, our problem is:

1. We've made an error in selling.
2. Our customer is uncertain about elements of the deal.
3. Our business case isn't good enough to be a priority.

> If your deal is stuck, you've made an error in your sales process, your business case isn't good enough to be a priority, or our customer is uncertain about something in the deal.

You're about to discover a bunch of strategies to unstick deals, but every one of them will trace back to one of these three things.

Simpler than you thought right?

A Word on Diagnosing Root Cause

I have a friend that owns a rather large bakery. It's a big operation and very successful. Because of the long lines, he was receiving complaints about the considerable wait times to receive product. To address the complaints, my friend spent a lot of time and money renovating and doubling his number of pick-up and checkout stations.

Weeks after all this was completed, the lines hadn't changed at all. All the time and money renovating and doubling the check-out stations had accomplished nothing.

Frustrated, my friend invested in a consultant to help him analyze and fix the problem. After taking a close look, they discovered that it was the process the bakers were using that was the constraint - not the number of pick-up and checkout stations. After changing their process and hiring additional bakers, not only was the problem of long lines solved, but customers were much happier, and revenues improved by almost 40%.

What's the point?

It's important to solve the right problem. Solving the wrong problem (even if done perfectly) doesn't help.

Peter Drucker says it this way - "There is nothing quite so useless, as doing with great efficiency, something that should not be done at all." - Peter Drucker

> "There is nothing quite so useless, as doing with great efficiency, something that should not be done at all."
>
> – PETER DRUCKER

In order to unstick deals it's important to know the root cause of WHY they are getting stuck in the first place. Solving the wrong problem won't unstick your deal. In fact, solving the wrong problem will further the delay and in some cases, make the problem even worse.

Within each of these three areas there are a small number of issues or sticking points.

This gives us a frame of reference that we can use for the rest of the book.

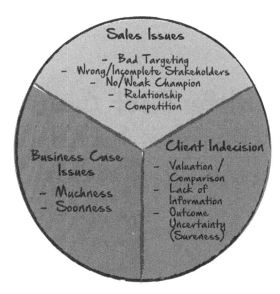

Figure 9–4: The 3 Causes of Stuck Deals

Identifying
root cause
is not
an exact
science.

Identifying Root Cause is Not an Exact Science

As we get to identifying root causes, let me point out that identifying root causes is not an exact science. In many cases it's obvious. In other cases, it's less clear.

Unfortunately, deals are not like lab tests. We can't just take a sample, run a test, and get the answer. In many cases, our client has gone silent, and we can't even illicit feedback to know where we are.

For those reasons, when we examine our stalled opportunities, we look at indicators that are both internal and external to help us identify the root cause. Taken together, these give us a clear picture of the root cause of our stalled opportunity. And these root causes tell us which strategies to use.

The 3-Step Stuck Deal Checklist

There are just three simple steps to follow to unstick your deals:

1. Identify the root cause of your stuck opportunity.
2. Brainstorm which strategy to employ.
3. Decide and execute your unsticking plays.

These are the steps we'll be taking to unstick your deals.

1. Identify Root Cause
2. Brainstorm Strategies
3. Decide & Execute Plays

Figure 9-5: The 3-Step Stuck Deal Checklist

Summary

The rest of this book is about dissecting these three areas, their root causes, and sharing with you the strategies to jump-start your currently stalled deals. Once you've mastered these, not only will you be able to jump start deals, you'll also be able to prevent them from ever sticking in the first place.

In Part 4 we will dive into the details of the root causes, dynamics and indicators that tell us the reasons our deal has stalled. We then arm you with the strategies you need to address each one.

We begin by addressing the most preventable of all three reasons – Sales Issues.

PART 04

Strategies for Unsticking Deals Caused by Sales Issues

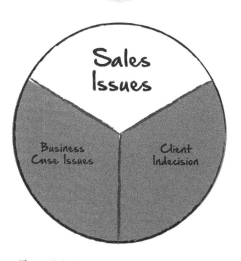

Figure P4–1: The 3 Causes of Stuck Deals

CHAPTER 10

UNSTICKING DEALS CAUSED BY BAD TARGETING

"Know who your target market is. Know their language. Know the words they use."
- EUGENE SCHWARTZ

The Big Ideas:

- Targeting is primarily a prevention strategy. Don't target non-ideal customers.
- Define your Ideal Customer Profile and target only ideal customers.
- Just because we have a load of unsticking strategies we can employ, doesn't always mean we should.

Targeting is mostly a prevention strategy so maybe it belongs in the list of prevention strategies in Part 1. However, most sales professionals have control over who they choose to engage in their sales efforts, and for that reason I have included it here in the section on sales issues. When conducting opportunity reviews, an enormous percentage of stuck deals can be attributed to bad targeting. It's probably the #1 sales issue with some estimating as much as 67% of lost deals being attributed to bad targeting. [1] And, as my friend Jeb Blount likes to say, "A lot of stuff that we called 'stalled' was never going to close to begin with."

Bad Targeting

What is the single biggest thing you can do to improve sales?

That's the question one of my clients asked me. And as the author of a best-selling book on closing sales you might imagine that my answer to this question would be closing – but it isn't.

The single most effective thing you can do to increase sales is to sell to only ideal candidates. That's what the data shows.

The reason for this is because everything else is downstream from there. No amount of brilliant messaging, computer automation or brute force effort can compensate for selling to the wrong prospect. Because with the wrong prospect all our efforts will fall on deaf ears. It's Garbage in - Garbage Out.

This is such a big problem across all businesses, all industries, and all professions, that as a bonus we're going to spend a little extra time on it.

One of the biggest crimes in all of selling (in fact, all of business) is selling to the wrong prospect. Selling to the wrong prospect is the biggest waste of time ever.

Non-ideal prospects:

- Have more objections.
- Have the longest, slowest sales cycles.
- The lowest margins and commissions.
- They're the biggest headaches after the sale, and
- In some cases, they actually become anti-references.

Have you ever sold an account that you regret selling?

The Pareto Principle dictates that 20% of our opportunities will consume 80% of our time. So it is absolutely critical that we make sure that the 20% of opportunities that are consuming 80% of our time are ideal candidates with a high-probability of closing.

Groundhog Day

Let me tell you about a challenge I see over and over as a manager.

I see reps engaging anything that moves - good or bad - and then in a downward spiral, they continue to pour their valuable time into weak prospects. This is especially true for new reps that don't know what an ideal customer looks like yet and are desperate to get anything into their pipeline and prove they were a good hire.

Then what happens, is when they get towards the end of the sales cycle when these deals have stalled out, they call me hoping there's some magic thing they can say or do that will turn their bad prospect into a good one.

It won't happen.

Discipline needs to be applied at the very beginning of the process to protect your precious time. Only work with good prospects and refuse to work with weak prospects. Instead, invest that time engaging ideal targets. You're better off finding an ideal prospect than continuing to waste time on non-ideal customers. Let that sink in for a minute because I know it's tough medicine.

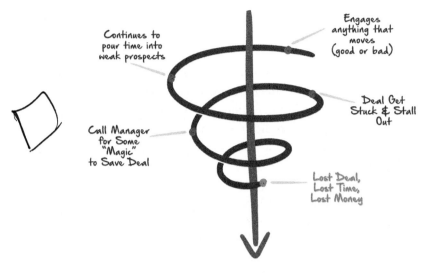

Figure 10-1: The Downward Spiral of Bad Targeting

Even though you have an engaged prospect on the line - if it's not an ideal prospect - you're better off making them a lower priority and going out and FINDING an <u>ideal prospect</u>.

So, it's shifting the effort from engaging (which I know is a lot more fun) to prospecting. (Which most salespeople consider less fun)

The highest leverage of your time is to focus on ideal, high-probability prospects to begin with. If you allow yourself to work on garbage accounts, you'll get garbage results.

> *You're better off finding an ideal prospect than continuing to waste time on non-ideal customers.*

Getting this one principle right – all by itself – can make you massively successful. And the reason for that is because focusing on ideal, high-probability prospects is statistically the highest leverage strategy you can employ. Period. That's what the data shows. All other strategies are downstream from this one. They are all dependent on it.

My good friend Mark Hunter says it this way - "You can't take a Walmart prospect and turn them into a Nordstrom's customer."

Now, that begs the question - How do I know what an ideal customer looks like? And to not distract us from our main conversation I have included the answer to that question along with a famous case study for you in Appendix 1.

How to Know if You're the Victim of Bad Targeting

So how can we tell if our deal has stalled because of bad targeting? We want to ask ourselves questions like these:

Targeting Assessment Questions
• Have we engaged in a suitably ideal client?
• Is the business case weak for this client?
• Does this client match our Ideal Customer Profile (ICP)?
• If it doesn't match our ICP, how far does it deviate from our ICP?
• Is this opportunity the best use of my time right now?
• Am I engaging at the right level according to our ICP?

Figure 10-2: Targeting Assessment Questions

Targeting Assessment Questions
- Have we engaged in a suitably ideal client?
- Is the business case weak for this client?
- Does this client match our Ideal Customer Profile (ICP)?
- If it doesn't match our ICP, how far does it deviate from our ICP?
- Is this opportunity the best use of my time right now?
- Am I engaging at the right level according to our ICP?

By the way, it's ok to engage non-ICP clients. We just need to go into it knowing that non-ICP clients are simply:
- Riskier.
- They have longer sales cycles.
- And generally, they have poorer returns.

That's why they're not ideal. So don't be surprised when they get stuck. Just know what you're getting into.

Lastly, even if an opportunity does fit our ICP, there are still lots of ways we can mess it up. But in this context, where we're talking about targeting, the question we want to ask is: Are we engaging at the right level, according to our ICP? That is, did we not only target the right type of client, but did we also target the right entry point?

Now, if the concept of an Ideal Customer Profile is new for you, quickly turn to Appendix 1 and come back. It will make a huge difference for you.

Strategies For Addressing Bad Targeting

What's the solution? I don't think this is going to surprise anyone, but the basic strategy is just to target better. We want to explore both prevention and unsticking strategies.

In that vein, we want to ask ourselves:

Targeting Improvement Questions

- How can we define or improve our Ideal Customer Profile (ICP)? Can we can do a better job of defining our profile so we're engaging higher probability opportunities?
- How can we perform or update the problem inventory of problems we solve? This will allow us to target ideal accounts better.
- How can we leverage better tools to more accurately identify customers that fit our Ideal Customer Profile (ICP)? (i.e., Tools like ZoomInfo and Lead scoring)
- How can we reevaluate our current pipeline against our updated Ideal Customer Profile and eliminate or re-prioritize mismatched accounts?

Figure 10-3: Targeting Improvement Questions

Targeting Improvement Questions:

- How can we define or improve our Ideal Customer Profile (ICP)? How can we do a better job of defining our profile so we're engaging in higher probability opportunities?
- How can we improve or update the problem inventory of problems we solve? This will allow us to target ideal accounts better.
- How can we leverage better tools to more accurately identify customers that fit our Ideal Customer Profile (ICP)? (i.e., tools like ZoomInfo and lead scoring)
- How can we reevaluate our current pipeline against our updated Ideal Customer Profile and eliminate or re-prioritize mismatched accounts?

Narrowing Your Target Market

The first and most important thing you can do to improve your targeting is to conduct a problem inventory and accurately define your Ideal Customer Profile (ICP). Most organizations can greatly benefit from narrowing the focus of who they are targeting. In general, there are four market targeting strategies.

- **Undifferentiated** – Targeting the masses, reaching as many people as possible.
- **Differentiated** (segmented) – Targeting key market segments.
- **Concentrated** (niche) – Targeting to a single small niche.
- **Microtargeting** – Often confused with niche targeting, this strategy targets even smaller segments all the way down to the individual level.

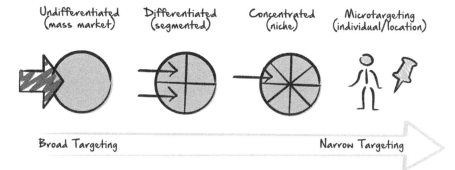

Figure 10-4: The 4 Types of Targeting

First define your ICP and then evaluate market segments. It would be impossible to do justice to the topic of segmenting in the few pages we have here, so I refer the reader to my favorite book on the topic: **Market Segmentation Analysis: Understanding It, Doing It, and Making It Useful** by Sara Dolnicar, Bettina Grün and Friedrich Leisch.

Because all other strategies are downstream from targeting, it is the single biggest thing you can do to improve sales. Do not ignore it.

The Big Question

I recommend you ask one more question every time you review a stuck opportunity: Is this deal still worth pursuing? Is it still worth our time and energy?

If not, maybe it's time to refocus our efforts elsewhere. Before investing a lot of time trying to unstick a stalled deal that perhaps shouldn't have been pursued in the first place, take stock, and scrutinize the deal closely using your newly updated ICP. Just because we have a load of unsticking strategies we can employ, doesn't mean we should.

Ask yourself the zero-sum thinking question: Knowing what you now know about this opportunity, if it were brought to you fresh today, would you still pursue it?

If the answer is no, then cut your losses and move on. (Remembering to target better next time) If the answer is yes, then buckle-up, poorly targeted deals get stuck a lot. Precisely because they're not the best match for what we do. You may end up employing multiple unsticking strategies multiple times.

> Just because we have a load of unsticking strategies we can employ, doesn't mean we should.

In terms of unsticking poorly targeted deals, we are going to use the unsticking strategies that you will learn in Parts 2 through 6, knowing that they just happen more often for poorly targeted deals.

Qualifying

No one should be reaching out to non-ICP customers. But despite our best efforts, we will sometimes end up engaged with a potential customer that does not fit our Ideal Customer Profile. How do we protect our precious time?

> The best remedy for bad targeting is strong qualification.

The best remedy for bad targeting is strong qualification. By ensuring that prospects meet our minimum standards we can protect ourselves from one of the biggest time-sucks in sales – pursuing bad opportunities.

Qualifying is different than discovery. Qualifying is about making sure the client meets your minimum specifications, while discovery is about understanding the details and nuances of their challenges. That said, qualifying happens during discovery. That makes discovery a bit of an art because clients can tell when you are qualifying them and that sometimes leaves a bad taste in their mouth. How to conduct an excellent and mutually beneficial discovery is a large and important topic and beyond the scope of this book. Our purpose here is to cover the qualification aspects of discovery.

How to Qualify in a Nutshell

In general, qualification is very straightforward. We're simply going to use our Ideal Customer Profile to create a checklist we can use to qualify accounts. If they pass, they're in. If they don't, they're out. And if it's borderline, we make a judgement call.

There are three levels of qualification:

1. **Account** – Does the client meet our minimum ICP standard?
2. **Stakeholder** – Will this person be our Executive Sponsor, Champion, or Coach?
3. **Opportunity** – Is there enough value to both us and the client to make this worthwhile?

At the account level we are mostly identifying if the account meets the minimum demographic standard set forth in our ICP.

At the stakeholder level we are determining if the person we are talking to is willing to act as an Executive Sponsor, Champion or Coach and a get us access to all of the other stakeholders that might be involved in the sale. In the next chapter you will learn the exact language you can use to get access to these stakeholders.

At the opportunity level we are going to determine the quality of the opportunity being presented to us. I recommend that you use the simplest methodology that matches your type of sale. There are many methodologies out there including:

- **BANT** – Budget, Authority, Need, Timeframe
- **ANUM** – Authority, Need, Urgency, Money
- **CHAMP** - Challenges, Authority, Money, and Priority
- **FAINT** – Funds (different than budget), Authority, Interest, Need, Timeframe
- **MEDDIC** – Metrics, Economic Buyer, Decision Process, Decision Criteria, Identify Pain, Champion
- **MEDDICC** – Same as above with the addition of "Competition"
- **MEDDPICC** – Metrics, Economic Buyer, Decision Process, Decision Criteria, Paper Process, Identify Pain, Champion, Competition

By now you've discovered that they are all fairly similar in their elements. My favorite for complex sales is MEDDICC and MEDDPICC.

Sidebar on MEDDICC & MEDDPICC

It is important to note that when using many of these frameworks and especially whichever flavor of MEDDICC you might choose to use, don't treat them as checklists to just gather lots of information. Instead, treat them as deal management tools. When you look at each letter, ask yourself, "Do I have the proper information, is my depth of knowledge in this area complete, and have I validated my assumptions with my prospect?" One of the biggest mistakes sellers make is they use these tools to check boxes, instead of treating them as guides to think critically about their deals. Oftentimes you are stuck because you made an assumption in one of these areas that was actually wrong, and the key to unsticking your deal lies in your ability to challenge those assumptions and find the truth.

Let's use MEDDPICC to briefly analyze a deal. Ask yourself the following questions, and where you have answered no, think about what you could do to get that no to a yes.

Metrics: Ask yourself, have I uncovered metrics that the client cares about that I can impact? Have we agreed upon the degree of impact? Does it tie to an executive priority? Have the metrics been turned into a financial business case? Has that case been pressure tested, had risk been removed, and agreed upon by all needed stakeholders including an economic buyer? — The difference here, is that it isn't about the metric, it is about the answers to these questions related to the metric. Deal Management vs. Checklist.

Economic Buyer: Do I have access to power? Have they agreed to sponsor my deal? Have they blessed the business case? Are they willing to allocate budget? Do they see this as a priority?

Decision Criteria: Do I know what they want in a solution? Are we well aligned with what they want?

Decision Process: Do we have a mutual action plan in place? Are we tracking to that plan?

Paper Process: Have we amended our mutual action plan with the legal process? Are we tracking to that revised plan?

Implicate Pain: Have I spoken to all needed stakeholders and understood all their unique pains? Do we understand the ripple effects of the pain across the business? Have we tied pain to metrics? Are there enough people with pain that the problem is hard to ignore?

Champion: Do I have a champion? Do they have access to power? Have I tested them? Have they stayed consistent in their commitment to drive this change?

Competition: Have they agreed on the desire to change? Have they agreed to change now? Do they have resources to implement my solution? Do they have a budget? Do they see my solution as the best fit? Have they stated we are vendor of choice?

My friend, David Weiss has a tool for this called DealDoc where it will ask you questions like these, color code your deal based on your answers, and show you where you have gaps and I highly recommend it.

Whatever Deal Management method you choose to use think critically about each part of your deal and ensure you have pressure tested your assumptions and moved from "I think I know" to "I know". This means asking the tough questions to yourself and your prospects, but therein lies the difference in your ability to remove the barriers that cause deals to stick.

At the minimum I recommend you consider the following elements when qualifying opportunities:

- **Value** – Is there enough value to both of us to make this opportunity worthwhile?
- **Solvability** – Does our solution address the client's challenges and goals?
- **Timeframe** – Does the projected timeframe for closure make this opportunity worth our time and effort?
- **Competition** – Do we have a good chance of winning given the competition involved?

Value

There is a simple way to monetize the value of your offering on your very first call using the 5 Golden Questions you will learn in Chapter 23. This will help both you and your client understand the scope and value of their challenge and allow you to easily qualify them in or out. It also eliminates pricing pressures at the end of the sale.

Solvability

Here we are assessing whether or not our company's solution can actually address the client's challenges and goals. We're not a match for everyone. Can we meet their requirements? Can we deliver in the countries/regions that is required? Do we have the technical and operational resources to implement and support the client? Etc.

Timeframe

Does the projected timeframe for closure make this opportunity worth our time and effort? When do they want to have the solution in place? What is driving that date? What we are looking for here is some outside pressure or impact that is driving the date. It is a concern if the date is too soon or too far out.

Competition

Given the alternatives the customer has, do we have a good chance of winning? Maybe the client is interested in one of your minor offerings that is highly commoditized. Is it going to be worth the time and energy to compete on this low margin opportunity? More on competition in Chapter 15.

If the opportunity does not qualify you may still have a chance to make it worthwhile. Is it possible to change the scope, timeframe, or our competitive position? If so, maybe they qualify now. The best strategy for accomplishing this is to deliver insight to the client in a way that shifts their paradigm and by extension changes the opportunity.

Using our example above, perhaps the client looking for your highly commoditized offering is unaware that new trends or regulations are going to make that solution alone no longer viable and that additional considerations are warranted. If this insight triggers an "ah-ha" moment, they may be willing to consider your other offerings that are more highly differentiated.

These types of insights are the number one way you add value to the selling process itself and we have discussed this at length in Chapter 9 of The Perfect Close.

How to Withdraw Gracefully

If you've concluded that it's time to walk away, do so politely and professionally. It's a very small world. Disengage in a way that still leaves your relationship intact. Here are some tips:

- Thank them for their time.
- Let them know you've enjoyed working with them.
- Let them know why you are going to pass for now.
- Keep it brief.
- Leave the door open.

Here's a verbal example:

"I appreciate our time together just now. Based on what you've shared, I don't think we'd be a good match for what you're looking for. [optional – I do think you might be a good match for ABC or XYZ company. So, you might want to explore that.] I've certainly enjoyed getting to know you and it would be great to work together, so if things change just let me know. I'd be happy to help."

And here's an email example:

"Craig, thank you so much for your time. It has been wonderful getting to know your team. It's been an enjoyable experience for me. After careful reflection with my team, we feel like given the current circumstances it will be challenging for us to craft a solution for you that works for everyone. So for that reason, we are going to pass on this opportunity for now. Things always change, so please keep us in mind for any future opportunities. It would be wonderful to work together with you and your team."

You can see these are completely devoid of drama. The reasons we are withdrawing are generic in these examples. Replace these with the more specific reasons for your specific circumstances.

Sometimes clients will come back after you deliver the message. If the client can somehow change the situation so that it becomes a win for you – great. But that's not what these are intended for. You learned how to create disengage messages in Chapter 8.

In this case, we are sending this message precisely because this opportunity is a bad use of our time. It might be bad for numerous other reasons as well. The client's willingness to engage us is not the issue. It's about us recognizing that we only want to invest in opportunities that create great value for both parties.

Summary

Targeting is primarily a prevention strategy. We can't un-target a stuck opportunity. By the time we have a stuck opportunity and realize that it is an opportunity we shouldn't have been pursuing in the first place, the horse has already left the barn. We can plan better for next time, but for now, we'll have to evaluate this deal for what it is and that is usually a combination of the other three reasons deals get stuck.

That means we take the deal at face value and evaluate it based on what you'll learn in upcoming chapters.

Deals that are stuck because of bad targeting are prone to having issues around Client Indecision and Business Case. And we will dive into that in detail in Parts 5 and 6.

In the next chapter will discuss a massive cause for stalled deals in complex sales and give you the key insights for succeeding in sales with multiple stakeholders.

If your type of sale is less complex and does not involve multiple stakeholders, I encourage you to skip to chapter 14.

CHAPTER 11

UNSTICKING DEALS CAUSED BY STAKEHOLDER MANAGEMENT

"Today's sales environment is one of managing for stakeholders. The professional's task is to create as much value as possible for stakeholders without resorting to trade-offs."

- JAMES MUIR

The Big Ideas:

- Stakeholder management issues are a huge contributor to stalled deals.
- Know how to identify the right stakeholders, how to access those stakeholders, and how to be comfortable having conversations with them.
- Two critical concepts essential for good stakeholder management are: Win-Win and Win-Results.
- Business Results create Personal Wins. Know how to uncover Personal Wins for stakeholders.

Wrong or Incomplete Stakeholders

For complex sales, engaging the wrong stakeholders, or not engaging all the appropriate stakeholders is a massive cause of stalled deals. It's right up there with bad targeting for being the top cause of stalled deals. If your type of sale has only one or two stakeholders and can be completed in one or two meetings move on to Chapter 14 now.

For complex sales, however, not knowing or engaging all the appropriate stakeholders is a big deal so we are going to drill down on this a bit.

5 Things That Make Sales Complex

What makes a sale complex in the first place? There are many things actually. Here are the top 5:

1. The client has multiple stakeholders.
2. The organization's buying process is complex.
3. The client has many options.

4. The client has many priorities.

5. The seller has many options & nuances.

All these things are important factors. Multiple stakeholders is the number one item on the list. And that's because it's the biggest, and very often the most difficult.

Deals are very often won or lost based on the quality of our stakeholder management. That is why it is vital that we hone our stakeholder management skills. Managing stakeholders can be challenging sometimes. It can be hard to identify who all the key stakeholders are. It can be hard to gain access to them. And it can sometimes be hard to have conversations with them.

> It is not hyperbole to say that complex selling literally is stakeholder management.

It is not hyperbole to say that complex selling literally is stakeholder management. I estimate that in complex sales, somewhere around 80% of all stalled opportunities can be traced back to this one thing. We will address all three of the above challenges coming up. Before we do, however, let us cover some foundational principles of complex sales.

NOTE: Again, if you are not involved in complex selling, simply skip to the next chapter.

Managing Stakeholders – Foundational Principles of Complex Selling

The average number of stakeholders in a complex sale is between 6 to 10 stakeholders and can often go much higher. [1] This is one of the key differences between simple and complex sales and has a new set of rules that you may not be familiar with if you started your career with less complex sales. This is not a book on how to manage complex sales from A to Z. But complex deals frequently stall out because of the issues unique to complex sales. For that reason, I will briefly cover some of the foundational principles of complex sales.

For those interested in a more comprehensive approach you will find several recommendations in the Recommended Reading section at the back of this book.

Principle 1 – Organizations don't buy things. People buy things.

And the first key point is that Organizations don't buy things. People buy things. Each stakeholder will need to be evaluated independently.

In complex sales we often speak of selling to an organization (like Dell, IBM or Banner Health). And that's ok. It's a convenient way of referring to

the opportunity. We might even characterize their culture by saying, "Oh ABC company is cheap." Or something like that. But the truth is, we're NOT really selling to an organization. We are selling to the stakeholders within that organization.

So, it's important that we think about the individuals within an organization rather than the organization itself.

Principle 2 – Risk/Reward decisions are made by each stakeholder independently.

Our next principle is that risk/reward decisions are made by each stakeholder independently. We'd all love it to be true that we could just pile all stakeholders into the same room and with a single presentation persuade all stakeholders at once. But in reality, each individual stakeholder has their own unique perspective on the opportunity and what their personal risk and reward will be. That means that we need to manage and sell to each stakeholder independently and make sure that each one is winning, and that all risks and uncertainty issues are addressed.

Principle 3 – Each stakeholder has differing perspectives and degrees of influence.

Our next key principle is that each stakeholder has differing perspectives and degrees of influence. This means that the wins for each individual stakeholder will be different and personal. Reduced human resource costs may be a benefit for the CEO and CFO but may be perceived as a loss by the COO if that means they have to do more with less resources.

This difference in perspective, and the differing roles that each stakeholder has, also means that the power stakeholders have to cause a deal to succeed, or stall can be wildly lopsided. Which brings us to our next key principle.

Principle 4 – Any sufficiently influential stakeholder can cause a deal to stick.

Regardless of title or role, any sufficiently influential stakeholder can cause a deal to get stuck. This is why we need to manage all stakeholders. Don't assume you know the degree of influence a stakeholder has based on their title alone. An operational stakeholder that may be using your product or service daily may have more influence than the CEO. A nearly invisible stakeholder may have a disproportionate level of influence because of a relationship with others in the organization.

This dynamic works both ways. We might have a stakeholder who is an adversary and opposes our offering, but if we have support of the key stakeholders with more influence, we can often drive the deal through anyway.

But don't count on it. Today's management is very consensus-driven, so a stakeholder with a surprisingly low degree of influence can often hang a deal. The best strategy is to evaluate and sell to each stakeholder independently.

While there are many more dynamics when it comes to complex selling, these four foundational principles will take you a long way toward understanding stakeholder management and the dynamics that cause complex sales to get stuck. Ahead, we will discuss in detail the challenges associated with Client Indecision and Business Case issues.

Foundational Principles of Complex Selling	
Principle 1	Organizations don't buy things. People buy things.
Principle 2	Risk/Reward decisions are made by each stakeholder independently.
Principle 3	Each stakeholder has differing perspectives and degrees of influence.
Principle 4	Any sufficiently influential stakeholder can cause a deal to stick.

Figure 11-1: Foundational Principles of Complex Selling

How to Know if Stakeholder Management is Your Root Cause

To assess whether or not wrong or incomplete stakeholders is the root cause of your stalled opportunity ask yourself questions like these:

Stakeholder Management Assessment Questions
- Do I know all the key stakeholders relevant to this opportunity?
- Am I able to freely navigate to all stakeholders?
- Have I engaged and spoken-to every stakeholder?
- Is my initial/primary contact the correct, ideal entry point?
- Are there any new or hidden stakeholders I should be aware of?
- Do I know the role and degree of influence each stakeholder has?
- Do I know the attitude of each stakeholder for this opportunity?
- Do I know the Win-Results for each stakeholder for this opportunity?
- Have I identified any other red-flags or concerns for individual stakeholders?

Figure 11-2: Stakeholder Management Assessment Questions

Stakeholder Management Assessment Questions

- Do I know all the key stakeholders relevant to this opportunity? If we are not confident that we know all the key stakeholders involved, that is a major risk and a cause for concern.
- Am I able to freely navigate to all stakeholders? If not, this is a cause for concern. We will discuss how to get to those stakeholders ahead.
- Have I engaged and spoken to every stakeholder? If not, then this is a major risk and a cause for concern.
- Is my initial/primary contact the correct, ideal entry point? If not, we may be operating with a handicap. How we enter a deal, and who sponsors us around makes a big difference.
- Are there any new or hidden stakeholders I should be aware of? Again, if you're not confident, that is a concern.
- Do I know the role and degree of influence each stakeholder has? You should know both things. If this is a new concept for you, we will explore both in just a moment. What we're really asking here is who has the juice here and what is their perspective on your initiative?
- Do I know the attitude of each stakeholder for this opportunity? You need to know this for each stakeholder.
- Do I know the Win-Results for each stakeholder for this opportunity? (i.e., what are their criteria for a personal win) All stakeholder wins are personal. If you do not know this for each stakeholder, it is a cause for concern.
- Have I identified any other red-flags or concerns for individual stakeholders? There are many things that can be issues of concern for stake-

holders. It is important that we take the time to explore this for each stakeholder.

If our deal is stuck, and we have negative answers in any of these areas, that suggests that we probably have a wrong or incomplete stakeholder issue as our root cause.

Strategies for Wrong or Incomplete Stakeholders

We just discussed the five primary things that make deals complex. At the top of that list is having multiple stakeholders. That is why it is vital that we hone our stakeholder management skills.

Complex selling is stakeholder management. I estimate that in complex sales, somewhere around 80% of all stalled opportunities can be traced back to this one thing.

The 3 Core Challenges of Stakeholder Management

There are three core challenges professionals face when dealing with stakeholder management.

1. **Can't Identify** - We're having challenges identifying who our stakeholders are.
2. **Getting Blocked** - We know who our stakeholders are but we're getting blocked from having interactions with them.
3. **Uncomfortable** - We're uncomfortable when working with certain stakeholders so we tend to avoid interacting with them.

Let's address each one.

Figure 11-3: The 3 Core Challenges of Stakeholder Management

How to Identify Stakeholders

Identifying all the appropriate stakeholders in a complex sale can be a big challenge. The larger the organization, the more challenging it becomes.

As challenging as this can be at times, when you boil it all the way down, there are really just three approaches or strategies to address this challenge.

1. Ask The Stakeholder Directly - When we have access to stakeholders, we can ask them directly if they are involved in the process or initiative. You'll always get a direct answer. "Yes, I am." or "No, I'm not." If they say "yes", great, mission accomplished. If they say no, then we use this opportunity to turn this stakeholder into an executive sponsor and get introductions to the other key stakeholders.

As I was writing this chapter, this just happened to me with a large university on the west coast. The person I asked was not directly going to be involved in the process, but they were going to be kept apprised of the process and he agreed to introduce me to the correct stakeholders. So just by asking directly, he became an executive sponsor for me and possibly a coach – time will tell.

2. Ask Our Champion or Coach - When we have established a champion or coach, we can simply ask them who all the stakeholders are. This is a great approach and probably the most common. All we need to do is ask something like: "In addition to yourself, who else will be impacted by this initiative?" There's also a version of this question where we ask, "Who, in addition to yourself, will be involved in the decision-making process?" That's a good question, but in my experience, it's better to ask "who will be impacted" because it will get you a broader list of stakeholders that could affect the outcome. Then, as a second step, we can ask which ones will be part of the decision-making process. Either way, asking our Champion or Coach who the stakeholders are is an excellent approach.

"In addition to yourself, who else will be impacted by this initiative."

3. Infer or Guess - The last, and least desirable approach, is that we can infer by a stakeholder's title, or guess based on what we see in tools like LinkedIn, ZoomInfo and other specialized tools. As undesirable as this approach is, I would say that it is very common. Sometimes justifiably so. When most of our lead generation is coming from cold outreach, the inference or guessing is taking place at the targeting stage and before we've had any contact. So it's not surprising that it's hard to identify the correct stakeholders when we guessed in our outreach to begin with. (See how targeting affects everything?)

Once we do gain access to someone, the goal will be to turn them into a coach or sponsor and have them introduce us to the rest of the appropriate stakeholders.

A Tip That Will Make You Incredibly Successful

Would you like to eliminate this problem forever and improve your close ratios 400-500% ? Here›s how...

If you begin your sales process with a referral or introduction, you will always have that initial stakeholder you need to get the introductions to everyone else. Not only that, a referral, or even just an introduction is an implied endorsement so you will have all the benefits of a built-in reference right at the beginning.

Here are 17 reasons why referrals and introductions are positively the best lead channel:

1. Information from referral sources is trusted far more than other sources.
2. Referrals, convert to opportunities far better than any other source (700-800% better - nothing else is even close)
3. Referrals convert to sales better. (400-500% better)
4. Referrals and introductions come with an implied endorsement.
5. Referrals are far more likely to result in appointments (500% better)
6. Referrals, on average, have higher deal value (13% more than non-referred)
7. Referrals have shorter sales cycles.
8. Referred customers are more loyal than non-referred customers.
9. Referred customers have higher lifetime value (16-25% more than non-referred)
10. Referred customers object less.
11. Referred customers are less likely to ask for concessions.
12. Referrals and introductions typically eliminate competition because we are the ones creating the timing (as opposed to the client)
13. Getting referrals trains clients to give referrals.
14. Referrals are one of the lowest-cost lead generation strategies there is.
15. Receiving referrals strengthens client relationships by reminding them of why they chose to go with us in the first place.

16. Data shows that referrals are the #1 driver of consumer purchase decisions at every single stage of the purchase cycle, across every single product category.

17. Referrals are the most enjoyable way to generate new business.

Exactly how to leverage referrals to generate the majority of your business will be the subject of a future work. The point here, is that we could add an 18th item on this list if we include that leveraging a referral or introduction to begin your sales process, will eliminate the challenges of guessing who stakeholders are - because you'll have an executive sponsor right from the beginning.

How to Access Stakeholders When You Are Being Blocked

Sometimes we're able to identify the stakeholder we want to engage, but we're getting blocked from meeting with them. There are lots of ways this happens. In most cases, the root that is causing us to get blocked is lack of trust and some sort of fear. That is, the person blocking us fears some possible outcome of our connecting with the stakeholder, even if that's just wasting the other stakeholder's time.

Interestingly, regardless of the root cause, there are just three approaches we can take when we're getting blocked:

1. Show the Blocker How to Win - The first approach (and by far the best) is we can show the blocker how to win. That is, we explain why it's in their best interest for us to meet with the stakeholder. And I'll give you some ways to do this in just a second.

2. Go Around the Blocker - The second option is to go around the blocker. Sometimes this is the only option if the blocker won't budge. When considering whether we want to go around the blocker, the key question to ask is: "What's the risk?" Will our blocker become an enemy? Or is it possible they will be relieved? I've seen both happen. In most cases we don't want to go around the blocker unless we have nothing to lose. But if you've got some skills, there's an exception to this. Here it is:

If you can arrange for a random circumstance where you happen to encounter the stakeholder you're being blocked from, your engagement will appear as a coincidence, and it won't raise the ire of your blocker.

I remember getting blocked from being introduced to an Executive Director at a large multispecialty group in CA. So, I did some homework and uncovered a state society meeting that the executive director was attending. In fact, the executive director was speaking. So, I had us attend the event as a sponsor, we listened to her talk and went up and talked with her after their session. And after we complimented her on her session, we tied her message back to the fact that we were working with her team. She said she was aware of the initiative, so we asked what her goals were regarding the project, and she gave us some very valuable information right then and there.

Here's the funny thing, when we told the COO who had been blocking us that we bumped into the Executive Director at the show, instead of freaking out, he said, "Oh, that's awesome! I'm so glad. What did she say?" He was actually relieved! So, with a little finesse, it's not a given that going around the blocker is going to burn a bridge. They might just be afraid for some reason.

3. Go Along With the Blocker - The third and last option is just to go along with the blocker. Again, the key question here is: "What›s the risk?" If the risk here is high, (for example, you might lose a departmental deal, but still maintain your ability to sell throughout the enterprise) it might be worth living with and just operating with a handicap on this deal, and not having the input and feedback from this stakeholder.

Tips & Tricks

Option #1 is the best. How can we show the blocker how to win?

There are many ways. Here is my favorite: Ask the blocker a question that only the stakeholder can answer.

Here is a real-world example: I was working with a large hospital system in the northwest and a clinic they had acquired was already a client and wanted to bring on another clinic with different specialties that would essentially double their size. Rather than allow me to speak to the new clinic executives, I was forced to talk to a purchaser. If you're not familiar with what I'm talking about, in healthcare, and other industries a purchaser is someone who negotiates with vendors on behalf of the system to purchase materials and supplies at the lowest price.

So, I took this as a good sign because it probably meant that the system was going to make the purchase, they were just trying to give me a haircut. The problem was this guy knew nothing about complex IT systems.

I did make an appeal to talk to the new clinic executives, but this guy wasn't having it. So, we talked, and we explored all the different areas they might save some money on the proposal. And I was honestly looking for ways to save them money on each line item on the proposal. For each line-item I'd say

> Just ask the blocker questions that only the stakeholder can answer. Then the blocker will either liaison for you or cave-in and schedule a meeting with your stakeholder.

something like: "Oh, we might be able to save you some money there. Tell me how you are doing X? Maybe we can use what you are doing now." To which he would not know the answer and would say he'd have to get back to me. This went on for dozens of items on the proposal until he finally got embarrassed and suggested, "Why don't I set up a time for us to talk to [so and so, and so and so - the executives at the new clinic] and then we can bang this all out at once."

You're a genius! I thought. (with a smile on my face) And I ended up getting access to the stakeholders I wanted.

Now, technically, I wasn't really showing him how to win here – I was just showing him how not to lose. Because making any one of those decisions incorrectly could have been very costly for them.

Let me simplify this for you a bit: Just ask the blocker questions that only the stakeholder can answer. Then the blocker will either liaison for you or cave-in and schedule a meeting.

Another similar approach, that uses the same psychology is to say, "This seems like an important project. Is there any chance the [CEO, CFO, COO, or whatever] is going to want a say on this? Does it make sense to schedule a couple of minutes with them so we can get their input and feedback?"

This simple question has worked for me to get meetings with key executives 90% of the time.

What to Do When You're Uncomfortable

The third stakeholder challenge is that sometimes we feel uncomfortable or intimidated by meeting with certain stakeholders. The basic strategy is simple: Get

> "This seems like an important project. Is there any chance the [CEO or other stakeholder] is going to want a say on this? Does it make sense to schedule a couple of minutes with them so we can get their input and feedback?"

comfortable having conversations with all types of stakeholders. Experienced professionals tend not to have this problem, but just in case you're new, here are some considerations that will help.

First, just remember that all stakeholders, regardless of title or demeanor, are still just human beings. Focus on the things you have in common. We are all more alike than we are different.

Next, know what this stakeholder is interested in professionally. What are the typical issues, challenges, and goals of a stakeholder in this role?

Have a Valid Business Reason to meet. Why is it important that you meet with this stakeholder? How does your meeting with this stakeholder help them achieve their goal?

Be prepared and don't waste time. Get right to your valid business reason. At this level, stakeholders are not looking for a relationship. They have tons of relationships already. At this stage it's all business. It might develop into a relationship over time, but initially, be prepared and get quickly to the relevant issues.

Understand the stakeholders Win-Results. (more on that below) Remember, all wins are personal. Consider what the personal wins will be for this stakeholder.

Feeling uncomfortable about meeting with certain stakeholders usually manifests itself when we're selling to a title we don't fully understand. So, the key is to simply understand all our typical stakeholders. Know their typical issues, challenges, and goals.

It will help dramatically if you learn the language and buzzwords for each stakeholder role.

And to help you with that I'm going to recommend two books for you. The first is: **Selling to the C-Suite: What Every Executive Wants You to Know About Successfully Selling to the Top** by Nicholas A.C. Read. And the second is: **The Key to the C-Suite: What You Need to Know to Sell Successfully to Top Executives** by Michael J. Nick

Both books are phenomenal, and I recommend reading them in this order.

Finally, always remember that the only reason we are meeting with them is because we're trying to help them achieve their goals. That is a noble purpose and something to be proud of. If you remember this and focus on serving well, it will make all your meetings much more enjoyable.

Win–Win and Win Results

The concept of win-win and win-results dates to the 1960s. Mirriam-Webster lists its first recorded use in 1962 by Victor Branco, but the concept did not become generally popular until the publishing of **The 7 Habits of Highly Effective People** by Stephen R. Covey in 1989. (Think Win-Win is habit #4) The concept was applied specifically to selling in Miller-Heiman's landmark book, **Strategic Selling** which I highly recommend. In today's current selling environment, the concepts of Win-Win and Win-Results are absolutely vital and more important than ever. So we will cover them both here briefly.

Win–Win

A Win-Win arrangement is a situation where all parties benefit. There are no losers. There are times when it is possible to close business that is Win-Lose. That is, either the customer or we end up losing in some way. All professionals operate on a Win-Win basis.

> **Win–Win** - An arrangement or situation where all parties benefit. There are no losers.

Here's the truth: All forms of Win-Lose eventually deteriorate into Lose-Lose.

For example, a business arrangement that is Win-Lose where we win, but the client loses still creates feelings and attitudes. Our relationship will be affected. We may get what we want now, but will our client be willing to do business with us again? And what will the ongoing relationship be like? We've all sold deals we wish we hadn't because of how difficult the client can be. And sometimes these clients even become anti-references and make trouble for us wherever they go. Our short-term win will actually become a long-term lose.

What about Lose-Win? Again, when we allow a client to win at our expense, we are planting the seeds of failure in some form. Not only may our feelings and attitude be affected, but there may also be genuine business ramifications that make the business relationship unsustainable. The client may appear to get what they want for the mo-

All forms of win–lose eventually deteriorate into lose–lose.

All forms of win-lose eventually
deteriorate into lose-lose.

Figure 11-4: All forms of win-lose eventually deteriorate into lose-lose.

ment. But how will a loss on our part impact our willingness and ability to fulfill the contract on an ongoing basis? So we are at Lose-Lose again.

All forms of win-lose eventually deteriorate into Lose-Lose and Lose-Lose isn't viable in any context.

Win-Win is the only viable scenario. We must consider our client's situation and point of view in both the sales process and solution creation. If it's not a win for both of us, we both lose. This is why all professionals operate on a Win-Win basis.

So the rule is: It's Win-Win or no-deal. We'd rather walk away, than accept an arrangement where someone loses on either side.

Does this make sense? We'd rather walk away than accept an arrangement where someone else loses because any form of win-lose will eventually deteriorate into lose-lose.

The Rule Win-Win or No Deal

Here are the rules for playing Win-Win with clients:

- Be completely open and transparent in communications.
- **Both sides need to play win-win.** If you're playing with a win-lose prospect, walk away. All forms of Win-Lose eventually deteriorate into Lose-Lose.
- **Our solution must genuinely be a fit**. If it's not, then introduce partners so it becomes a fit. Or walk away. We would never sell something that won't address the customer's issue or help them achieve their goal.
- <u>You</u> **are the one responsible to make sure everything is Win-Win.** Clients sometimes don't know better. As the change agent, it's <u>your</u> job to make sure everyone wins.
- **It's Win-Win or no deal.** We don't involve ourselves in win-lose opportunities.

With this background you are now ready for the next concept.

Win-Results

All wins are personal.

Even though we are producing results for the company (usually financial results), the wins that each stakeholder experiences are personal. This is an extremely important concept and the reason why we need to consider and manage each stakeholder separately. Many stuck opportunities can be traced back to this exact issue. We need to make sure that the solution is going to be Win-Win for each stakeholder.

Win-Results Dynamics

What follows are the basic dynamics of Win-Results. Once you understand and leverage these dynamics, your success will go way up.

First, each stakeholder is looking for a **business result** that gives them a **personal win**. An important distinction here is that **businesses get results, stakeholders get wins**. Said another way, stakeholders selfishly, look for business results that create personal wins for themselves.

The next key concept is that stakeholders win in their own individual ways. It differs from individual to individual. I know this seems obvious, but in workshops people get confused with this concept all the time. **Your win** is different from the **stakeholder's win**. Don't project your win onto stakeholders.

Next, successful sales require more than just focusing on results. The human element cannot be ignored. (Companies don't buy things, people buy things. Remember?) We need to understand what the personal wins are for stakeholders. In fact, understanding and creating personal wins for your stakeholders is a critical part of your sales strategy. And when you combine these two things, you'll be coming from a very strong position of strength.

Next, when we connect our solution to our stakeholder's personal wins, it becomes differentiating - at least for that stakeholder. Because

> Successful sales requires more than just focusing on results. We need to understand the personal wins for each stakeholder.

they see our solution as a means to attain their personal win.

I just boiled down several hours of training into one short section. You can read more about these dynamics in **Strategic Selling** and the other titles in the Recommended Reading section. These are the dynamics that make the stakeholder machine work. If you apply what you see here, it will make a big difference for you.

The Key Stakeholder Management Question

This brings us to our key stakeholder management question. As you are reviewing each stakeholder in your opportunity, I want you to ask yourself this question: What are the specific **business results** I need to produce, to create a **personal win** for this stakeholder?

Creating a win for each stakeholder is the key to long-lasting relationships. By answering this key question, you are literally tying these two critical sales strategies together - Business Results and Personal Wins.

> What are the specific business results I need to produce, to create a personal win for this stakeholder?

Business Results

I know you will be shocked by this, but Win-Results are made up of two parts: Wins and Results. Lol. Or perhaps to clarify even further, maybe we should say "Personal Wins and Business Results". Results are the Business Results that our solution delivers.

Our solution may consist of tools, expertise, resources, insights etc. that a customer can invest in. Those tools and expertise are then applied to the customer's processes to deliver improved results. And those results are typically manifested in terms of improved Time, Money, or Resource utilization. (see the graphic below – you'll see why it flows from right to left in a moment.)

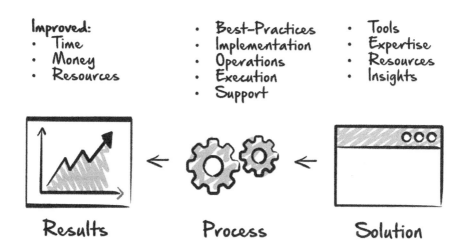

Improved:
- Time
- Money
- Resources

- Best-Practices
- Implementation
- Operations
- Execution
- Support

- Tools
- Expertise
- Resources
- Insights

Results   **Process**   **Solution**

Figure 11–5: Our solution delivers improved results typically measured in terms of time, money, or resources.

It's important to remember here that customers invest in results – not products. The product is simply a means to an end.

Personal Wins

Then we have Wins. Again, perhaps a clearer way to say this is "Personal Wins". A Personal Win is the condition that appeals to the stakeholder's self-interest. They are, in fact, the reason why stakeholders buy.

> **Personal Win** – A condition that appeals to the stakeholder's self-interest.

So, we have our various stakeholders. (CEOs, CFOs, COOs, etc.) And each of those has their own selfish, personal self-interests. These include things like security, ego/status and importance, being recognized socially, a feeling of belonging, a desire to avoid loss, a desire to serve others, and more. You get the idea.

A Personal Win is when a condition is created, that appeals or satisfies, our stakeholder's self-interest.

As outside agents, we create those conditions by producing business results. Said another way: Business Results create Personal Wins. And you can see that illustrated here by the arrow that flows from Results to Personal Win.

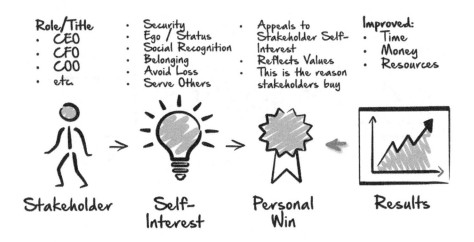

Figure 11–6: A Personal Win is when a condition is created, that appeals or satisfies, our stakeholder's self-interest.

One of the biggest tools in our stakeholder management toolbox is to enhance our **offer** so that it delivers a result that creates a Personal Win for each individual stakeholder. I'm getting ahead here, but it is one of the strategies we can use to unstick deals.

The challenge is, personal wins are sometimes hard to identify, precisely because they are personal. And stakeholders are sometimes cautious or uncomfortable sharing. More on this in a moment.

Personal wins tend to fall into categories like: achievement, autonomy, belonging, ego, loss avoidance, mastery, order, power, recognition, security, status, etc.

Win-Results

Here you see the whole formula all together where the right side meets the left.

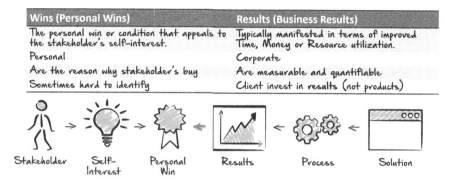

Wins (Personal Wins)	Results (Business Results)
The personal win or condition that appeals to the stakeholder's self-interest.	Typically manifested in terms of improved Time, Money or Resource utilization.
Personal	Corporate
Are the reason why stakeholder's buy	Are measurable and quantifiable
Sometimes hard to identify	Client invest in results (not products)

Stakeholder → Self-Interest → Personal Win ← Results ← Process ← Solution

Business Results Create Personal Wins

Figure 11–7: Business results create personal wins.

The key takeaway here is that Business Results Create Personal Wins. And if we have identified that stakeholder management is the root cause of our stuck deal, one of the biggest tools in our stakeholder management toolbox is to enhance our offer so that it delivers the result that creates a personal win for each individual stakeholder. And I'll give you some examples of that coming up.

Discovering Stakeholder Personal Wins

Here's how to discover what each stakeholder's personal win is. You basically have three options:

1. Ask the Stakeholder Directly
2. Ask Our Coach or Champion
3. Infer Based on What we Know About the Stakeholder

"Just curious, this seems like a big project, what's the win in it for you? Personally..."

By far the best strategy here is simply to ask the stakeholder directly. This is where your interpersonal sales skills are going to come into play, because it is the trust and relationship part of what we're doing that makes the stakeholders want to share these personal details.

An approach that works very well, is simply to act slightly surprised or confused about why a stakeholder would even want to be involved in a project like this and then ask something like: "Just curious, this seems like a big project, what's the win in it for you? Personally..."

However you decide to word your question, the basic gist is: Man, from a personal perspective, why would you want to even pursue something like this? So, it's a "why" question without the "why".

After listening to their response, we can ask: "Well, what **would** make this a personal win for you?" with the emphasis on the "would". We're basically asking what scenario or outcome creates a personal win for you. We're just asking in a way that is more diplomatic. If your rapport is high enough, you might just ask it that way, "What scenario or outcome makes this a personal win for you?" A lot of times stakeholders that have had some experience in sales respond very well to this more direct approach.

These questions are best done in a one-on-one conversation and not in a group because in a group people tend not to share this type of stuff. There are political dynamics interfering. But in one-on-ones, I have gotten spectacular information with these questions.

Discovering Personal Wins – Real–World Examples

I have combined several of the sometimes-mind-blowing responses I've gotten in the past here so you can see how valuable this question is. My apologies if they are overly healthcare related since that is my background. I think you'll easily see how they can be applied to your type of sale. Here are half-a-dozen real-world examples of how this question works.

As you read through these, ask yourself these questions:

- What is the personal win for this stakeholder?
- What else does this response tell us about the dynamic of our deal?
- How might we change our offering to meet this stakeholder's need (i.e., create a win)?

These are all responses to this question: "Just curious, this seems like a big project, what's the win in it for you? Personally..."

Example 1

- **Comment:** "We HAVE to make this work. If we don't improve our A/R they're going to outsource the whole thing."
- **What's the personal win for this stakeholder?** [Security]
- **What else did we just learn?** [this is make or break, a lot of people's jobs might be affected, support across all stakeholders is probably high,

there is a strong desire to make this work]

■ **How might we change our offering to meet this stakeholder's need (i.e., create a win)?** [Guarantees, responsibilities given to stakeholder (sidebar – isn't it interesting how in one context giving a stakeholder additional responsibility is bad (increased workload) but in another context it is good? (job security)]

Example 2

■ **Comment:** "There isn't one. If anything, it just means more work for me. I really don't have much say anyway."

■ **What's the personal win for this stakeholder?** [Nothing]

■ **What else did we just learn?** [this person is an opponent, but doesn't have much influence]

■ **How might we change our offering to meet this stakeholder's need (i.e., create a win)?** [perhaps explain that it will be less work, not more, maybe they will learn a new skill which will make them even more valuable and provide additional influence and job security, ask them what *would* make this a personal win for them]

Example 3

■ **Comment:** "Look, they hired me to turn this place around and I'm looking for any way I can do that."

■ **What's the personal win for this stakeholder?** [Ego, Status, Importance, Security, Social Recognition]

■ **What else did we just learn?** [this person's job is to produce the result our solution affects greatly, they were hired specifically for that purpose, security is on the line as well]

■ **How might we change our offering to meet this stakeholder's need (i.e., create a win)?** [Maximize Muchness, Soonness & Sureness]

Example 4

■ **Comment:** "This thing is going nowhere just like every other initiative. Honestly, it would make my life much easier, but these kinds of things never get completed."

■ **What's the personal win for this stakeholder?** [Reduced Workload (and whatever impact that brings)]

- **What else did we just learn?** [this person is an advocate, but something internally tends to kill these types of deals]
- **How might we change our offering to meet this stakeholder's need (i.e., create a win)?** [Make them a coach, get help navigating organization, explore the impact of making "life much easier"]

Example 5

- **Comment:** "I might actually be moving to a different organization soon, so it's not that big a deal. But a success here would be a nice thing to put on my resume."
- **What's the personal win for this stakeholder?** [Land New Job – Increased Income, Ego/Status/Importance, Security]
- **What else did we just learn?** [this person is disengaged and apathetic, they are not an enemy but not an advocate either]
- **How might we change our offering to meet this stakeholder's need (i.e., create a win)?** [Succeed and give them some resume eye-candy, maybe turn them into a coach]

Example 6

- **Comment:** "We catch all this stuff already. I really don't see the point. We should focus on X."
- **What's the personal win for this stakeholder?** [None, they may even be a threat]
- **What else did we just learn?** [this person doesn't see value in the initiative, it's possible our solution is a threat to them]
- **How might we change our offering to meet this stakeholder's need (i.e., create a win)?** [Ask: What *would* make this a personal win for you? Discover a personal win. Explain differences between how they are "catching all this stuff already" and what we do. Position solution as enhancing their personal value.]

Strategies for Managing Stakeholders

To this point we've discussed strategies for identifying and engaging stakeholders, we've covered Win-Win and Win-Results at length, with just a touch of how to apply some of these concepts to create wins for our stakeholder using our offer. This following chapter applies primarily to complex sales with many stakeholders. If your sale typically has less than two stakeholders, you are welcome to skip the next chapter.

If your sale involves multiple stakeholders, then I briefly remind you that 80% of complex sales stalls are due to stakeholder management issues. So a major strategy we are about to apply, is adding some rigor to our stakeholder management process.

Summary

In this chapter we begin to answer the question, "How do I know which play or plays to use for my stuck deal?". The key to selecting the right play or plays is identifying the root cause and, in this chapter, we discussed the top sales-related issue that causes stalled deals for complex sales: Stakeholder Management.

We have invested a significant amount of time discussing stakeholder management because it is such a huge contributor to stalled deals. We've discussed how to Identify the right stakeholders, how to access those stakeholders when we get blocked and what to do when we're uncomfortable having conversations with them.

We've reviewed two critical concepts that are essential for good stakeholder management - Win-Win and Win-Results. We've uncovered the important principle that Business Results create Personal Wins for stakeholders and discussed how to uncover the Personal Wins for stakeholders.

In the next chapter we will expand our understanding of stakeholder management and learn some powerful tools for managing stakeholders and how to use those tools to unstick our stalled deals.

CHAPTER 12

CREATING STAKEHOLDER MAPS AND WORKING THE GRID

"If we cannot identify, engage, and align all key stakeholders, the most likely outcome
- and our strongest competitor - is often a decision to simply stick with the status quo.
It's no wonder that fewer than 50% of forecasted deals close as predicted."

- BOB APOLLO

The Big Idea: Stakeholder Maps are useful tools for improving the quality of your stakeholder management.

Creating Stakeholder Maps

One of your top strategies for both managing and unsticking deals is creating a stakeholder map. A stakeholder map identifies all your possible stakeholders, their role and degree of influence, their attitude toward your initiative, their win-results and our strategy to help them win. You can see an example of a stakeholder map in the figure below.

We use the stakeholder map to systematically review our standing with each stakeholder in our opportunity. This helps us align better with each stakeholder, add new stakeholders when needed, and most importantly it helps us clearly see gaps in our understanding and strategy that are easy to miss when we try and keep this in our heads. Gaps in understanding and strategy cause stuck and lost deals. Our stakeholder map will help you prevent both and identify strategies you can employ to unstick your opportunities.

Working The Grid

Because a stakeholder map tends to look like a spreadsheet, my mentor Mahan Khalsa affectionately referred to creating and completing the stakeholder map as "Working the grid". We will now use a de-identified example of an actual stuck deal to teach you working the grid. The solution being sold here was a healthcare IT system that improves financial performance and reduces risk.

Creating Your Stakeholder Map

There are both software and pre-printed forms out there to help you create your stakeholder map. If you like these, by all means, use them. All you really need is a pen and paper or a spreadsheet. We will be using the pen and paper method in our example.

To create your stakeholder map you will need eight columns. Those columns are:

1. Stakeholder Name
2. Role
3. Influence
4. Attitude
5. Rating
6. Win-Results
7. Date Met
8. Strategy

The number of rows you need depends on the average number of stakeholders in your type of sale. You probably won't need more than a dozen, but you will need room enough to add notes in the "Win-Results" and "Strategy" columns.

Here is an example of working the grid.

Stakeholder	Role	Influence	Attitude	Rating	Win-Results	Met	Strategy
Michael Firkins	CEO	High	Growth	7	Improving financial results will accomplish something his predecessor was unable to do and help new CEO validate the board's recent hire of him. (Ego, Security)	1/25	Share the story of Marty at ABC and how his success with our solution there generated $X and got him coverage in the local news and Becker's.
Jake Lee	CFO	High	Trouble	6	Jake was here with the previous CEO and is concerned that the focus is now on him. Improving financial results will deliver the job security he's looking for. (Security)	1/13	Position solution as a fail-proof strategy to generate a decent amount of revenue in a short amount of time. Share story of Vai at XYZ and how quick the turnaround was.
Rob Beach	COO	Medium	Content	5	Rob recognizes the challenges and growth goals on the table but feels that everything will right itself shortly. Is the chairman's son so he feels very secure. (???) Need to find a win-result.	1/13	Discover a win-result. Possibly get him to recognize that there is much more risk than he realizes.
Jennifer Batten	Director of AR (Coach)	Low	Trouble	8	Jennifer is ambitious and has risen quickly through the ranks, but recent issues threaten to end that. A win here will position her for a COO or CRO position. (Ambition, Ego)	1/13	Position solution as a fail-proof strategy to generate a decent amount of revenue in a short amount of time. Share story of Vai at XYZ and how quickly turnaround was. Suggest that success here will create opportunities with other clients we have.
Vito Brata	CIO	High	Over-confident				
Nita Strauss	Director of Integrations	Low					
	Director of Quality						

Figure 12–1: Working the Grid

Along the left side we have all our stakeholders and then a column for Role (which is basically their title). After that we have Influence, Attitude, and our overall Rating of how they see our initiative (the higher the better here). Then we have Win-Results, the date we met them, and our Strategy for that stakeholder.

This is a stuck deal. We've had virtually no progress for several months. As we go through this example ask yourself, "For which of the primary reasons (sales issues, client indecision or business case) might this deal be stuck?" Then ask, "What is the likely root cause?"

Stuck Deal Stakeholder Map and Analysis

Michael Firkins, CEO - We can see we met with Mike Firkins the CEO, and he has a High degree of influence. His attitude is "growth", which means that his perspective and goals are around growing the business. We've given him a rating for our initiative of 7 because while he does see it as a way to grow the business, it's not quite as much growth potential as some other initiatives he's looking at.

Our win-results say: "Improving financial results will accomplish something his predecessor was unable to do and help this new CEO validate the board's recent hire of him." So, we're playing to Ego and Security here.

Our strategy says: "Share the story of Marty out at ABC and how his success with our solution generated $X millions of dollars and got him coverage in the local news and Becker's Healthcare."

See how this works? In the context of this one stakeholder, let's ask ourselves the two questions:

For which of the primary reasons might this deal be stuck? - For this stakeholder, all three reasons are possible. Because we know this stakeholder is looking at other initiatives, competition is involved. That means Sales Issues could be a primary reason. Business case is certainly an issue because this stakeholder has communicated that our initiative does not have the same growth potential as some of the other initiatives they are looking at. Finally, it's possible that our stakeholder is having a hard time comparing these different initiatives, making Client Indecision a possible candidate as well.

What is the likely root cause? - There are three possible root causes: 1. Sales Issues (Competition), 2. Client Indecision (Valuation/Comparison), 3. Business Case (Muchness)

Strategy Commentary - Clear as mud, right? There is nothing conclusive here, but we can already see gaps in our information with this stakeholder. Our current strategy has us accentuating the muchness of the return and a play to Ego. To help with possible competition and business case comparisons, we need to understand exactly what the other alternative initiatives are that our stakeholder is considering. Since our communication channel is still open with this client, Play #1 - Inquiry is the most straightforward option. Let's just ask the CEO what other initiatives he's considering and how they compare. From there we can help facilitate comparison as needed.

Let's do the next one.

Jake Lee, CFO - We've met with Jake Lee the CFO who has a High degree of influence, but instead of being in growth-mode like our new CEO, his attitude is "trouble". We've rated his view of our solution as a 6 out of 10 because he is very skeptical of the returns being promised.

Our Win-Results says: "Jake was here with the previous CEO who was let go, and he is now concerned that the focus is now on him." (Because he's part of the old guard). Improving financial results will deliver the job security he's looking for. So, the win-result here is straight-up Security.

Our Strategy for Jake the CFO reads: "Position our solution as a fail-proof strategy to generate a decent amount of revenue in a short amount of time. Share the story of Vai at XYZ and how quick the turnaround was there."

For which of the primary reasons might this deal be stuck? - This one is very straightforward. This stakeholder is suffering from Client Indecision. He is skeptical about getting the returns being promised.

What is the likely root cause? - Specifically, he is suffering from Outcome Uncertainty or (Sureness).

Strategy Commentary - Our current strategy is to use a reference client to increase the CFOs confidence, and this is a great step. It is proof coming from an objective 3rd party source. But is it enough? Clients suffering from indecision have an insatiable thirst for proof that they will get the return being promised. Remember, credibility and proof are delivered in dump trucks - not shovels. All the strategies that address Outcome Uncertainty will work here. And that includes references, case studies, 3rd party industry reports, project plans, and guarantees. We can do more. With the right level of confidence, this CFO can be changed into a Champion.

Let's do the COO.

Reb Beach, COO - We met with Reb Beach the COO back in January. He has a medium level of influence, and his attitude is "content" (which means he's happy with how things are now). We've rated his view of our solution as a 5 of 10 because of that. He's not really against it, he just doesn't see the need.

Our Win-Results for Reb reads: "Reb recognizes the challenges and growth goals on the table but feels that everything will right itself shortly. Reb is the chairman of the board's son, so he feels very secure. We need to find a win-result."

Our Strategy for Reb reads: "Discover a win-result. Possibly get him to recognize that there is much more risk than he realizes.

For which of the primary reasons might this deal be stuck? - This stakeholder could be affected by all three reasons. Not having a Win-Result for this stakeholder is a Sales Issue. However, it's clear that this stakeholder has no urgency to grow or address current challenges. These can both be Client Indecision and Business Case issues when the stakeholder is unaware of the implications of doing nothing.

What is the likely root cause? - 1. Sales Issues (Stakeholder Management), 2. Client Indecision (possibly Lack of Information), 3. Business Case (possibly Muchness or Soonness)

Strategy Commentary - We don't have a win-result for Reb Beach, and that's a big problem with for someone with this much influence that we've rated so low. Our stated strategy is to discover a win-result for him. And certainly, that's what we need to do, but that's not much of a strategy is it? Additional work uncovering and sharing insight with the stakeholder about the risks of doing nothing, and the upside (and personal wins for the stakeholder) of moving forward with the initiative needs to be done. The good news is that the communication channel is open so all this can be easily accomplished.

Let's continue.

Jennifer Batten, Director of AR (Coach) - Jennifer is the Director of Accounts Receivable and she's our Coach! That means she's helping is navigate this deal. Unfortunately, because she's newer and she's lower on the totem-pole she doesn't have as much influence as we'd like. (if she did, we would label her as a champion) Jennifer's attitude is "trouble" which means she's motivated. We've rated her view of our solution as an 8 of 10.

Her Win-Results reads: "Jennifer is ambitious and has risen quickly through the ranks, but recent issues threaten to end that. A win here will position her for a COO or CRO position either internally or outside the organization." So, we're playing to Ambition and Ego here.

Our Strategy reads: "Position our solution as a fail-proof strategy to generate a decent amount of revenue in a short amount of time. Share story of Vai at XYZ and how quick turnaround there was. Suggest that success here will create possible job opportunities with other clients we have." (Can you see what we're doing with that one?)

For which of the primary reasons might this deal be stuck? - Jennifer is not the reason our deal is stuck. There is perhaps only one of the three reasons that could be contributing to the stall and that is Sales Issues.

What is the likely root cause? - Specifically, Weak Champion could be contributing to our deal being stuck. That is, our coach does not have enough influence to address all the other issues stalling our deal.

Strategy Commentary - Our current strategy focuses on keeping our coach happy and ensuring she has a win. When a coach lacks influence the best strategy is to garner additional coaches. In this context, I think our CEO and CFO both make good candidates to develop into additional coaches because they are both highly motivated.

Let's talk about Vito Brata the CIO.

Vito Brata, CIO - What about Vito Brata the CIO? Does he have a high degree of influence? Absolutely. Because this is IT related, this guy can kill our deal all by himself. The problem is, we haven't even met him yet. But by all reports Vito is hugely over-confident (meaning he thinks they are doing better than they really are). And because we haven't met him, we have no idea what would be a win for him and that makes it very hard to create any sort of strategy. This is a huge risk to our opportunity.

For which of the primary reasons might this deal be stuck? - This could very well be the exact reason our deal is stuck. Right now, this is a Sales Issue. Once we meet with Vito, we may uncover other issues.

What is the likely root cause? - At this point, this is specifically a Stakeholder Management issue. However, once we meet with Vito, because of his over-confidence, we may uncover issues with business case and client indecision.

Strategy Commentary - Clearly the most immediate next-step is to meet with Vito and get his perspective. We can best do this by leveraging Jennifer (our coach) to arrange an introduction, or perhaps do the same leveraging our CEO or CFO.

Next.

Nita Strauss, Director of Integrations - We have the same problem with Nita Strauss the Director of Integrations as we do with Vito Brata. The only difference is that Nita seems to have a low degree of influence. Other than that, we don't know anything about her and that is a risk to our opportunity.

For which of the primary reasons might this deal be stuck? - It is a Sales Issue to not know anything about this stakeholder.

What is the likely root cause? - This is specifically a Stakeholder Management issue. With such a low degree of influence it seems unlikely that Nita is the cause of the stall. But how would we know for sure? We haven't even met with her.

Strategy Commentary - The next most immediate next-step for Nita is to meet with her and get her perspective. Again, we can best do this by leveraging Jennifer (our coach) to arrange an introduction, or perhaps we can have Vito arrange the meeting after we meet with him.

Finally...

Unknown, Director of Quality - Finally, and perhaps worst of all, in our type of opportunity we usually end up dealing with the Director of Quality. But in this case, we don't even know who that person is yet. This is a tremendous risk because this person usually has a high degree of influence.

For which of the primary reasons might this deal be stuck? - It is a Sales Issue to not know who this stakeholder is or anything about them. This could very well be the reason our opportunity is stuck.

What is the likely root cause? - This is specifically a Stakeholder Management issue (i.e., Wrong/Incomplete Stakeholders). Since this stakeholder typically has a high degree of influence it seems very likely that this stakeholder could be contributing to our stalled opportunity.

Strategy Commentary - The most immediate next-step is to identify and meet with this person and get their perspective. We can best do this by leveraging Jennifer (our coach) to arrange an introduction, or perhaps do the same leveraging our CEO or CFO.

There is some good and bad with this opportunity. The good news is we have access and open communication channels with three of the five most important stakeholders. We also have a coach who is willing to help us facilitate our deal. This real example is actually fairly simple. Stakeholders are communicating with us, and we don't even seem to have any stakeholders that are antagonistic and oppose the solution. If this seemed like a lot, then welcome to the world of complex selling.

An Interesting Pattern

When coaching on opportunities using stakeholder maps, an interesting pattern emerges. Most of the time, the problem we uncover is that we really don't know as much about our deal as we thought we did. Huge gaps in our understanding become apparent immediately. The root of this phenomenon is simply that this is all too much information to keep track of in our heads. We need a system or process to help us.

At a high level, using stakeholder maps and "working the grid" is very straight forward. We simply map out what we know about stakeholders and then fill in the gaps when they emerge. And the good news is our uncertainty and these gaps in understanding readily suggest strategies and next steps.

> When we serve stakeholder self-interest, we are serving our own self-interest.

An Important Reminder

As we conclude this chapter let me leave you with a very important reminder. When we serve stakeholder self-interest, we are serving our own self-interest.

You may have heard the Zig Ziglar version of this concept: 'You can have everything in life you want, if you will just help enough other people get what they want.'

You may have just been surprised by how much work it can be to manage a complex opportunity. If so, just remember this: This isn't a game or a trick. This is a true principle and something to remember during stakeholder management. All we're trying to do here is genuinely make sure that everyone wins. And when you approach it with this attitude and mindset, you will find the process very enjoyable. You'll be able to communicate your authentic desire to make sure everyone is getting their needs met and clients will value you and respect you for it.

Summary

This chapter on stakeholder maps and "working the grid" is starting to introduce you to a systematic approach to stakeholder management. We did not explore all the possible strategies to influence each stakeholder. And a comprehensive system for managing sales is beyond the scope of this book. You'll find the best resources that I have encountered for that purpose in the Recommended Reading section of this book. Rather, what we did was touch on some possible strategies to stimulate your thinking and understanding on the subject. In the upcoming chapters we will explore even more strategies.

I intentionally spent extra time in these last two chapters focusing on addressing stakeholder management issues because they are one of the top sales reasons why deals stall. In the next chapter we will continue our exploration of how to unstick deals that are caused by Sales Issues by discussing one of the most important elements to successfully closing any deal – coaches and champions.

CHAPTER 13

UNSTICKING DEALS CAUSED BY CHAMPION MANAGEMENT

"A coach is someone who tells you what you don't want to hear,
who helps you see what you can't see, so you can succeed."
- Tom Landry

The Big Ideas:

- Engage and develop new coaches and champions.
- Develop your solution to include wins for your coaches.
- Learn and leverage the keys to gaining trust.
- More client contact shortens the sales cycle.

We have all worked with someone who wants the sale as much as we do. These individuals serve as useful guides giving us insight into other stakeholders, internal challenges and more. These individuals, as it turns out, are a major key to success – especially in complex sales.

What is a champion or coach?

It is not our intention to create a comprehensive approach to complex sales, but just in case the whole concept of a champion or coach is unfamiliar to you, let's briefly cover what a champion or coach is.

A **Champion** is defined as someone with access to power, that is selling for you when you are not there. They must be tested consistently.

A **Coach** will carry a lot of the same markers of a champion, except they lack access to power.

Dynamics

There is also an interesting change in power dynamics related to the champion when dealing with budgeted and unbudgeted expenses. As an example, if you are selling to HR, your economic buyer may appear to be the head of the function, the CHRO. They have been given a budget for a variety of solutions and they are choosing to spend some of it with you. In this scenario, one step below the CHRO would be your champion, likely a VP of HR. A coach would fall one step below them, or possibly someone sharing relevant information in a different department.

However, say the CHRO has used their budget for the year. In this scenario, your champion turns into the CHRO and the economic buyer flips to a CFO/CEO, the person who the CHRO would go to if they needed additional budget. In this case, your coach becomes the VP of HR.

This is very important to understand, and it is one of the main reasons deals get stuck. You think you are selling to the right people and driving the right end results with the correct stakeholders, and then are puzzled when you can't get funding, or the deal gets deprioritized. It is often because you didn't understand the power dynamics related to getting a project funded and weren't selling at the right levels.

With that said, lets talk more about the role of champions and coaches.

Roles

Champions and coaches act as a guide and internal seller for your deal. They provide and help interpret internal information and dynamics related to your deal. They share information with you whether it is good, bad, or ugly. This includes information about:

- Other Stakeholders
- Challenges & Initiatives the Organization Has
- Relevant Business Metrics
- Decision Criteria
- Decision Process
- Contracting Process
- Competition & Alternative Options
- Coaching on Your overall Strategy

There is a specific set of criteria that determines whether you have a coach or not.

- The first is you have established trust and credibility with this individual. Without trust they don't share information.
- Your champion or coach should act as a guide and internal seller for you. If they're not doing this, then they are not champions or coaches.

- Champions and coaches have a vested interest in your success. They want your solution. They're not being agnostic. They want you to win.
- Champions have credibility, power, and influence with other stakeholders.

This is where the difference between Coaches and Champions comes in. For all intents and purposes Coaches & Champions are the same. The only difference is that champions have power and influence, and coaches may not.

Friendship is not a requirement to have a coach or champion. But it is very common for you to be friends with your coach or champion.

Criteria	Coach	Champion
You Have Established Trust & Credibility	Y	Y
Acts as a Guide & Internal Seller	Y	Y
Has Vested Interest in Your Success	Y	Y
Has Power & Influence	N	Y

Figure 13-1: Coach and Champion Criteria

The focus of the coach or champion is the success of *this* proposal. They are always asking: "How can we make this happen?" And the rule is to always develop at least one champion and/or coach. The more the better.

How to Know if Champion Management is Your Root Cause

The third sales-related cause of deals sticking is not having a champion or coach to help you navigate your deal. A similarly related challenge is when the champion or coach we do have is weak. Because they are similar, I have combined these challenges here to simplify.

To identify whether this is our root cause, we want to ask ourselves these questions:

Coach/Champion Assessment Questions
• Have you established trust and credibility with this stakeholder?
• Does this stakeholder act as a guide?
• Does this stakeholder have a vested interest in our success?
• Does this stakeholder act as an internal seller?
• Does this stakeholder share important details about challenges the organization is experiencing?
• Does this stakeholder share relevant business metrics?
• Does this stakeholder share important details about other stakeholders?
• Does this stakeholder share important details about the decision criteria?
• Does this stakeholder share important details about the decision process?
• Does this stakeholder share important details about the contracting process?
• Does this stakeholder share important details about the competition and alternative options?
• Does this stakeholder have power and influence within their organization?

Figure 13–2: Champion/Coach Assessment Questions

Champion/Coach Assessment Questions

- Have you established trust and credibility with this stakeholder?
- Does this stakeholder act as a guide?
- Does this stakeholder have a vested interest in our success?
- Does this stakeholder act as an internal seller?
- Does this stakeholder share important details about the challenges the organization is experiencing?
- Does this stakeholder share relevant business metrics?
- Does this stakeholder share important details about other stakeholders?
- Does this stakeholder share important details about the decision criteria?
- Does this stakeholder share important details about the decision process?
- Does this stakeholder share important details about the contracting process?
- Does this stakeholder share important details about the competition and alternative options?
- Does this stakeholder have power and influence within their organization?

If we are getting negative answers in any of these areas, then either our champion or coach is weak, or we don't really have one.

Champion and Coach Unsticking Strategies

The basic strategy for deals that are stalled because of champion management is very straightforward: Engage and Develop new Champions and Coaches.

Engage and Develop new Champions and Coaches.

Continually, consistently developing your Champion and Coaches is one of the most powerful way to strengthen your opportunities. This is both a prevention as well as an unsticking strategy.

If the assessment we performed uncovers a pattern that that your stalled deals have no coach or that your coaches tend to be weak, then consider the following:

Can we identify and engage a new champion/coach earlier in the process?

What is the process you are using to identify and develop coaches now? Sometimes professionals struggle with developing champions and coaches simply because they haven't identified all the stakeholders, leaving them with very few options for developing coaches. I have seen very large opportunities lost because they were being managed completely through a single stakeholder. And when that stakeholder is removed from the picture for some reason, there's no other stakeholders to engage and we're starting from scratch.

The rule is this: Engage high and wide.

This means we engage as **high** on the executive ladder as we can, and we have as **many** contacts as we can. You can think of each stakeholder as a strand connecting you to your successful, closed deal. Do you want to have a strong cable with many reinforcing strands, or do you want your deal hanging by a single thread?

In the context of developing champions and coaches, the more contacts and stakeholders we have, the more opportunities we have to develop coaches. And the *higher* those contacts and stakeholders are in the executive hierarchy, the better likelihood we can develop them into champions.

Repeating the prevention play we discussed in Chapter 3 (Secure Executive Sponsorship), I strongly recommend that you engage as high as you possibly can on the executive ladder and turn those executives into Executive Sponsors who will introduce you to everyone you need. If you do this right from the start, you'll have many good opportunities to develop champions and coaches.

Can we do a better job of engaging stakeholders that have credibility, power, and influence?

We just invested a lot of time on stakeholders and Win-Results, so I won't belabor this here, but what is the quality of your engagement with stakeholders? Especially those with power and influence? Are you speaking their language? Are you focusing on the right areas? Are you bringing them valuable insights in those areas? And do those insights and the opportunities you bring create personal wins for them? What is the quality of your interpersonal and professional sales skills?

> Where domain knowledge and sales expertise intersect, tremendous value is created for all parties.

Improve your interpersonal and professional sales skills. These are all learnable things. Invest in yourself. Both in terms of your skills as a professional, but also in your knowledge of the domain you sell in. Where domain knowledge and sales expertise intersect, tremendous value is created for all parties.

Study and master the industry resources for the domain you sell in, and then improve your ability to effectively engage stakeholders. There are many excellent resources for this, and you will find many of the best resources outlined for you in the Recommended Reading section of this book.

Can we do a better job of identifying key issues and creating Win–Results to identify a new or additional Champion/Coach?

Sometimes folks have tremendous interpersonal skills, but still find it hard to be relevant to certain stakeholders simply because they aren't aware of the key issues that are relevant to that stakeholder. It is important that you master the domain that you are selling into. You must know more than just your product. You need to understand your client's industry, the trends and challenges they are facing, how those trends and challenges affect each stakeholder, and then finally how your solution specifically addresses those issues for each individual stakeholder. You need to have the entire picture.

When you master this, your credibility, competence, and the value you can bring your clients will be over-the-top.

This means understanding your whole solution at a much more granular

> Mastering the domain you are selling into will raise your credibility, competence and the value you add to clients to almost irresistible levels.

level than you may have today. Invest the time to do this. Spend time understanding how each stakeholder is measured, how they perform their work and where their joys and frustrations come from. I've had some folks ask me, "How will I know when I've learned enough?" The short answer is, you'll never have learned enough. But a good rule of thumb is that if one of your stakeholders had to take a leave of absence for some reason, and that they asked you if you could fill in for them while they were gone, that you could competently do it. Then you know enough about that stakeholder's role. And I'm happy to say that I've enjoyed this opportunity several times in my career.

Can we develop another stakeholder into a Champion or Coach?

Remember our primary strategy - Engage and develop new champions and coaches. We are continually strengthening our opportunity by developing additional Champions and Coaches. Our primary method of doing this is to leverage our existing stakeholders and/or our Executive Sponsor to get to other stakeholders that might make better champions or coaches.

But once we get introduced to someone, how do we actually develop that stakeholder into a coach or champion? By leveraging what you know about that stakeholder's goals and challenges, you align your solution to create a personal win for them. If that sounds familiar, it should. It's the same basic strategy we use for every stakeholder. Where you have creativity is in crafting a solution that creates a strong personal win for each particular champion and coach. Remember, champions and coaches **want** your solution to win. They are biased. You can help develop this bias in several ways. The two most important ways are:

- Craft a solution that benefits them
- Gain trust and respect

Crafting Solutions that Benefit Stakeholders

I alluded to this strategy earlier. Do you know what would make this a personal win for this stakeholder? Then just build that into your solution. The opportunities here are limitless. Let me give you an example to stimulate your thinking.

In working with a large healthcare organization, we had a long-tenured and very influential CIO as an important stakeholder. Because we knew this was going to be an important stakeholder, we intentionally met with him later in the process so we could get impressions and guidance from all the other stakeholders. By all accounts the CIO was a kingdom-builder and expected to oppose our solution because he favored different technology. So we crafted a strategy that we thought would help sway this stakeholder to our side. When we finally met and the issue of technology came up, we explained that we required that someone in the organization have a professional certification in the technology we were using, but since we've found that many companies don't have someone with this certification on staff, we include in our proposal providing that training for someone in the organization to become certified.

I'm sure you see the strategy here. We hoped that our CIO would see this professional training as a way to increase his influence and net worth even further and build his kingdom even bigger. It worked. Our CIO felt he was the best candidate to receive the certification and it completely neutralized his bias against our solution.

By the way, it was completely true that we wanted a certified professional within the organization. We just didn't typically include the cost of someone getting certified into the offer. This is a fantastic tool that you can use to create wins for stakeholders. Since you are the one that controls the offer, you can build whatever stakeholder wins are necessary into your offer. This bypasses any ancillary approval processes within the larger organization because it is bundled into your solution. Again, there are unlimited ways you can apply this to win over stakeholders and create personal wins for them.

Gaining Trust and Respect

In Stephen Covey's outstanding book, The Speed of Trust, he says this, "Trust always affects two outcomes: speed and cost. When trust goes down, speed goes down and cost goes up."

The corollary to this very insightful dynamic is that when we increase trust, we also increase speed, and decrease cost.

Champions and coaches, like all stakeholders, see uncertainty as risk. This, in fact, is exactly why mistrust slows things down. We will discuss this in more detail in Part 5 on Client Indecision. Uncertainty causes us to tread

> "Trust always affects two outcomes: speed and cost. When trust goes down, speed goes down and cost goes up."
>
> – STEPHEN COVEY

cautiously. Developing trust and respect, in contrast, eliminates risk and speeds everything up.

Clever crafting of solutions can win over stakeholders, but developing champions and coaches requires trust.

We need to be mindful of both needs. Invest time into building trust and rapport with each stakeholder. We also need to thoughtfully craft solutions that are genuine wins for them. This builds the trust and rapport required to develop champions and coaches.

Much has been written about the interpersonal aspect of selling and relationships, and you will find some of those resources in the recommended reading section of this book. I want to take a moment and point out a couple of sometimes counter-intuitive dynamics when it comes to building trust, respect, and relationships in general.

First, from a financial perspective, we all want to close business as quickly as possible. In fact, it's our job. However, a very common mistake is to assume that cutting out steps we might perceive as unnecessary (on our part), will speed up the sales cycle. Less steps = shorter sales cycle right? Not necessarily. This is a classic case of efficiency vs. effectiveness. What is efficient isn't always effective. This is especially true of relationships.

Here's an example: Let's say that you have an opportunity that is moving along fine and that you and one of your stakeholders are both going to be at a trade show at the same time. Since things are moving along fine, is it important to meet with this stakeholder while you're together in the same place at the same time? Could your sale close without meeting at the show? Probably. Would the most efficient use of your time be to meet with someone new while at the show? Maybe. Will your opportunity close at the same **time** it would have without meeting? Probably not. Here's why:

Trust affects speed. Lack of trust creates uncertainty and risk.

What you have here is an opportunity to create greater trust and certainty, and by extension, shorten your sale cycle and increase your chances of a successful close. It's more effective to meet than to not meet.

Now, let's take it one step further. In the Chapter on "LIKING", the second lever of influence, in Robert Chaldini's outstanding book **Influence: The**

Psychology of Persuasion, we learn that familiarity is a powerful factor in persuasion and influence. We also learn that increased exposure increases likability. The more the better. On this basis, it is my recommendation that you create as many opportunities to interact with your stakeholders as is practically possible.

This is counter-intuitive to our natural proclivity to speed things up by removing steps. Rather, I am recommending that you create as many interactions and touchpoints as you possibly can without becoming annoying, because each interaction improves trust and rapport. And that speeds things up. More contacts = shorter sales cycle. Ironic, isn't it?

The Key to Gaining Trust

Jean Giraudoux is reputed to have said, "The secret of success is sincerity. Once you can fake that you've got it made." I absolutely love the irony in this joke. Because faking sincerity isn't sincerity, is it? And the truth, which we have covered at length in The Perfect Close, is that sincerity cannot be faked. There are mirror neurons, micro-expressions, and paralanguage, that are beyond our control, that reveal what our true intentions are - whether they be good or bad.

> In order to communicate good intention, you actually have to have good intention.

The lesson here is that in order to communicate good intention, you actually have to HAVE good intention. It cannot be faked.

And so it is with gaining trust and respect. If you want to be trusted, you must actually be trustworthy. If you want to be respected, you must actually be respectable. That means being honest, and reliable. It means being committed to always doing the right thing, as opposed to doing the expedient or self-serving thing. It means having the knowledge and experience that causes others to respect and value your advice. It means doing what you say you'll do, when you say you'll do it.

> If you want to be trusted, you must actually be trustworthy. If you want to be respected, you must actually be respectable.

Without belaboring it, I will just note that these are personal attributes. And I'm not ashamed to say that there is something divine going on here. These attributes are about being a better person. Becoming a better person will make you a better sales-person. And you will find joy in both.

There's more to gaining trust and rapport and I recommend that you further your studies because it will benefit you in both your personal and professional life. You can read more about the trust equation in Charlie Green's excellent book **Trust-Based Selling**.

Developing Champions

Developing champions and coaches is intimately interwoven into stakeholder management. They are directly related to each other. Today's complex sales are sufficiently complicated that it is a severe handicap to sell without a champion or coach.

So, the rule is: Always develop at least one champion or coach. Or as one of my friends likes to say: No champion, no sale.

> Always develop at least one coach or champion. No champion, no sale.

If we already have a champion or coach, and we're still having the issues outlined in the assessment, then it's time to face the fact that our current coach or champion isn't cutting it and we need to take the steps to secure additional coaches or champions.

Conclusion

After having done thousands of deal reviews I can tell you that having a solid champion or coach is a major determinant of sales success.

Salespeople often convince themselves that they have a champion or coach when they don't. There is a specific set of criteria that determines whether we have a coach or not. Be objective using the assessment questions above to determine the quality of your coaches.

Get good at turning stakeholders into coaches. The two most important keys to accomplishing this are to craft solutions that benefit them and earning their trust. Trust affects speed and the more client contact you have the shorter your sales cycle will be.

Your ability to develop champions and coaches is an enabling skill that will enhance every other aspect of your sale. To a large extent, the quality of your champion or coach determines the quality of your sale. There is no limit to the number of coaches you can develop. And quality coaches and champions will shorten your sales cycle, increase your probability of winning and prevent deals from sticking in the first place.

In the next chapter, we will discuss one of the most easily fixable causes of deal stalls – relationships.

CHAPTER 14

UNSTICKING DEALS CAUSED BY RELATIONSHIP ISSUES

"Rapport is the ultimate tool for producing results with other people. No matter what you want in your life, if you can develop rapport with the right people, you'll be able to fill their needs, and they will be able to fill yours."

- TONY ROBBINS

Big Idea: All things being equal, people do business with people they know, like and trust.

Chemistry and rapport are the special connection two people have with one another. Rapport is largely about mutual understanding and trust. When two people trust each other and are comfortable communicating openly rapport has been established. You should be aspiring to find these kinds of connections on both a personal as well as a professional level.

In the business world we adopt standard protocols for interacting with one another that sometimes make it hard to identify when we have established genuine rapport. This can cause us to assume there is chemistry and rapport when there sometimes isn't.

I once had a rep that had been working on a deal with a large clinic in the western US that had gone on for over a year. By chance I encountered one of their executives at a trade show. I said, "You guys have been evaluating solutions for a long time now. How are you making out on your project?" To which the executive told me, "Oh we love you guys. We decided months ago. You're our vendor of choice."

"Really, I hadn't heard that. That's good news. What's the next step?" I asked. She hesitated uncomfortably and then said, "Well, our COO doesn't care for your salesperson." Surprised, I said, "Really? Why is that?" To which she said with a minor chuckle, "She says every time she's with him her 'spider sense' goes off. She just can't bring herself to work with him."

So this big deal had been stalled for months because of a relationship issue between the COO and my sales rep. This is exactly what we are trying to avoid.

How to Know if Relationship is Your Root Cause

The fourth sales-related cause of deals sticking is not having good relationships with stakeholders. Again, risk/reward decisions are made independently by each stakeholder. And each stakeholder has a different perspective and degree of influence. Any sufficiently influential stakeholder can cause a deal to stick. So, do not dismiss relationships as the root cause of your problem. This is often a blind spot and tough medicine for individuals with big egos or a lower EQ (Emotional Quotient) – i.e., empathy.

> "All things being equal, people do business with people they know, like and trust."
>
> – BOB BURG

All things being equal, people do business with people they know, like and trust. Part of our job as professionals is to make sure that things are **not** equal. But, until that has been successfully communicated to the client, if rapport is low, then we are operating at a huge disadvantage.

In order to assess whether or not relationships are the root cause of our stuck deal, we want to ask ourselves these questions:

Relationship Assessment Questions

- Do you feel you have good chemistry and rapport?
- Do you detect a negative change in tone?
- Is the stakeholder withholding information?
- Do the questions the stakeholder asks suggest mistrust or poor rapport?
- Does the stakeholder interrupt or act impatient?
- Does the stakeholder's body language suggest mistrust or poor rapport?
- Does your pacing & leading with the stakeholder suggest incongruence or poor rapport?
- Does the stakeholder jump right to discussions about price?
- Does the stakeholder refuse to disclose budget?
- Does the stakeholder refuse to introduce you to others?
- Does the stakeholder keep putting you off?
- Has the stakeholder gone "radio silent"?
- Has the stakeholder asked to speak to someone else in your organization?

Figure 14-1: Relationship Assessment Questions

Relationship Assessment Questions
- Do you feel you have good chemistry and rapport?
- Do you detect a negative change in tone?
- Is the stakeholder withholding information?
- Do the questions the stakeholder asks suggest mistrust or poor rapport?
- Does the stakeholder interrupt or act impatiently?
- Does the stakeholder's body language suggest mistrust or poor rapport?
- Does your pacing & leading with the stakeholder suggest incongruence or poor rapport?
- Does the stakeholder jump right to discussions about price?
- Does the stakeholder refuse to disclose budget?
- Does the stakeholder refuse to introduce you to others?
- Does the stakeholder keep putting you off?
- Has the stakeholder gone "radio silent"?
- Has the stakeholder asked to speak to someone else in your organization?

If we're getting negative answers in any of these areas, this suggests that we may have a relationship problem with the client.

Unsticking Deals Caused by Relationship Issues

When we identify that we do have relationship issues, what is the solution? How do we fix it? The basic strategy is simple: Improve the relationship.

Sometimes deals get stuck because the rapport between us and stakeholders just isn't there. I am a very agreeable guy, but I have had this happen to me several times in my career. The key is to remove all emotion and ego from the situation and do whatever it takes to get the ball rolling again. In my case, somebody other than me needed to go be face-to-face with the client.

Chemistry Rapport Strategies

There are really only two strategies to consider when it comes to chemistry and rapport:

1. Can we improve our style to improve chemistry and rapport?
2. Can we change our engagement team to improve chemistry and rapport?

Maybe we're coming across too aggressively. Or maybe you're getting right to business when certain stakeholders want to spend more time establishing rapport before we dive in. There are a million reasons why chemistry

> Feedback is the breakfast of champions.

can go wrong. Whatever it is, it's very possible that just a simple tweak to our style will improve things.

Study yourself. See yourself from the other person's perspective. Ask your team and your clients for feedback about your style. And how you might improve your style. Identify how you are coming across and then tweak and improve your interpersonal skills as needed. This takes humility. Suck it up and be teachable. Feedback is the breakfast of champions.

Tips for Establishing Rapport

A detailed discussion of how to establish chemistry and rapport has been covered in many books and is beyond the scope of this work. Here I offer a few of my favorite tips for those seeking to improve their rapport skills.

Be Authentic and Genuine

Your intentions are judged in the first few seconds of any interaction. The top two attributes judged in that time are warmth and competence. [1] The warmth attribute displays traits related to perceived intent, friendliness, helpfulness, sincerity, trustworthiness, and morality. Whereas the competence attribute reflects traits that are related to perceived ability, intelligence, skill, creativity, and efficacy. [2] Judgements about warmth are judged first and carry more weight than competency. [3] When a client decides that a salesperson's intentions are not aligned with their best interest, in most cases the deal is off. [4]

Be authentic and genuinely interested in others. Be 100% present. Listen actively. And seek to understand before you are understood.

Smile

When we see a smiling face, our brains release endorphins which make us feel happier and calmer. The part of your brain responsible for unconscious responses is called the cingulate cortex and will actually cause you to copy someone else's facial expressions. When you see a facial expression, you recreate that expression in your brain. This is fancy science-talk for saying: Smiles are contagious.

People consider you more trustworthy when you make eye contact with them and smile. They will naturally smile back which releases their endorphins and makes them feel happy and calmer as well. It's a virtuous cycle. It's a powerful effect. Don't dismiss it.

We Are the Same

Rapport is largely about the other person concluding that they can predict your intention. When we find similarities between us, we feel more aligned. Find the commonality between you and your stakeholders. It improves rapport. We are all more alike than we are different.

Pacing and Mirroring

When we are genuinely in rapport with another person, we begin to match each other's language, pacing and body language. There is a lot of material on this concept that I don't care for because it often advocates mimicking the other person. When truly in rapport with another person this happens automatically. That is, rapport precedes matching.

When I was young, I worked on a ranch in Idaho with an Australian ranch hand whom I became close friends with. And I was amazed that without even thinking about it, I would naturally slide into aspects of his Australian accent. That is rapport.

However, science is clear, this works in reverse as well. You can build rapport by matching and pacing the other person. So, if you're from New York, consider slowing your pace a bit when speaking with someone from Texas. But don't try to be something you're not. That's not being authentic.

Adapting to Personality Types

A lot has been written about how to adapt to different personality types when selling. And I must confess that analyzing personalities is something of a hobby. There are many good models for deciphering personalities and communication styles including: DISC, Meyers-Briggs, the Hartman Color Code and more. I encourage you to explore these further. I am going to briefly simplify these into the three personality types I have encountered the most often in my career.

Executive – These are pragmatic, goal-seeking individuals who enjoy control. Their focus is on getting things done and often prefer getting right to business. Adapt by getting right to the details and benefits of the business case. These are often CEOs and Executive Directors.

Analytical – These are logical, process and detail-oriented individuals that are methodical and skeptical. Their focus is on making sure no detail is missed. They don't like vague statements, risk, or surprises. Adapt by having all the details they need and be patient with them. It takes time to digest the details. These are often finance people and engineers.

Social – These are empathetic individuals that are highly consensus-driven. They care about how decisions will affect their team. They are social and tend to want to get to know your human side before getting down to business. These are often COOs and managers.

Don't change your personality when interacting with these different personality types. Rather, just be flexible and focus on what they want. Executive types don't want lots of idle chit-chat and social types do. Be flexible enough to make their interactions with you great experiences for them.

Changing Your Team

When our deal is stuck because of relationship issues, sometimes it's easiest just to ask: Can we change our engagement team to improve the relationship? If someone on our team isn't getting on well with the client, maybe we can just swap them out for someone who will have better rapport. If we can, change it right away. This may be the *easiest* unsticking strategy in this book.

My team and I used to have to work with an assigned systems integrations guy at our company who was the kiss of death to any sale. His personality affected so many sales that we eventually hired a salesperson to be our dedicated client-facing contact with the integrations team so that no one would have to work with this guy. This change-up worked like a charm. It solved all our issues almost immediately. A personality transplant wasn't possible, but a personnel transplant was.

> A personality transplant may not be possible, but a personnel transplant is.

When it comes to relationship and rapport issues, prevention is clearly the best strategy. But I have found that introducing new faces is just straight-up a good strategy. Just introducing your boss, because they have a title, is sometimes all it takes to jumpstart a stuck deal. So don't ignore it.

Swallow your pride, introduce some new bodies, and see if that solves the problem. If it does, consider yourself lucky because this is an easy fix.

This is exactly the approach I used in the opening story of this chapter. I simply traded out my rep with a new personality and within weeks our deal was closed. (I still took care of my original rep on the deal by the way. They just had to split the deal between them.)

We need good relationships to maintain progress. If a deal is stalling, it probably has at least a little bit to do with chemistry. We can't control who is on the client's team, but we can certainly manage what we do on our side. And that includes changing out our team members when needed. Even if that team member is you. You can always coach from the sidelines.

Conclusion

Poor relationships stick deals. But it is sometimes difficult to detect this. Objectively ask yourself the questions above about each stakeholder in your deal remembering that any sufficiently influential stakeholder can cause a deal to stick.

Stalls due to chemistry are almost always avoidable. Continually improve your communication style and be flexible in your approach with different stakeholder personalities. And when required, don't be afraid to change your team members even if that team member is you.

In the next chapter, we address deals that are stalled due to competition and the strategies for unsticking them.

CHAPTER 15

UNSTICKING DEALS CAUSED BY COMPETITION

"Don't knock your competitors. By boosting others you will boost yourself. A little competition is a good thing and severe competition is a blessing."
- Jacob Kindleberger

The Big Ideas:

- The number one tool in your arsenal for addressing competition is you.
- Greater value creation is the shortcut to addressing competition.
- Never bad-mouth your competition.

The fifth most common sales-related cause of deals sticking is competition. Deals sometimes get stuck because competition of some sort has become involved.

There are three types of competition:

1. **Status Quo** - This is competing with the customer just continuing to do what they have always done. This is the dreaded "no-decision" and is the number one "competitor" for most businesses.
2. **Alternative Investments** - This is the use of the money that might fund your project for other potentially dissimilar projects.
3. **Category Competition** - This is a competitor in the specific solution category you are selling in.

How to Know if Competition is Your Root Cause

Regardless of the type of competition you might be facing there are some common signs that a competitor might be influencing your deal. Use these signs to assess if competition is at the root cause of your stuck opportunity.

Competition Assessment Questions
• Stakeholder asks you why this would be the best investment of their time and money?
• Stakeholder asks you how you compare to your competitor.
• Stakeholder uses your competitor's terminology.
• Stakeholder communication is inconsistent.
• Stakeholder is asking for things we don't have, or that don't address their outcome goals.
• Customer asks you to participate in an RFP process.
• Customer or stakeholder is not really collaborating.
• There's been a recent change in stakeholders. (merger, acquisition, promotion, retirement, etc.)
• Stakeholder objects—to or overplays insignificant differentiators.
• Stakeholder gives you misinformation.
• An existing customer starts complaining about lots of trivial things and is slow to pay.

Figure 15–1: Competition Assessment Questions

Competition Assessment Questions

I feel a bit like Jeff Foxworthy, but a competitor might be influencing your deal if...

▪ A stakeholder asks you why this would be the best investment of their time and money right now? (Suggesting that they have alternative investments they could pursue.)

▪ A stakeholder asks you how you compare to your competitor. This does not guarantee that a competitor is involved, but what made them curious enough to ask?

▪ Your stakeholder uses your competitor's terminology. "Do you guys have SuperFlash?" (or any term trademarked by your competition.) Sounds like they've been talking to competitor ABC.

▪ Your stakeholder's communication is inconsistent. Maybe because they're spending time with their preferred vendor – and that's not us.

▪ Our stakeholder is asking for things we don't have, or things that don't even address their key outcome goals. Sometimes this suggests there's some internal comparison going on or posturing to exclude you based on some minor differentiation.

▪ The customer asks you to participate in an RFP process. One of my friends likes to say, "If you didn't help write the RFP the odds are stacked against you."

▪ The customer or stakeholder is not really collaborating. They're not really helping move the process along. This is a form of passive-aggressive resistance. In healthcare sometimes we call this the "slow no".

- There's been a recent change in stakeholders (merger, acquisition, promotion, retirement, etc.). If our deal suddenly stalled, they might have introduced their buddies they›re used to working with at the competition.
- The stakeholder objects to or overplays insignificant differentiators. This is sometimes an indicator that there might be some secret comparison going on or posturing to exclude you based on some minor differentiation.
- The stakeholder gives you misinformation. It is a very bad sign when a stakeholder intentionally gives you bad information. You can be sure they are working against you. You need to explore how deep the infiltration goes. Is it just one stakeholder or have they gotten to several stakeholders?
- If we're talking about an existing customer, and the customer starts complaining about lots of trivial things and is slow to pay. This suggests that they may be reevaluating their relationship with you and that a competitor may be involved with them.

If we're seeing a number of these things all at once, then it is an indicator that a competitor may be influencing our opportunity.

Your Number One Tool for Addressing Competition

> The number one tool in your arsenal for addressing competition is you.

If we think our deal has stalled because the competition has somehow gotten in there, what do we do? Once again, the basic strategy is simple: Improve our position against the competition. But the number one tool in your arsenal for addressing competition is you.

Entire books have been written on improving competitive position and you'll find some in the additional reading section. My favorite is Anthony Iannarino's **Eat Their Lunch** which I highly recommend. Improving your position against the competition is really not as complex as you might think.

Product Parity Over Time

Over time, all solutions tend to reach parity where all solutions are considered roughly equal or equivalent by customers. This is especially true for solutions in mature product categories. Even when it is not true, customers often erroneously presume that all products in mature categories are roughly equal. This can, unfortunately, lead to something called "profitable deception" where vendors exploit consumer's misperception of parity. [1]

Customers rarely have a complete understanding of a solution along with the full spectrum of risks and pitfalls. This is especially true of complex sales. The more complex a solution is, the more buyers rely on trust and outside validation. They realize they can never fully assess all the proportions of the solution, so they utilize shortcuts in their consideration of alternatives.

How you sell is a sample of how you solve.

Customers see the time they spend with us during the sales process as an indicator of what their experience will be like after the sale. Each interaction with us is a "sample." They are sampling their experience with **us** as much as they are evaluating the solution. In many cases (especially with service offerings) the experience during the sale is weighed far above anything else. Because this experience sample is relatively small, clients are prone to a cognitive bias known as extrapolation bias—a form of availability bias where we overestimate probabilities of events associated with memorable or dramatic occurrences.

With extrapolation bias we extrapolate what we think future events will become based upon a narrow sampling of current events. For example, if a stock is going up, we may extrapolate that it will continue to go up. Or if our experience at a restaurant is good, we extrapolate that it will always be good.

In general, prospects will take the sum of their experiences with us and extrapolate them into what they think all future experiences will be. This can work for you or against you.

Have you ever lost a deal to a competitor that was clearly inferior? How did that happen?

Customers make decisions with imperfect knowledge. Your prospect's narrow sampling from your compet-

> How you sell is a sample of how you solve.

> "Prospects will take the sum of their experiences with us and extrapolate them into what they think all future experiences will be."

itor may have been exceptional while their sampling of you may have been sub-par. Because prospects can never really get a sample adequate enough to fully understand all the dimensions of each offering — they extrapolate. If clients are not given sufficient opportunity to sample each solution, they will extrapolate based on the narrow experience that they <u>do</u> have—and sometimes come to the wrong conclusion.

> How you sell is more important than what you sell.

It is certainly unfortunate (for both us and customers) when they end up making poor decisions. But rather than complain about it, accept that this dynamic exists and embrace it. Leverage it. This dynamic can work for you or against you.

Why am I sharing this with you?

Because in the long run, **how** you sell is more important than **what** you sell.

Still don't believe me?

You Are the Biggest Factor

Numerous studies have been done over the years to examine which sales factors are most influential in the buying process. Two of the most noteworthy and extensive come from HR Chally and Corporate Executive Board (CEB). Between the two, they span over two decades and exceed 100,000 interviews. They examine many factors including company and brand, quality of offering, total solution, total value, the salesperson, and price. All this was done to determine which factors have the most influence on purchase decisions.

Independently, both studies concluded that far and away, the most influential factor is the salesperson. The salesperson is, in fact, two to four times more important than any other factor. [2]

Let me point out three important conclusions from these important studies:

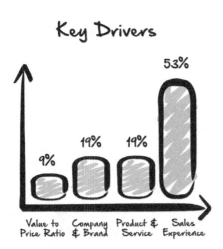

Key Drivers

- 9% — Value to Price Ratio
- 19% — Company & Brand
- 19% — Product & Service
- 53% — Sales Experience

Figure 15-2: The salesperson is 2-4 times more important than any other factor in selling.

1. You cannot rely solely on your solution, your brand, or your price. **You are the number one influence.**
2. You have far more control and influence than you may have previously realized. How you sell matters more than anything else.
3. This can work for you or against you.

This last point reminds me of a joke you may have heard. Two hikers see an aggressive bear off in the distance who comes barreling at them at high speed. One of the hikers quickly bends down and begins changing his shoes to the running sneakers he has in his pack. The other hiker exclaims, "Are you crazy? You can't outrun a bear!" To which the other hiker says, "I don't have to outrun the bear. I only have to outrun you."

So it is with this sales dynamic. You don't have to be perfect in your sales execution. You just have to be better than your competition.

This all paints a very clear and empowering picture that applies directly to how we deal with competition and sell more deals. Because all solutions tend toward parity over time, the number one strategy or tool in your toolbox is how you sell.

Master your skills and your execution of those skills, because they are the biggest factor. You will find many outstanding resources for this in the recommended reading section of this book.

The Inevitable Stall

Even with perfect execution, stalls due to competition are not completely avoidable. Again, addressing this issue is not as complex as you might imagine. Competition is an excellent example of how the reasons deals stall out are often interrelated.

What causes competition to stall a deal in the first place?

Competition is a Sales Issue that causes Client Indecision.

We cover Client Indecision extensively in Part 5 of this book. When competition is introduced into the mix, if our positioning against that competitor is not clear, it creates Client Indecision. When clients are unsure of how to compare solutions, they become concerned that they don't have enough information, and they are uncertain about which solution (if any) will produce

> Competition is a Sales Issue that causes Client Indecision.

the outcomes they are looking for. Everything you will learn in Part 5 is now at play.

The good news is that all the strategies we discuss in the next chapter about addressing Client Indecision apply to unsticking deals due to competition. For now, here are some insights for unsticking strategies we can explore for dealing with competition.

The Surprising Secret About Competition

"Outselling the competition" is always a popular topic when surveying sales professionals. I'm going to share a surprising secret about competition that I think will make your life much easier.

> Greater value creation is the shortcut to addressing competition.

Competition is about creating the greatest value.

You can't control your competition or how they choose to compete. You can only strive to create the greatest possible value for clients.

And regardless of how they choose to compete, properly informed clients choose the solution that delivers the greatest value. Said another way, value creation is a shortcut to addressing competition. The biggest win-win wins the deal.

Focus on delivering greater value.

Differentiation

Focusing on greater value will indeed, ultimately, drive you to a conversation about differentiation – but probably not the differentiation you are thinking of.

> Customers do not buy solutions – they buy outcomes.

Most folks spend an inordinate amount of time differentiating their solution. This is a trap. Customers do not buy solutions – they buy outcomes. The vast majority of salespeople spend too much time trying to differentiate their solution when they should be differentiating their outcomes.

Your solution is only relevant in the sense that it produces a result. It is a means to an end – not the end.

> Most salespeople spend too much time trying to differentiate their solution when they should be differentiating their outcomes.

And I know you know this. But be honest, are you spending more time differentiating your solution or the outcome it produces for your client?

When the conversation is about the value of your solution and the outcomes it delivers, your conversations will be far more impactful. And, ultimately, your focus on outcomes and results will force your competition to focus on results as well.

When you shift the conversation to outcomes, many times your competition's salespeople are not prepared for this. They are used to fighting the solution battle. When you shift the battle to endgame results that they are not prepared for, they often get eliminated right there. This will come into even greater focus for you in Part 5.

You're Working Too Hard

Let me ask you a question. How well do you know all your competitor's solutions? Do you know every nuance? Every detail? Have you ever been surprised by something new from your competition?

If it's difficult for you, a professional 100% focused in this area, to keep current on all the details of your competitors' solutions, imagine how hard it is for your clients to know.

You're working too hard. Differentiating your solution is orders of magnitude more difficult than differentiating your outcomes. Selling outcomes is easier.

Positioning Against Your Competition

The battle is for value. And we go into detail on ways you can increase your value in Part 6. But how do we take the conversation there? Customers are often hyper-focused on the solution. How do we shift the focus from solution to results?

I recommend you say something like the following which I have adapted from Anthony Iannarino's **Eat Their Lunch**.

Example Positioning Transition to Value Statement:

"You should know that the investment for our solution is going to be 7-9%

more than our competitors on average. But you want that. And if you'll allow
me to, I'll explain that even though we're in the same segment as some other
companies, we have radically different ideas on how things should be done and
why they should be done that way to achieve the best results. Are you ok with
me sharing that with you?"

Can you see the power? There is a lot going on here from a psychology
perspective:

- **Framing** – We've set the expectation that our solution comes at a premium.
- **Curiosity** – We piqued curiosity by sharing that it's a good thing that our solution costs more and that we have radically different ideas of how things should be done and implied they produce the best results. It's almost irresistible.
- **Permission** – We've asked for their permission to reveal our secrets.

This takes us to a conversation that shifts the focus to the results we produce for clients and how we get them there.

This shifts the battleground to results and value which is easier to sell and far more impactful. And once you've applied what you'll learn in the chapters about Business Case and Client Indecision, it will amp up your effectiveness and your ability to unstick deals tenfold.

Before concluding, here are a few more thoughts on unsticking deals stalled by competition.

Can trustworthy summary analyses, comparisons or references be used to position against the competition? Can we leverage a strong 3rd party source for our superiority?

When dealing with competition, you are going to be using a lot of Play #2 - Introduce New Information that you learned in Chapter 8. Remember, the best approach to introducing new information is to use Judo or "the way of gentleness" and the "Yes-And" formula we learned in that chapter.

It is important to remember that in the context of positioning against competition, your credibility with the client is at an all-time low. This is because the client sees your positioning and new information as selfish and self-serving. They think you will only share information that serves your selfish purpose of getting their money. Regardless of whether this is true or not, this is the dynamic at play. And it means that to create compelling messages, you must use what your client considers to be objective 3rd party sources for the information you introduce.

This mistrust dynamic is so strong, that you should be continually developing your 3rd party validation assets. Your clients will never tire of seeing them.

Reference clients fall into this category. They are not you, and they use your solution. Even on your best day, a referenceable client will be ten times more effective than you are - precisely because they are not you.

Comparisons and any kind of summary analyses also fall into this same category. Again, if coming from a 3rd party objective source it will be far more effective than anything you can create yourself. Having said that, if you don't have such resources, then stand where you are and use what you have. A well-done comparison or analysis can still be very effective.

Keep in mind that different types of information solve different sticking issues. Comparisons will help with Valuation/Comparison issues. Case studies and references are better at addressing Outcome Uncertainty (Sureness). And all your information will help with Lack of Information issues. More on that in the next chapter.

Can conversation, demonstrations, references, or site–visits be used to position against the competition? Can we take them to a customer site where we replaced our competition?

Any information you provide, including demonstrations, references and site-visits are forms of proof. When dealing with competition the strongest proof comes from what the client sees as reliable 3rd parties. And the strongest proof of all comes from clients who have used your competitor's solution in the past but have now switched to your solution. Absolutely keep track of the solutions each of your new clients are coming from. These are extremely powerful assets for positioning against competitors.

Can we uncover any insights that can help us position against the competition?

What are the insights or "dirty little secrets" about alternative solutions? This was the strategy we were forced to use in the story I shared in Chapter 8. We presented new paradigm-shifting information from a reliable 3rd party to position against a competitor that was being less than forthright. But be careful with this, because it is risky.

Never bad-mouth your competition. Never.

Not only is it unprofessional and which reflects badly on you, but research also shows it doesn't work anyway. It's all downside. Trashing the competition always backfires.

Let me share an experience with you. As an individual contributor I was working with a mid-sized clinic in Arizona. As fate would have it this clinic was considering a system from my previous employer with whom I had spent 10 years. I knew that system inside and out.

At one point the client said they were interested in a specific feature. I let them know that we had the feature they were looking for and then, hoping to get some extra credit and knock out my competition, I mentioned that I had worked at ABC company for 10 years and that their system could not do this.

Despite my amazing qualifications for making that statement, instead of agreeing with me, they looked at me strangely and said, "Yes, it does. I just saw it last week."

I could tell I just took a huge credibility hit. But, rather than playing it off and leaving an opening for that to be true, I instead doubled-down and explained in detail how it might "look" like it was doing what they wanted, but in fact, it could not do that. (I was such an idiot.)

My lengthier explanation didn't help. In fact, it made things much worse. I could tell the client no longer trusted anything I said after that. It won't surprise you to discover that my poor handling of that feature caused a moderately important feature to become the #1 criteria for system selection and ultimately caused me to lose my deal.

Guess what? They DID have that feature. In the few months I had been gone they had developed it. Despite my good intentions, my trashing my competition made me look like a lying snake oil salesman. It utterly destroyed my credibility. It was unrecoverable.

Here's the irony, later when I learned in detail about my old company's new feature, I discovered that they were handling the whole process in a very clunky way. It worked, but poorly. Our solution was easily three times better. But that didn't matter. The mistrust I created by trying to comment on my competitor's system completely knocked me out when I could have won in a straight-up contest.

All this could have been prevented if I had simply acknowledged my competition rather than trying to suggest to the client that they were being fooled.

How to Position Against the Competition

So how are we supposed to position ourselves against our competition without bad-mouthing them? Here are some communication tips:

- **Position against the competition by referring to them abstractly as "other solutions".** This won't be perceived as being combative.
- **Compliment the competition.** When pressed, for a direct comparison say something like, "XYZ is a good company. For organizations looking for A, B and C they do great work. If that is your goal, then I think they might be a good option for you. In contrast, our focus is more on organizations looking for D, E and F." All you're really doing here is sharing the differences between your business' philosophy and your solution's focus. You're making it easy for them to compare.
- **Remain agnostic.** If you're not familiar with the competitor then remain neutral and say something like, "We don't compete with them often. I really don't know much about them. What is your perception?"
- **Share client experiences diplomatically.** Do not share your own personal experience - even if you worked for your competitors and know everything about them. Sadly, the data shows that it just doesn't work. Clients will only see your comments through the lens that you are selfishly trying to gain. You can, however, share client experiences if you do so diplomatically. If you have a client that previously used the solution, you now have the potential for a 1-2 knockout punch. You can graciously share your client's experience and plant the seed for a reference call or visit. For example: "I really don't know anything about this personally, but our client ABC used to use them and said that they had some issues with XYZ which impacted their cash flow. I don't really know the whole story, but I'd be happy to connect you if you'd like to see what their experience was."

Have we explored how we might improve our business case to position ourselves better than the competition in terms of muchness, soonness and sureness?

We will address this in more detail in Part 6, but maybe we can make the business case so compelling stakeholders can't ignore it. In this context, where we are specifically addressing competition (whether it is a similar solution or an alternative use of funds) we can always modify our offer to make it more compelling than other alternatives using the three universal comparisons.

Beware of Info-Dumping

When it comes to positioning against the competition, don't just dump all the information you have on clients. They cannot absorb it all. It must be rationed to them strategically. Remember what you learned in Chapter 4. We need to deliver the right information, to the right person at the right time. To do otherwise will be counterproductive and hurt your sale. Info-dumping can be especially tempting once you've built up a lot of assets that help with selling. Exercise restraint and remember to keep the focus on outcomes.

Summary

Even though competition seems like a special scenario, competition is actually just a combination of all three of the stall areas we're already covering. Sales Issues, Customer Indecision and Business Case. And that means that all our unsticking strategies for those areas will help us position against competitors. While we haven't covered Customer Indecision & Business Case yet, when it comes to addressing competition, it just boils down to execution of the strategies in each area.

Another important thing to remember is that Competition doesn't permanently stick deals. It just slows them down while clients gather more information on business case and personal risk. Which are coming right up.

In the next chapter we will address the strategies we can use to unstick deals that are stalled because of Client Indecision.

PART 05

Strategies for Unsticking Deals Caused by Client Indecision

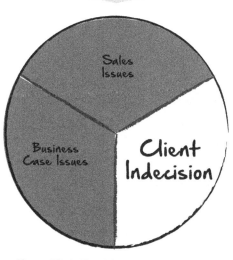

Figure P5-1: The 3 Causes of Stuck Deals

CHAPTER 16

WHY DEALS STALL DUE TO CLIENT INDECISION

"Buyer anxiety is real."

- DARRYL PRAILL

The Big Ideas:

- Three things cause customers to suffer from indecision: Valuation/Comparison Problems, Lack of Information, and Outcome Uncertainty.
- Once clients become convinced of the value of changing, they pivot to concerns about the risks of making a decision.
- Indecision and preference for the status quo are different and require different strategies.
- Know when to pivot with customers by accentuating the safety of making a decision.

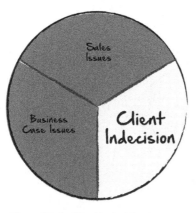

Figure 16–1: Client Indecision

The second biggest (and perhaps the most challenging) root cause of deals getting stuck is Client Indecision.

While client indecision is by no means a new concept, one of the things recently discovered is that the problem of client indecision is really a much bigger problem than had previously been thought. [1] A whopping 87% of sales opportunities suffer from moderate or high levels of indecision. [2] This means that the vast majority of sales include some challenge of client indecision. Most sales have it.

We already know that 40-60 percent of sales are lost due to no-decision. [3] What has been recently discovered is that on average, 56% of those losses are actually caused by customer indecision as opposed to preference for the status quo. [4]

There is a strong negative correlation between win-rates and indecision. As indecision increases, win rates plummet. [5]

This is an important finding because traditionally, strategies to address "no-decision" deals have typically revolved around the business case and creating a greater desire for change. This new understanding now suggests that in 56% of cases, the traditional approach to combating "no-decision" actually makes the problem worse, not better.

Why Customers Suffer From Indecision

So, the big question is WHY? Why do clients suffer so much from indecision?

Customer indecision is driven by a psychological effect called **omission bias**, which is driven by the customer's desire to avoid making a mistake. And it accounts for more deals lost than does any preference for the status quo.

> **Omission Bias** – The preference to do nothing rather than risk actively making a mistake.

Omission bias is the preference to do nothing, (even if it means missing out on some gain) rather than taking on the risk of actively making a mistake.

This is an important point.

Customers are much less worried about missing out than they are about messing up. That's what the data shows.

This dynamic is extremely important to understanding why deals stall, and why so many deals are lost to no-decision. The reason for this importance is because it means that improving the business case (that is, showing them that they are missing out on something) doesn't work on these guys. That's not what they're worried about. They're more worried about not making a mistake. To win these stakeholders over, we have to use different strategies.

Messing Up > Missing Out

Figure 16-2

Again, for these stakeholders, messing up (or the fear of actively making a mistake), *is a stronger force* than the fear of missing out on gaining some benefit. They'd rather do nothing, even if it means things going up in flames, rather than *being the person responsible* for making the decision that causes some problem.

Hold on to this thought...

It Gets Worse

Unfortunately, to make things worse, omission bias is empirically more difficult for salespeople to overcome. There are several reasons for that.

First, it's hard to detect. Many times, customers don't want to share that they're suffering from indecision. Other times, they are not even aware that they're suffering from indecision. Either way, we end up in the dark so it's hard to fix.

This sometimes causes professionals to unknowingly address the wrong issue. That is, rather than address the indecision, they sometimes double-down on improving the business case – which, as we just learned, doesn't work on these guys.

And this will make more sense in a minute, but an easy way to remember it is this: Business Case & Pricing Issues are not Risk & Indecision Issues.

They're completely different. And require completely different strategies.

And, as it turns out, the problem of client indecision is getting worse. Environmental factors, the number of options available, and the sheer quantity of information available are all increasing. And this is driving up the number of deals lost to no decision. [6]

Omission Bias

Omission bias is a rich and interesting topic that can get academic very quickly. My mission is to make the complex simple for you, so I have simplified things here.

In a nutshell, omission bias is a form of **loss aversion**. And if you don't know what that is, Nobel prize winners Daniel Kahneman and Amos Tversky demonstrated that people value the ability to minimize loss more than the ability to maximize gain.

This is extremely important for us to know in sales and entrepreneurship because we tend to project ourselves onto others. And as sales professionals and entrepreneurs, we are attracted to gain. That's one of the reasons we're entrepreneurs and salespeople. So, we sometimes project our attraction to gain onto others in the way we sell.

But what Kahneman and Tversky discovered is that Customers are two to three times more likely to make a decision that enables them to avoid a loss than they are to make a decision that enables them to realize a gain. Or said another way, People hate losing much more than they like winning. 2-3 times as much.

This has huge ramifications on the approach and messaging we use in selling.

The Key to Why Deals Stall From Indecision

We now know that people want to avoid losses. Let's go deeper.

As it turns out, not all *types* of losses are equal. And this is the crux of why and how deals stall because of no-decision.

We place more weight on losses that are "errors of commission" (where we actively do something wrong) than we do on losses that are "errors of omission" (where we passively fail to do something at all). This is the technical definition of omission bias.

Or said another way: People feel more regret when bad things result from their actions, as opposed to when bad things happen because of their inactions.

> People feel more regret when bad things result from their actions, as opposed to when bad things happen because of their inactions.

An Example:

I've spent most of my career selling complex information systems and services to large healthcare organizations. These solutions are very expensive.

When a healthcare organization makes this type of investment it can change the course of their whole business. The new solution can generate additional revenue as well as lower labor costs. Let's hypothetically say that the combined gain is $20 million dollars. If the customer does nothing, and chooses not to make the investment, they don't get the $20 million gain.

Now consider the worst-case scenario. The customer does decide to make the investment, but instead of it generating $20 million in gain, the project fails and instead it turns into a $20 million loss.

What choice would you make?

> Customers fear the bad things that happen when they do something more, than the bad things that happen when they do nothing.

When presented with these two options, virtually everyone chooses the first option where they forego the $20 million gain. Even though objectively speaking, the quantifiable loss is exactly the same in both circumstances. This is what Kahneman and Tversky discovered.

All customers want to avoid loss. But what they really want to avoid is losses that are the **direct result of an action they took**.

I know I'm repeating myself, but I really want you to get this.

Customers fear the bad things that happen when they **do something** _more_ than the bad things that happen when they **do nothing**. This is what we're up against.

Much more could be said here but I want to keep this simple.

Status Quo Preference vs. Desire to Avoid Making a Mistake

Now let's apply this to identifying root cause and the strategies we'll use to unstick our deal. The root cause of our stalled deal will determine the strategy we use to unstick it. And in this context, it is very important to understand the difference between preference for the status-quo and a desire to avoid making a mistake. A customer's preference for the status quo vs. their desire to avoid making a mistake are two _very_ different things. Each requires very different strategies.

Using status quo strategies when working with someone who is trying to avoid making a mistake makes the problem worse. We need to know what problem we're dealing with. We need to know the root cause of our stall.

The challenge here is that the symptoms for both can often look the same. And in the pages ahead you'll discover how to tell the difference. Before we do, let's briefly review the three reasons customers suffer from indecision.

> A customer's preference for the status quo vs. their desire to avoid making a mistake are two very different things. Each requires very different strategies.

Three Reasons Clients Suffer from Indecision

There are just three reasons that customers suffer from Indecision.

1. **Valuation / Comparison Problems** – where they're worried about choosing the wrong option and struggling with how to compare all the options and trade-offs.
2. **Lack of Information** – where they're worried, they haven't done enough homework to make an intelligent decision.
3. **Outcome Uncertainty** – where they're worried, they won't get the outcome they're paying for and that you're promising.

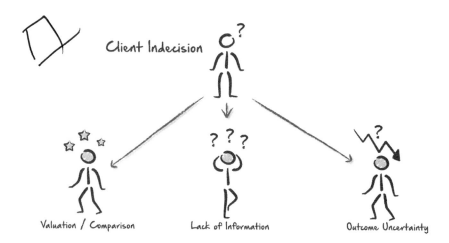

Figure 16-3: The 3 Reason Customers Suffer from Indecision

The Pivot

Now let's discuss how we can incorporate this important insight into our sales process.

Many sales professionals don't realize that every sale actually includes two key elements:

- Overcoming the Status-quo, and
- Overcoming Indecision

The precarious thing is that the weight of these two things shifts over time as the sale progresses. At the beginning of our sale, we are selling "Why Change". We have to defeat the status quo by creating a Valid Business Reason for changing. So, we're fighting inaction. Then at some point, our efforts are successful, and the customer becomes convinced of the value of the change.

> Somewhere in the middle of the sale, the rules flip, and we have to go from selling the cost of doing nothing, to selling against the risk of doing something.

Then a twisted thing happens.

The customer switches from thinking about the <u>value</u> of the change, to thinking about the <u>risk</u> of change.

They start asking themselves, "What if I take action and decide to change and it doesn't work out?" They are worried about making an error of Commission. So now, we're literally contending with the very same change we were selling moments before. We are now selling against the **risks** of that change.

Crazy right?

Somewhere in the middle of the sale, the rules flip, and we have to go from selling the cost of doing nothing, to selling **against** the risk of doing something!

We now have to overcome Omission Bias. And where defeating the status quo is about showing customers how they can succeed, defeating omission bias is about showing the customer they cannot fail.

To avoid a stall, we have to transition our messaging focus as the sale progresses.

> Defeating omission bias is about showing the customer they cannot fail.

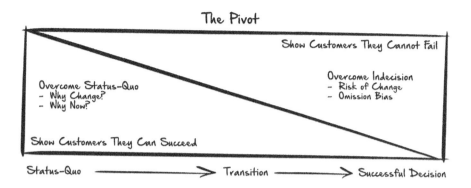

Figure 16-4: The Pivot

Knowing When to Pivot

How do we know when to pivot? Well, it's possible to start incorporating the "no risk" messaging right from the beginning. You can't ignore the business case, but great messaging has guarantees and risk-reversals built right into it.

Conversationally, the tell that someone is transitioning to risk mitigation is when stakeholders start changing their questions from: Will it solve? How much? and How soon? to concerns around points of failure. Or when they say things like: "I know we need to change but..." THAT'S when you've overcome the status quo and they are transitioning into considering the risks of making a decision.

Each stakeholder will transition independently. When you hear this type of language, that's when it's time to ask some simple questions to test the transition. You can identify when it's time to pivot for a given stakeholder with two simple yes/no questions.

1. "Do you feel like this will actually address the issues we've been talking about?".

If we get an affirmative response, then we ask something like:

2. "And do you feel like the return is big enough to warrant making some kind of a change?"

Adapt as needed to fit your style. If they say yes to both, then it's time to pivot your messaging towards addressing uncertainty and risk mitigation for that stakeholder. If not, then it's time to go back to work on our business case.

Pivot Strategies

When it comes to pivot strategies, the strategies for preventing deals from sticking and unsticking deals are essentially the same. The only difference is that one is proactive and the other reactive. What I mean by that, is we can be proactive and begin our risk mitigation messaging early, and transition to it more heavily at the appropriate time, or we can wait until deals stick and then we can use them.

The actual things we're going to do are exactly the same. The only difference is when we employ them.

Conclusion

Client Indecision is an extremely important and often overlooked dynamic in selling. Knowing when to pivot from selling the value of changing to the safety of making a decision can mean the difference between a stuck deal or a closed deal. Failure to address indecision issues can cause endlessly long sales cycles.

There are three different flavors of Client Indecision - Valuation/Comparison Problems, Lack of Information, and Outcome Uncertainty. In the chapters ahead we will uncover how to know which form of indecision our clients are suffering from and the strategies to help them through it.

In the next chapter, we begin with one of the most common issues – Valuation and Comparison problems.

CHAPTER 17

UNSTICKING DEALS CAUSED BY VALUATION / COMPARISON ISSUES

"The simpler we make things, the richer the experiences become."
— STEVE HOUSE

The Big Idea: Simplify Comparisons.

Valuation / Comparison

Figure 17–1: Valuation / Comparison

How to Assess if Valuation / Comparison Issues are the Root Cause of Your Stalled Deal

How can we tell if a stakeholder is suffering from Valuation / Comparison issues, and how do we address it if they are?

Valuation/Comparison Assessment Questions

On the assessment side, we want to consider things like this:

- Can the stakeholder quickly describe what they want, or do they seem to want everything? If they seem to want everything because "it all looks good" they may be taking a mental shortcut because they are having trouble comparing things. Wanting everything is a safe way not to miss out on anything.
- Does the stakeholder continue to focus on differences between packages or configurations? Do they frequently ask things like: "Can you explain the difference between X and Y?"
- Does the stakeholder openly express confusion about which option(s) to go with?
- Does the stakeholder get easily distracted by new discoveries and options they didn't know about before?

Valuation/Comparison Assessment Questions
• Can the stakeholder quickly describe what they want, or do they seem to want everything?
• Does the stakeholder continue to focus on differences between packages or configurations?
• Does the stakeholder openly express confusion about which option(s) to go with?
• Does the stakeholder get easily distracted by new discoveries and options they didn't know about before?

Figure 17-2: Valuation / Comparison Assessment Questions

Answering yes to many of these questions suggests that our stakeholder is suffering from Valuation and Comparison problems. And that may be the cause of your stalled deal.

Valuation / Comparison Strategies

When we correctly identify that valuation and comparison issues are the problem, what are our options?

The basic strategy can be summed up in a single word - Simplify. Clarify and reduce options as much as possible.

There are two basic categories of comparisons and valuations customers make that professionals need to be aware of:

1. Valuation and Comparisons of our own packages and offerings.
2. Valuation and Comparisons of competing solutions.

More choice makes people miserable and causes deals to stall. Barry Schwartz outlines this well in his excellent book, **The Paradox of Choice: Why More is Less**. More choice increases risk for customers in two ways. First, as the number of choices increases so does the customer's risk of making the wrong choice. And second, it creates uncertainty around the impact or outcome that each individual choice will have.

In the context of our own packages and offerings, it's important that we don't shoot ourselves in the foot. Offering too many options and choices paralyzes customers. We don't want to be the cause of our client's stall.

From the perspective of our own offering, we need to simplify. Create packages that cli-

> The basic strategy against valuation and comparison issues can be summed up in a single word - Simplify.

ents can easily assess and compare. An exhaustive exploration into the creation of solution packages is beyond the scope of this work, but in general, you want to have three packages - 1. An entry level offering, 2. The main offering (the one you want most customers to take) and 3. A high-end offering. [1, 2]

The high-end offering creates something sometimes referred to as the "decoy effect". It basically turns bargain hunters into value seekers.

To aid with valuation and comparison, you will also need a matrix that makes the differences easy to compare for each package.

	Package 1	Package 2	Package 3
Feature 1	✓	✓	✓
Feature 2	✓	✓	✓
Feature 3	✗	✓	✓
Feature 4	✗	✗	✓

Figure 17–3: Comparison matrices make it easy to compare differences.

Comparing Competition

To the degree we can, we need to create comparisons against the competition. In the context of creating comparisons, you basically have three types of competition that you learned about in Chapter 15.

1. **Status Quo** - This is competing with the customer just continuing to do what they have always done. This is the dreaded "no-decision" and is the number one "competitor" for most businesses.
2. **Alternative Investments** - This is the use of the money that might fund your project for other potentially dissimilar projects.
3. **Category Competition** - This is a competitor in the specific solution category you are selling in.

To be successful in addressing Comparison / Valuation issues you will need comparisons in all three.

Status Quo - For the status quo you need to develop a business case for change. The comparison being made here is the upside, risks, and trade-offs of doing something new versus continuing to do what they are already doing. Create some generic examples that fit a wide range of your target market so your clients can see themselves in the examples you use. Show upside, risks, and trade-offs. The goal here is to make the analysis easy. You may consider using this collateral to offer a deeper and more specific analysis that is unique to the client.

Case studies of other clients that examine these same elements also aid clients in making comparisons. They are not as effective as a specific analysis for the client, but are a shortcut to the data gathering side of that process and are still very helpful.

Depending on your sales model, you may even want to offer return on investment calculators. These can be used as lead generating devices or mid-sale value-add assets.

Alternative Investments - We touched briefly on this in Chapter 9. Any two investments can be compared using three business case criteria:

Muchness – Muchness is how much benefit or revenue will the project return.

Soonness – Soonness is how soon that return will materialize.

Sureness – Sureness is how certain they are to get the return being promised.

We generally do not have a complete picture of all the alternative investment opportunities a client has. So the comparison you're going to be doing here is essentially teaching them how to compare these dissimilar projects while supplying your own metrics in terms of Muchness, Soonness and Sureness. We will cover this in depth in Part 6.

Category Competition - These are the other companies competing in your solution space. Sometimes it is easy to compare solutions against each other and sometimes it isn't. The fact that it can sometimes be difficult to compare competing solutions is exactly what is triggering your client's indecision and stalling your deal. So when it comes to Category Competition, commit to developing good comparisons that you can use to help your client compare offerings. It can be difficult sometimes. And if it's difficult for you, just imagine how difficult it is for your clients. These are important and valuable assets to develop.

Sometimes, you can find a good, objective 3rd party source that compares solutions in your category. If so, consider yourself lucky and leverage it. Objective 3rd party sources are weighed much more heavily by stakeholders. I often find, however, that 3rd party comparison services don't always incorporate all the most important and differentiating categories that clients should be looking at when comparing solutions. When that happens, we need to create our own supportive comparisons as an adjunct to our 3rd party sources.

Type of Competition	Asset to be Developed
Status Quo	• Compare upside, risks and trade-offs vs the status-quo • Case Studies • Offer deeper, unique analysis for client • Consider return on investment calculators
Alternative Investments	• Teach clients how to compare alternate investments in terms of Muchness, Soonness and Sureness
Category Competition	• Leverage 3rd party comparison services when possible • Create your own comparisons that include important points of differentiation

Figure 17-4: Competition Comparison Asset Matrix

Bonus Play - The Reverse RFP Scorecard Play

One way of simplifying is to create a scorecard for your client. This bonus play comes from Davis Weiss. He calls it this The Reverse RFP Scorecard Play.

> We often see a buying team can't figure out which solution to buy, they all look the same. In this situation buyers become fatigued and can't see the nuance differences between solutions. This leads to stuck deals and indecision, because there is no confidence on the correct path forward. The worst outcome is that price becomes the deciding factor, and the cheapest solution wins. We want to avoid this at all cost.

The Reverse RFP Scorecard Play:

In this play, you will develop a comprehensive Excel spreadsheet or other visual outlining the problems your solution addresses and the key features and functions it offers.

As you create these, emphasize your solution's competitive differentiators to highlight your unique strengths. Don't make it so different from the space that people can't compare apples to apples but do highlight specific areas of differentiation in the solution, how the product works, and how you position it.

Incorporate separate columns for "nice-to-have" and "need-to-have" elements, as well as designated spaces for ticking off these criteria and scoring the completeness of each offering.

Once your spreadsheet is ready, review it together with your prospective buyers. Engage them in a discussion to determine which features they consider "nice-to-have" and which are deemed essential. Encourage them to use this scorecard throughout their evaluation process.

This approach enables them to objectively compare your solution with others in the market. In addition, it provides a helpful checklist to keep track of the challenges you address and the benefits your solution offers relative to others.

By using the "Reverse RFP Scorecard Play," you assist buyers in re-ducing decision fatigue and bolstering their confidence in making an informed choice while stacking the deck in your favor.

From the Sales Tactician's Playbook by David Weiss.

Remove Friction From Your Sale

It can sometimes take a long time for clients to even identify all the vendors they might want to consider. And it can take even longer for them to compare the differences between them even after they have been identified.

When clients can't compare things – whether that be solutions, offerings, or business cases, it extends our sales cycle by the amount of time it takes them to complete those comparisons. Without your help, clients will try and make these comparisons on their own – or worse, they will get help from your competition.

Remove the friction from your sale by developing comparison assets for:

- Your Own Offerings
- Your Business Case
- Your Competition (all three types)

Applying the Strategy

Deals stuck from Valuation / Comparison issues are among the easiest to fix. When clients struggle making comparisons – simplify and make comparisons easy for them. Get the right asset into their hands. Develop all the assets your clients need to make these comparisons quickly and easily.

Conclusion

When it's difficult for clients to compare things, whether that be solutions, offerings, or business cases, it stalls deals and lengthens the sales cycle.

There is no big mystery in how to address this challenge. The answer is to simplify. Take the friction out of your sale by making these comparisons easy for them. When you do, you will shorten your sales cycle and you will be able to unstick stalled deals caused by Valuation / Comparison issues at-will.

In the next chapter, we will address the second cause of Client Indecision – Lack of Information.

UNSTICKING DEALS CAUSED BY LACK OF INFORMATION ISSUES

"Without proper information consumers are unlikely to make good decisions when purchasing products and services."
- TIM HARFORD

The Big Idea: Anticipate the proof or assurances each stakeholder will need to be confident in moving forward.

??? Lack of Information

Figure 18–1: Lack of Information

How to Assess if Lack of Information Issues are the Root Cause of Your Stalled Deal

How can we tell if a stakeholder has become paralyzed because of what they consider to be Lack of Information?

Lack of Information Assessment Questions

Consider these questions:

- Does the stakeholder continue to ask for more and more input? (Whitepapers, demos, conversations with subject matter experts, reference calls, etc.) If they seem to have an endless thirst for information, they might be suffering from the Lack of Information cognitive bias. (Which is just fancy talk for Analysis Paralysis.)
- Does the stakeholder ever delay things in the name of collecting more information?
- Does the stakeholder ever say they feel overwhelmed by "all the information out there"?
- Does the customer ever express concern about "being in the dark" or being "still on the learning curve"?

Lack of Information Assessment Questions

- Does the stakeholder continue to ask for more and more input? (whitepapers, demos, conversations with subject matter experts, reference calls, etc.)
- Does the stakeholder ever delay things in the name of collecting more information?
- Does the stakeholder ever say they feel overwhelmed by "all the information out there"?
- Does the customer ever express concern about "being in the dark" or being "still on the learning curve"?

Figure 18–2: Lack of Information Assessment Questions

These are all indicators that our stakeholder may be suffering from the Lack of Information cognitive bias.

Lack of Information Strategies

Deliver the right information, to the right person, at the right time.

We alluded to the main strategy for addressing Client Indecision due to Lack of Information in Chapter 4. And that solution can be summed up in a single sentence.

Basic Strategy: Deliver the right information, to the right person, at the right time.

This applies to prevention as well as unsticking. When it comes to unsticking a deal that is already stuck, however, odds are good that we've already blown the "right time" part of this strategy. So what we need to do now is get that information to the right person right away.

When it comes to delivering new information, much of what has been mentioned previously in this book applies here. So we will focus primarily on elements we have not yet covered.

What is the "right" Information?

This begs the question, what constitutes the "right" information? This is an important question because "good information" is contextual and will vary from stakeholder to stakeholder. One man's trash is another man's treasure. And we cannot just dump all our information on the client and expect them to sort it out. Remember the paradox of choice. Too much information paralyzes clients. The wrong information paralyzes clients. [1]

If you look closely, I think you'll discover that these two are in fact, exact-

> **Too much information paralyzes clients. The wrong information paralyzes clients.**

ly the same thing. Too much information implies extra information that the stakeholder doesn't need. And what would we call that extra information? Wrong information. Any information beyond what they need is wrong information. Less is more.

I am reminded of the famous quip by Mark Twain, "Sorry I wrote you such a long letter. I didn't have time to write you a short one."

Clients value brevity and conciseness. In fact, the author has made a major effort to keep this work short, concise, and actionable for you for the same reason.

It's important that we correctly diagnose the information the client needs before delivering it. We need to know the bullseye because insufficient information is what got us in this mess in the first place, and too much information will stall the client as well. So how do we know?

Assessing and Diagnosing Information Needs

The best way to identify a stakeholder's informational needs is to simply ask. I have found the following question to be very effective.

"I don't want to bury you with information. What type of information would help you most as you go through your process?" If your sales process is less complex then just drop the last part and go with something like, "I don't want to bury you with information. What type of information would help you most?"

Listen closely to their response. Stakeholder responses will tell you a lot about where they are in their buyer's journey. From an information perspective, you will find that their requests will tend toward the other two categories of Client Indecision: Valuation / Comparison and Outcome Uncertainty. Requests for Valuation / Comparison information usually come first, and Outcome Uncertainty questions tend to come later.

Occasionally, you will bump into a person that is overwhelmed and talks about the tremendous amount of information there is out

> **"I don't want to bury you with information. What type of information would help you most?"**

there. For these scenarios consider developing an asset that simplifies understanding how to make a choice. One of my clients has a whitepaper titled, "Everything You Need to Know About Revenue Cycle Outsourcing in Six Easy Concepts". Another has one titled, "The Four Critical Steps to Selecting a Sales Acceleration Partner". You get the idea. These assets reduce overwhelm by simplifying things for the client. These also make good webinar themes.

Addressing Lack of Information When You Can't Communicate With the Client

If our deal is stalled, then it's possible that our client may not be actively communicating with us. In that case, we won't be able to just ask. We'll have to use other methods.

The best method is simply to engage our Executive Sponsor or Coach we learned about earlier. Get their coaching and feedback about the type of information they think each stakeholder needs. Once identified, you can use the Executive Sponsor or Coach to deliver the new information or use one of the plays we discussed in Chapter 8.

If you don't have an Executive Sponsor or Coach to rely on, then we're going to have to guess based on what we already know about the stakeholder's personality and title. Technical people tend to want specifications. CFOs and CEOs tend to prefer business cases and 3rd party proof. Once you've made your calculated guess as to what content is needed, use one of the plays we discussed in Chapter 8 to deliver the information.

Elevating the Quality of the Information You Deliver

Once again, quality is in the eye of the beholder. I recommend that you create informational content that is:

1. Aimed at a specific stakeholder or persona (i.e., CEO, CFO, CIO, etc.)
2. That speaks to that stakeholder's top business goals and concerns.
3. Has a very specific outcome goal.

Exit Criteria

We discussed Exit Criteria briefly in Chapter 4. Exit Criteria are the things that the stakeholder needs to see, hear, feel, understand, and believe before they can move to the next stage of their buyer's journey. Exit criteria can be hard or soft.

If our stakeholder is in the Evaluate Solutions stage, then a "hard" exit criteria might be: Database must support ANSI SQL. Either we meet this, or we don't.

An example of "soft" exit criteria might be: Believe that the technology solution is complimentary with their existing IT infrastructure. There is wiggle room there and a question of degree to consider.

When we don't meet the exit criteria for a given stakeholder, it dramatically reduces our chances of winning over the stakeholder.

Depending on circumstances it may or may not be beneficial for you to crystallize soft exit criteria into hard criteria. For example, if our exit criteria is "Believe support is excellent." and we offer a response time of 30 minutes or less, it may prove differentiating to ask, "What response time do you consider excellent?" That will drive to criteria that may differentiate you.

On the other hand, you may be able to address the exit criteria in other ways. For example, maybe your response time is below average, but your first call resolution rate is 99%. In that case it's better to leave the exit criteria as a general goal or ask questions about resolution rate.

In this context where we are discussing our information having a "Very specific outcome goal." We want to identify specifically what our stakeholder or persona needs to see, hear, feel, understand and believe to move to the next stage.

Again, this has been covered wonderfully in Mike Kunkle's **The Building Blocks of Sales Enablement** which I recommend.

Here are seven questions you can ask to help focus your content efforts and improve the quality of the information you deliver:

1. Where are we getting stuck? Is there a pattern to where deals get stuck most often?
2. Who is the intended recipient of this information? (i.e., stakeholder or persona)
3. What is this stakeholder/persona's business goals and top areas of concern?
4. How does your content help buyers address the "jobs to be done"? [2]
5. What is the outcome we want to achieve with this asset?
6. How can we make this content the best in this category for the customer? What is the value to the stakeholder?
7. What channels will we likely be using to deliver it?

Let's use these questions to create an information asset using a hypothetical scenario.

Let's say we've noticed a pattern that our deals tend to get stuck when we start engaging IT about integrations with existing systems. And let's say that we've noticed that the top challenges and concerns of CIOs are: 1. IT Overload - They just can't take on any more new projects. 2. Ease of Administration - They are concerned that any new system will create an additional load on the IT team that is already understaffed. 3. Uniform technology and the quality of integration with their current system.

And taking a page from what we learned about Win-Results in Chapter 11, we know that CIO and IT stakeholders tend to have business goals and concerns around maintaining stability, minimizing support requests, and developing fiefdoms that increase their level of control and influence.

IT team's Jobs to be Done (JBTD) [2] include: setting up systems, fielding support tickets, and fixing things when systems aren't working together properly.

The goal of this informational asset is to:

1. Simplify the details of the new system's administration so the stakeholder doesn't have to spend time researching it.
2. Show the stakeholder how the new solution will work with their existing systems.
3. Show the stakeholder that the new solution will actually free up resources rather than constrain them.

4. Show the stakeholder that the new system provides value to the C-Suite and the rest of the organization that will garner additional power and influence for IT.

We can make this piece most valuable to the stakeholder by using easy to understand visuals, using concepts and language the stakeholder already recognizes, and addressing any relevant areas outside our solution that impact their Jobs to be Done. This might include other vendors or even competition.

The value for our stakeholder is time saved researching details, and the hope of additional resources and influence.

This asset is probably best delivered as a whitepaper or video. (Or both)

Our asset might be titled something like: "How CIOs can Reclaim Valuable IT Resources by Implementing [solution category] - The 4 Key Questions & Answers to Know "

See how this works? This is straight-up Play #2 from Chapter 8. Now all we have to do is deliver the new information using one of the plays you learned there.

After completing this, repeat the process for each place you've identified that deals get stuck due to Lack of Information and you will eventually have a huge arsenal of high-quality informational assets that you can use to prevent and unstick deals.

Here are some additional areas to consider if you've identified that one or more stakeholder is struggling with Lack of Information:

- Can trustworthy summary analyses, comparisons or references be used to quickly address research needs?
- Can conversation, demonstrations, references, or site-visits be used to quickly address research needs?
- Can research needs be quickly addressed by developing and responding to a simple punch list of questions?

I used the term "quickly" in all three of these precisely because we're trying to unstick a deal. Having marketing take four months to create a glorious comparison whitepaper is not what we're looking for. We need the whitepaper **before** the deal sticks.

Now, we don't always have all the marketing assets we need. In fact, it's actually rare when marketing develops these types of resources because they just don't have much contact with this part of the sales process, and they don't understand the need. If you have any at all, count yourself lucky. If not, then it's time for you to start collaborating with marketing, your subject matter experts, and clients to develop this content.

When these assets are not created, your main strategy will be to rely on scheduling conversations with your subject matter experts and referenceable customers while marketing is building up your assets.

Having said that, it's important to remember that the personality types that tend to get stalled because of Lack of Information tend to value hard, physical information over conversations where they have to take notes. Stand where you are, use what you have and build for a better tomorrow.

Throttle Information

Carefully throttle information you deliver to each stakeholder. What we're really trying to do here is get them exactly the piece of information they need to take the next step along their buyer's journey. Hold back. You may foresee the next five steps the stakeholder will need to take, but they are still discovering. Throttling information has two very important benefits:

1. Increased Absorption
2. Increased Touches

Throttling information increases the speed that the stakeholder can absorb it. Deliver information in small, digestible bites. It's a simple pacing loop that delivers information at the optimal speed for each stakeholder.

Delivering information in this way increases the total number of touchpoints you will have with each stakeholder. And remember what we learned in Chapter 13 – more contacts = shorter sales cycle.

There are some common logical pieces of information that stakeholders need to progress to the next stage of their buyer's journey. You can review that progression for informational ideas and assets you may want to create in Appendix 2.

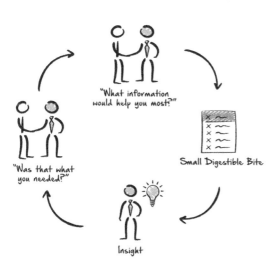

Figure 18–3: Client Information Loop

A Revealing Story

Years ago, our company rolled out an innovative workflow feature that moved tasks around to the appropriate parties within a healthcare organization, saving time and money by preventing errors and making the organization more efficient.

We were working with a mid-sized clinic on the west coast. We had been working on the deal for over nine months. This type of deal would typically have a 3-to-5-month sales cycle. We knew exactly where our trouble was. Amy, the operations manager, was stuck. She was not a good communicator. But despite having no objections about the solution or the offer, we just couldn't get her comfortable with all the change for some reason.

We sent her mounds of information. We sent her technical specifications. We sent her project plans. We had her speak with our trainers. We introduced her to several reference sites. Nothing seemed to work. This went on for months. We could tell she wanted the solution, but she couldn't seem to step over the finish line.

One day Amy was showing us these elaborate process diagrams she had been creating for the clinic. And after describing a particularly complex process, she pointed to a specific part of their business process and asked, "How would I do this in your system?"

We described the standard way we would handle that process. Amy patiently waited until we were done and then said, "No, I mean how will I set this up using your new workflow module?"

I am embarrassed to tell you that of the three of us that were there, none of us knew. We didn't know the answer. The product was too new. Naturally, we told her we'd get one of our experts to get an answer for us.

Guess what? Our subject matter expert didn't know either. Turns out it was a good question. Something no one in our company had thought of until this one client asked.

Ultimately, we brought in our engineers and improved the system to account for this unexpected process. That development was going to take months, however. So I also brought in one of our rock-star consultants and together they developed a workaround that Amy was comfortable with until the enhancement was complete. We closed the deal a couple weeks later.

There's a lot to unpack here.

1. First, the information Amy was lacking was how to implement her complex process using our new workflow module. Shame on us. We should

have figured that out instead of throwing everything and the kitchen sink at her to try and get things moving. We should have done a better job of asking her "What information would help you most?"

2. The information Amy needed didn't exist. We should have anticipated this informational need and created it before going to market with a new software module. It would have shortened our sales cycle.

3. We did ultimately adapt and created a solution that solved the immediate need and allowed us to move forward. We used this information to create a new asset for future sales that answered the question on a single sheet of paper.

The takeaway here is that lack of information creates client indecision and client indecision stalls deals. In contrast, anticipating informational needs and delivering them at the right time speeds up the sales cycle and prevents deals from stalling.

Conclusion

Preventing deals from sticking and unsticking deals that are stalled because of lack of information is a very straightforward play. Lack of information stalls deals. Too much information stalls deals. Anticipate the information, proof, and assurances that stakeholders will need as they travel their buyer's journey and throttle the information you deliver. The goal is to deliver the right information to the right person at the right time.

Be strategic about the informational assets you need and collaborate with your sales and marketing team to create them. Know how to read the signs that we have missed the mark in delivering information and use the pattern of stalls to prioritize the creation and delivery of those assets to clients.

If you follow this process, you will eventually prevent all stalls caused by informational issues.

In the next chapter, we will address the granddaddy of Client Indecision – Outcome Uncertainty.

CHAPTER 19

UNSTICKING DEALS CAUSED BY OUTCOME UNCERTAINTY

"The best reps know that dealing with the customer's outcome uncertainty isn't about making them more scared; it's about making them more confident."

- MATT DIXON

The Big Ideas:

- Defeating Client Indecision is about showing clients they cannot fail.
- All stakeholders suffer from Outcome Uncertainty. Outcome Uncertainty will be a factor in every sale.
- Anything that reduces risk helps address Client Indecision.
- The more precise your risk-reversal strategies are, the more effective they will be.
- Implement risk reduction strategies right from the beginning to prevent deals from sticking.

Outcome Uncertainty

Figure 19-1: Outcome Uncertainty

How to Assess if Outcome Uncertainty Issues are the Root Cause of Your Stalled Deal

This brings us to the granddaddy of the three – Outcome Uncertainty. Some experts argue (and I tend to agree) that the previous two – Valuation/Comparison Problems and Lack of Information Problems are really just symptoms of Outcome Uncertainty.

The argument goes like this: The reason some stakeholders get hung-up on comparisons and lack of information is because they are really suffering from Outcome Uncertainty, and they place a high value in comparisons, valuations, and information. In other words: Outcome Uncertainty is the true problem, and stakeholders try to address that uncertainty by using comparisons, valuations, and endless amounts of information.

This makes sense to me and if true, it means that the strategies that address outcome uncertainty are a shortcut to solving all three challenges.

It is a given that every stakeholder will face uncertainty. The real question is, do they get hung up on it and what can we do to alleviate it?

Outcome Uncertainty Assessment Questions
• Does the stakeholder press you for more and more project plans and detailed ROI projections?
• Does the stakeholder mention other investments they've been burned on in the past?
• Does the stakeholder talk about how big a risk or investment your solutions is for them or for the organization?
• Does the stakeholder ask for guarantees or assurance of results?
• Does the stakeholder express skepticism about achievability of their desired outcome?
• Does the stakeholder seek legal and contracting terms to limit liability and risk?

Figure 19-2: Outcome Uncertainty Assessment Questions

Outcome Uncertainty Assessment Questions

Here are some signs that a stakeholder is getting stuck on Outcome Uncertainty:

- Does the stakeholder press you for more and more project plans and detailed ROI projections?
- Does the stakeholder mention other investments they've been burned on in the past?
- Does the stakeholder talk about how big a risk or investment your solution is for them or for the organization?
- Does the stakeholder ask for guarantees or assurance of results?
- Does the stakeholder express skepticism about achievability of their desired outcome?
- Does the stakeholder seek legal and contracting terms to limit liability and risk?

All of these are indicators that the stakeholder doesn't trust the certainty of our promised results.

Outcome Uncertainty Strategies

All stakeholders suffer from outcome uncertainty. Every stakeholder will independently grapple with the risk/reward of your solution. It is always a factor. Plan on it and act accordingly.

The basic strategy to address Outcome Uncertainty is to Eliminate Risk. In any form.

> All stakeholders suffer from outcome uncertainty. Outcome Uncertainty is always a factor.

It's risk that's causing our stakeholders to stick. Eliminating that risk removes the friction and unsticks the deal.

How to Reduce Risk and Outcome Uncertainty

Just as there are a million ways to create risk, there are also a million to reduce it as well. There is a lot of mind-numbing academic literature on what creates risk for organizations and stakeholders, how they perceive and are affected by it, and approaches to managing it. I'm about to save you a ton of time and make this complex subject simple.

All risks, can be lumped into four simple categories:

- Trust Risk
- Internal Risk
- Financial Risk
- External Risk

That's it. Let's review each of these.

Trust Risk

Trust risk is the customer's perception of you and your company's trustworthiness to do what you say you will. They are asking themselves: Can I trust this person? (You.) Can I trust this company? Will this company make good on their promises? Is your company competent enough to deliver the promised results? Is your company financially viable enough to be around to support them after the sale? Can the solution actually do what you are claiming it will? All concerns related to you, your company and your solution fall into this category.

Outcome Uncertainty and risk issues tend to come up in a certain pattern. Issues of uncertainty about you personally, and your company tend to come up first. If clients come to the conclusion that you or your company are untrustworthy, or that your intentions are not in their best interest, in most cases the sale is lost. [1]

Fortunately, there are many excellent strategies for building trust and many great books have been written on the subject. You will find many of these in the recommended reading section of this book and a great place to start is Charlie Green's book **The Trusted Advisor**. I will highlight a subset of strategies for you here.

Trust and Heuristics

Heuristics are mental shortcuts that people make to simplify decision-making. Rather than expend enormous amounts of energy analyzing every dimension for decision-making, we all use heuristics to differing degrees. Heuristics are accurate and useful shortcuts most of the time. But not always. Sometimes heuristics fool us into making incorrect choices. These are sometimes referred to as cognitive biases.

A "frame" is a mental template we use to make sense of a situation or environment. It is a mental construct that helps us organize thoughts and make decisions.

Trust is a unique and very interesting aspect of decision-making because it is both a frame as well as a decision heuristic. [2] That is, if trust is already established, it then becomes the frame through which all future experiences are viewed. Once trust is established, **many** shortcuts in decision-making happen. However, if trust has not been established, then other heuristics are used to develop and establish the level of trust. That level of trust then becomes the frame through which we see future interactions.

This has a potential snowball effect for good or for bad. This is because the tiniest elements of experience with us and our company form the initial frame through which all future interactions are seen. The tiniest seeds at the beginning of the process can create a runaway train of trust or distrust.

The frames we and our stakeholders use are constantly being created and refined. Trust and reputations are like eggs. They are fragile. They may take a long time to develop but can be broken in an instant by a careless action. And once that happens, it is often difficult to rebuild.

Personal Trust Strategies

You are the face of your company and offering. Clients take a thin slice of their experience with you and extrapolate it into what they think the experience with your whole company will be. [3] You must be 100% professional and 100% reliable 100% of the time. Do what you say you will, exactly when you say you will do it. Your potential clients are watching you very closely. It is a test you must pass to win the sale.

Adopt the right mindset. You communicate your intentions with body language and paralanguage that is beyond your control. [4] The only way to communicate good intent is to actually have good intent. [5] Be objective. You are there to serve the customer and help them achieve their desired outcomes. You are a coach and trusted advisor. Sometimes that will involve you, and sometimes it won't. Once clients see that you can add value and they detect that you are not selfish, self-serving, or willing to do things at their expense, they will trust you greatly.

I have found this to be so true that occasionally clients over-trust to the point where they begin to take massive shortcuts. That is, they trust so much in the professional that they don't take the time to cover certain details because they are confident that they will ultimately be taken care of. This is valuable trust indeed and something that must be managed with great responsibility and care.

> Delivering unexpected value engenders trust.

Add value. Huthwaite research proved that based on the client's experience with the sales professional, there are four conditions under which they are willing to pay a premium for solutions.

- The seller identified an Unanticipated Solution for the buyer's problems.
- The seller identified an Unrecognized Problem the buyer was experiencing.
- The seller identified an Unseen Opportunity.
- The seller acted as more than just a vendor of products and services but instead served as a Broker of Strengths. [6]

We have covered this at length in Chapter 9 of The Perfect Close. A general observation here is that all of these are unexpected. And delivering unexpected value engenders trust.

There are seven primary ways to add unexpected value and gain stakeholder trust. Here they are in descending order of impact:

#1 – Deliver Insight
#2 – Employ Powerful Questions
#3 – Help Them Better Understand Their Needs
#4 – Help Them See the Path to Success
#5 – Share New Ideas
#6 – Deliver Education
#7 – Share News, Trigger Events & Trends from Their Industry [7]

Be a Consultant. Genuinely help customers make the right choice regardless of how much it affects your commission. Things like recommending that clients start with a smaller scope or make choices that do not necessarily benefit you engenders trust. Be personally accountable for the results you are promising. Your support as a professional is a strong form of purchase insurance.

Be Honest and Positive. Freely admit when your solution has gaps that need to be considered. Solve gaps in your solution by introducing other vendors when needed. This is what Huthwaite is referring to as being a "Broker of Strengths". Offer positive feedback on a competitor's solution when warranted. Sometimes, another vendor or solution may be better suited for this client. When that happens, recommend them. You are helping the client make the right decision, not just a decision in your favor. When clients realize this, your trust will go off the charts. I was once referred to a large health system by a prospect to whom I recommended go with a competitor. That referral ended up being worth millions of dollars to our company.

Company Trust

To simplify, when it comes to developing trust in your company, customers are looking for three things: 1. Stability, 2. Service, and 3. Cultural Fit. These three areas account for 90% of what is important to customers.

Company Stability - Unsurprisingly, clients want to know that the company they are working with is stable, growing and will be able to serve them long into the future. Some of the ways of communicating this include:

- **Years established.** Let them know you have been operating a successful business for a long time. If you are a startup, then you need to use other methods or focus more on the incredible amount of funding you›ve received that gives you more than enough runway to succeed. If famous or recognizable organizations are investing in your firm, you may want to invoke their names if you use this approach.
- **Size.** If you command a significant amount of market share, or your organization is very large, accentuate it. These are strong stability markers for clients.
- **Growth.** Consistent growth sends a message to clients that you are delivering for clients and have business scalability worked out.
- **Status.** If you have a premium brand that the client or outside parties recognize, consider leveraging your brand position.
- **Employee Tenure/Retention Rate.** Long-tenured employees are indicators of a good company that knows how to retain its most valuable

asset - its employees. If you have long-tenured staff or a significantly better than average employee retention rate, clients will see this as a strong indicator of stability.

- **3rd Party Validation and Awards.** If your company has won industry awards or is recognized by outside authorities as being noteworthy, leverage them. These are excellent indicators of stability.
- **Recognizable, Referenceable Clients.** Testimonials, case Studies, and large numbers of clients are useful social proof that your company is stable and delivers on its promises.

If none of these are particularly strong for you, you will need to focus more heavily on Service, Cultural Fit, and the other areas of trust while you develop these areas going forward.

Customer Service - The reason clients seek stable companies is because they want the quality service that a stable company implies. You can garner trust with clients by communicating high levels of customer service. Some of the ways of communicating this include:

- **Service Guarantees.** Guarantees in all forms are strong risk-reversal strategies and should be used wherever possible. If you guarantee fast response time, or any of the service KPIs mentioned below, leverage it heavily. Service guarantees are probably the best and strongest strategy for building company trust.
- **Service Metrics.** Prove your high level of service by sharing your customer service metrics. Some metrics to consider sharing include:
  - **First Response Time** - This is the time between when your customer inquiries and your support team responds.
  - **Customer Retention Rate** - This is the percentage of customers that renew contracts. Alternatively this can be measured by the percentage of revenue contributed by existing customers vs. new customers.
  - **Customer Satisfaction Score** - There are many different approaches to measuring customer satisfaction. One of the most popular is called the Net Promoter Score. This is a 1-10 ranking to the question "How likely are you to recommend this company to a friend or colleague?" 6 and lower are "detractors". 7-8 are "passives". And 9-10 are "promoters".
  - **First Contact Resolution** - This is the percentage of issues resolved on the first call.

- **Resolution Rate** - This is the percentage of support issues resolved.
- **Average Resolution Time** - This is the average time it takes to resolve an issue.
- **Open Cases** - This is the number of currently unresolved cases outstanding.
- **Customer Effort Score** - This is the customer rating of how easy it was to solve their problem. Typically rated 1-5 - Very Difficult, Difficult, Neither, Easy, Very Easy.
- **Abandoned Call Rate** - This is the percentage of calls abandoned because the wait was too long.
- **Dramatic Stories.** Due to a cognitive bias called vividness, a single dramatic story can often outweigh mounds of statistical data. If you have dramatic stories of customer service, collect, and institutionalize these stories and leverage them at every possible opportunity.

Every business is different. These are meant to spark your thinking. Every business should be leveraging service guarantees and dramatic stories.

Cultural Fit - Company stability and customer service are about the quality of work a company does. Cultural fit is more about being aligned with that company's value and how enjoyable those interactions are, and that you stand for the same things. Much has been written about company culture, and for brevity's sake we won't rehash that here. Rather, the important thing to remember is that clients want to know that your company has values you stand behind, and that their values are in alignment with yours. You should be able to articulate how your company's values positively impact your client.

Solution Trust

There are two questions stakeholders ask themselves as they are developing trust in your solution:

1. **Can** this solution actually do what I need it to? (And what you are claiming it will.)
2. **How** does this solution accomplish that?

Not understanding the difference between these two causes organizations and sales professionals to devolve off into endless discussion about the minutiae of their solution.

Clients buy results, not solutions. Your solution has no inherent value. Your solution is only a means to an end. It only has value in the sense that it can produce a result for the client. Most professionals and organizations

Clients buy results, not solutions. Your solution is only a means to an end.

could shorten their sales cycles dramatically if they focused less on their solution and more on the results they deliver.

Can This Solution Deliver?

When a stakeholder asks the question "Can this solution actually do what I need it to?", they are asking a result question. Will this solution produce the results I need? To answer this question, you need to know the results your stakeholder seeks. Do you know that? If not, it's time to work on your discovery skills and go back to "working the grid" that we learned about in Chapter 12.

Building trust in your solution is straightforward once you know the stakeholder's goals. Simply deliver proof that your solution achieves that stakeholder's win conditions. That proof typically falls into these now familiar categories:

- **Recognizable, Referenceable Clients** - This includes things like testimonials, case studies, references, market share and large numbers of clients. This is social proof.
- **Objective 3rd Party Endorsements** - This includes things like awards, studies in your solution category and reviews from objective 3rd parties.
- **Result Guarantees** - These are guarantees your company offers that clients will achieve specific results.
- **Demonstrations** - This is showing how your solution solves the customer's problem.

The first three on this list can be done without ever mentioning your solution. Compared to demonstrations, they are a massive shortcut to establishing trust in your solution. Demonstrations can be valuable, but most organizations jump right to demonstrations when they could be building trust far more quickly and easily using the first three methods. I have sold solutions valued in the millions without ever demonstrating the product. All these investors needed was the right proof.

You don't have that kind of proof you say? Start developing it today. It is the "Right" information we talked about earlier. The right information, to the right stakeholders at the right time prevents deals from sticking. The wrong information, to the wrong stakeholders at the wrong time will cause deals to stick every time. Demonstrations are indeed a form of proof. And startups often have no other choice than to use it. But for building trust in your solution, it is not the best choice. Recognizable, referenceable clients, objective 3rd party endorsements and result guarantees are superior for this purpose.

Did I mention that this form of proof comes in dump trucks, not shovels?

How Does This Solution Deliver?

Once a stakeholder becomes convinced that your solution **can** solve, that is, produce the results they are looking for, there is an immediate and natural reaction - skepticism. What they are saying to themselves is, "Right. So how do you manage to accomplish that?" They are now perfectly primed to receive your message about **how** you actually solve the problem or achieve the goal.

Most folks will immediately jump to suggesting a demonstration. And that may be appropriate at times. But let me offer you a suggestion that may speed up your sales cycle. When a stakeholder asks "how" you accomplish the goal, they are not asking for a demo. Rather, they are asking for the mechanism of action by which your solution produces the results. This is your secret sauce. Whatever it is in your solution that produces the result, that is what the client is asking for. They may not need a full demonstration. Rather they are curious about the proprietary thing in your solution that produces the result. Just describing that may be all you need.

Sometimes, skepticism does not end after understanding the mechanism of action. Often the next question going through their head is something like, "Sure. That would work, but I'll bet it's overly cumbersome or impossible to implement." You will usually get this from stakeholders that will work directly with your solution. This is essentially an operational question about ease of use or implementation and will almost always take you to some kind of solution demonstration.

Here are statistically the most common solution areas clients focus on and strategies for building trust in those areas.

- **Mechanism of Action** - This is the innovation that makes your results happen. You may have one or many.
- **Solution Quality** - Show the individual components that make up overall product/solution quality and reliability.
- **Scalability** - Prove your solution scales using case studies, references, 3rd party endorsements and performance guarantees. In the absence of these, demonstration and mechanism of action can also be used.

- **Time Savings, Simplification & Reduced Effort** - Show time savings, simplification and reduced effort using case studies, references, 3rd party endorsements and performance guarantees. In the absence of these, demonstration and mechanism of action can also be used.
- **Flexibility and Configurability** - Show that the solution can be configured and is flexible enough to handle current and future needs. You are answering the question "Will this work for us?" here.
- **Certifications, Specifications & Regulatory Compliance** - Show all specifications and certifications that you currently comply with.

Virtually all your company and solution trust is built using play #2 from Chapter 8 - Introduce New Information. This can be done using all forms of communication including collateral, whitepapers, presentations, video, etc.

Lack of trust or outright distrust, stalls deals. Lack of trust = Uncertainty. And Uncertainty = Risk. High levels of trust are arguably the biggest shortcut in selling. As trust goes up, sales cycle time goes down.

> As trust goes up, sales cycle time goes down.

Internal Risk Strategies

Initially, clients will be vetting you and your company, and you will be dealing with trust risks. Then as clients reach the pivot point discussed earlier, clients will switch to worrying about the risk of making a decision (omission bias).

> Client's distrust their own ability to execute.

Internal risk is the fear that the client does not have the wherewithal to implement and make the changes necessary to achieve their own goal. This can happen on a personal level as well as organizationally.

There are many risks that can cause a solution or project to fail. But when analyzed, about two-thirds of stakeholder risk concerns are not about you or your solution at all. [8] Rather, they are concerned about their own ability to make the changes needed to succeed. Clients distrust their own ability to execute.

This is an important insight. The average salesperson will continue doubling down on their company and solution when the root of the problem is that clients don't trust themselves. It has nothing to do with you.

The good news is that this same insight tells us exactly how to address the concern. They need a coach to help them make sure they succeed. And there are many strategies that fit into this category.

The Holy Grail of Addressing Internal Risk

The holy grail here is to sell outcomes. Selling the outcomes or results that clients seek, rather than the tool that enables that result, is a massive shortcut. Selling results, as a selling strategy, triumphs over every other strategy for these reasons:

- **Goal Alignment** - Our goals and the client's goals are the same. And that's the result we've agreed to deliver.
- **Solution Risk is Eliminated** - All the challenges around solution trust and risk are eliminated. We also have more latitude on **how** to solve, since the deliverable is the results not the solution.
- **Risk of Change Placed on Vendor** - Since the deliverable is the agreed upon results, the burden of change for the client is greatly diminished because the vendor becomes responsible for getting the client to implement the necessary changes.
- **Underperformance Risk Placed on Vendor** - Like the previous reason, since the contract is based on results, the risk of underperformance by the client is placed on the vendor.
- **Trust is Elevated** - Trust becomes greatly elevated because the vendor is willing to guarantee results.

There is an art to creating outcomes-based contracts. The vendor is taking on more risk in these models, and it is important to make sure that the arrangement is still truly win-win. Having said that, if you have the ability to offer results or outcome-based contracts, you will eliminate a huge number of potential deal-stalling issues.

This strategy can also be used to unstick deals. For example, changing your purchase model and offer from a straight licensed software purchase to a outcomes-based model can completely shift the client's paradigm and upend the competition.

Not every business can offer results or outcomes-based contracts. But most organizations can incorporate elements of the strategy into their current offering and significantly reduce the internal risk felt by stakeholders.

For those who cannot leverage outcomes-based contracts, the basic strategy here is simple: remove or lower the internal risk of failure due to change or implementation on the client's side. Here are some tools and strategies for that purpose:

- **Done For You Service** - Take over the responsibility that the client is afraid of messing up the most. Ironically, clients are usually willing to pay a premium for this service, so it increases the size of your deal while reducing internal risk for the client.
- **Consulting** - Offer best-practices implementation, optimization, and consulting. Again, clients are usually willing to pay for the service, so it increases deal size while reducing the client's internal risk.
- **Training & Implementation** - Like consulting, offer training and implementation services to ensure client success.
- **Customer Service** - Everything previously mentioned about strong customer service applies here. Strong support makes clients feel like they cannot fail.
- **Project Plans, Best Practices Docs & Checklists** - Project plans, best practices documentation and easy to use checklists show clients you have a proven recipe that if they follow, they cannot fail.

> The basic strategy for addressing internal risk is simple: remove or lower the client's internal risk of failure due to change or implementation.

All of these can be applied to various degrees depending on the dynamics in your business. For example, I have one client that delivered remote training on an as-needed basis for each client. After reviewing the training workload this was causing, they chose to offer regular weekly group training on the most common themes and made those sessions available for all clients at no charge. Training workload was reduced, and the company was able to offer "Unlimited Training" as part of their solution, which hugely reduced internal risk concerns for prospective clients. Sales increased and training costs went down - a win-win for everyone.

Financial Risk Strategies

Financial risk concerns basically boil down to two questions:
1. What if this costs more than expected?
2. What if the solution doesn't produce the promised return?

At its core, there are just two basic elements of the value equation: 1. The Input, and 2. The Output. The above questions cover these two elements in a simple way. These are both business case questions and we will expand on business case in the next chapter.

For such an important topic, the strategies for addressing financial risk are very straightforward. They basically boil down to accurate proposals and guarantees.

Cost Controls

If the price of what you sell is always fixed, then this is not an issue for you, and you can move on to the next section. If what you sell has variable components to it, then for managing the risk of cost overruns, you basically have 3 main strategies.

1. **Cost Guarantees** - Unsurprisingly, guarantees are our number one strategy.
    - **Cap Pricing** - Make sure you have sufficient margin for cost variability on your side, and then simply cap the price at a certain amount above which you are responsible for 100% of the costs.
    - **Guarantee the Cost Model** - When capping the price is not an option, you can estimate the price and then guarantee the cost model when it exceeds your estimate. For example, we might offer materials at 1% over cost once we exceed the agreed upon estimated cost. This is an example of "Sharing Risk" below.
2. **Accurate Detailed Cost Models** - Detailed costing models give stakeholders confidence that cost estimates are accurate. Consider including things like return on investment (ROI), Internal rate of return (IRR) and Total Cost of Ownership (TCO). The more logical and complete the model is, the more comfortable stakeholders will be that your estimates are accurate. This is easy and the lowest risk strategy in the list.
3. **Share Risk** - A shared risk agreement is simply an agreement where you and the client agree to split unexpected cost overruns using some formula.

If cost variability is a major factor in your industry, you may want to add a fourth strategy here, and that is leveraging references and testimonials that your projects come in on-time and on-budget.

Sidebar on Guarantees

We will discuss this more in the upcoming chapter, but when it comes to guarantees, many people get stuck thinking that a guarantee has to be a price guarantee, or a money-back guarantee. That is not the case. You have almost infinite options when it comes to guarantees. And they can be applied to almost every aspect of your business. For example, you may not be able to guarantee certain types of pricing because your project spans many months and includes resources that are market-dependent and ever changing. You can, however, guarantee that your pricing will follow a formula that is predictable and low.

If a guaranteed threshold is hit and you have to make good on your guarantee, you have many options. The guarantee does not have to be apples to apples. The remedy can be different than the trigger or the damage. For example, I have a client that guarantees that their customer will achieve or exceed a certain return when using their solution. This is a tremendous guarantee because the client is the biggest factor in their project's success, and their customers know that. If their customer does not achieve the expected return in the expected timeframe, my client doesn't just give them a refund. That's not what their customer wants anyway. What they want is success. So, the guarantee my client offers is to continue to train their customer on their solution at no expense until the expected return is achieved. So the impact of the guarantee to the client is very high while the cost to remedy, if they need to, is minimal.

Minimizing Investment Return Risk

The return the client gets from their investment is an important part of our business case and we will delve more deeply into business case in the next chapter. In the context of minimizing risk for stakeholders, the key question that stakeholders are asking is, "What if the solution doesn't produce the promised return?" And we need to be asking ourselves that question as well, because when stakeholders are uncertain about the return we are promising, they hesitate. And that hesitation often stalls deals.

When it comes to minimizing the client's fear that they won't achieve the promised return, we basically have just three strategies:

1. Guarantee Results

2. Minimize Impact

3. Offer Empirical Proof

Guaranteeing Results

Guaranteeing results is just what it sounds like. Carefully and accurately esti-mate the return the client will receive, and then assure stakeholders they will achieve those results with some form of guarantee. As mentioned above, you have many options here. And while our treatment here is aimed primarily at financial returns, all products and services deliver some kind of result. If you sell a health or affinity product, you may consider a satisfaction guarantee where the client can return the product for their money back. For example, a supplement company I work with offers a 30-day risk-free trial. If the supple-ment doesn't have the effect the customer is seeking, the customer can return the product for a full refund.

> **Strategy: Carefully and accurately estimate the return the client will receive, and then assure stakeholders they will achieve those results with some form of guarantee.**

Affinity products such as jewelry tend more towards quality and service guaran-tees. For example, Patek Phillippe guar-antees service and restoration for every watch since their founding in 1839. This sends a strong quality message to their clients. Similarly, Oris offers an unheard of 10-year warranty on their in-house watch calibres. To be fair, neither of these is actually guaranteeing results, which in the affinity world is very often sub-jective things like prestige, ego and re-spect. Rather, these types of warranties are measurable surrogates for the subjec-tive results that their clients are seeking to achieve.

Guarantees are powerful tools for combating client indecision because they remove risk and uncertainty from the decision-making process.

Minimizing Impact

Minimizing impact is simply another form of guarantee that minimizes the impact to the client while the solution is being implemented. Some solutions are sufficiently complex that it is difficult or impossible to accurately estimate returns. When this is the case, you can offer guarantees that minimize the impact on the client until the predicted return is achieved. A simple way of doing this is to offer payment terms that place most of the payment for the solution after the return is received. One of my clients offers a healthcare coding solution costing hundreds of thousands of dollars. They agree not to invoice their customer until after the solution has fully paid for itself. Since there is a significant up-front cost in implementation, this is a strong indicator of their confidence in their solution to produce the results their customers are looking for.

Offering Empirical Proof

Empirical proof does not guarantee results. Rather, it is proof that others have achieved the same results the client is seeking. And these will all be familiar to you at this point. These include market share, case studies, referenceable clients, testimonials, 3rd party evaluations and dramatic stories. Empirical proof is a very strong form of social proof. The heuristic being used is "If it works for others it will work for me." This messaging can be leveraged in many ways depending on what you have to work with. I have one client that says they are used by 90% of Fortune 500 Companies. An affinity example might be Rolex's "Worn by world leaders for over a century."

> The silver bullet in selling: Do great work for clients and have those clients help you get other clients.

Because of the vividness cognitive bias and the 3rd-party nature of references, your prospect speaking with an existing client trumps everything else on this list. Invest in maintaining relationships with existing clients so they are willing to share their experience with prospective clients. If there is a silver bullet in selling, this is it: Do great work for clients and have those clients help you get other clients.

Case studies are a very strong form of Empirical proof so long as your prospective client can see that they are similar to the client being used in the case study. Case studies from clients that are wildly different in size or are in different industries altogether will trigger a "It worked for them, but we are different." concern. Develop case studies for every client you sell. Make it part of your implementation process. You will never have enough case studies. Clients will never tire of seeing proof that you deliver.

Dramatic stories of how you delivered a return for a client can potentially trump everything if the prospective client can see themselves in the story. The psychology and impact of storytelling is irrefutable, and many excellent books have been written on this topic. Do not ignore it. You will find some excellent titles I recommend in the Recommended Reading section of this book.

External Risk Strategies

External risks are outside forces beyond the control of you and your client. They include things like economic conditions, regulations, and natural disasters. Neither you nor your client can control these things. Yet, the fear of the possible impact of these things can absolutely paralyze clients.

To understand external risks, you can do a PESTLE analysis. PESTLE stands for: Political, Economic, Socio-Economic, Technological, Legal, and Environmental. These are the most common categories of factors that are generally outside client control. You will find plenty of analyst coverage and resources for these conditions.

The solution is to mitigate client risk using two of the same three strategies we used for minimizing investment return risk. Those are:

1. Minimize Impact
2. Offer Empirical Proof

Minimizing External Risk Impact

This is the exact same strategy we just discussed above. We are just applying it to external risks.

Often, these guarantees look something like this: In the event that [external event] happens, we will [impact minimization guarantee].

For example, if your solution is affected by interest rates, then you might agree to offer fixed payment terms rather than financing. Or you might agree to finance the client directly. This is exactly how GE Capital started.

The specter of regulation can permanently stall deals. Creative thinking and problem-solving on your part can neutralize this. In one opportunity we were working on, there was a bill in congress that had the potential to severely impact the financial dynamic of our standard contract terms. In the end, after making sure all the client's goals were met, we created a second alternative model that would address the issues if the legislation passed. The standard agreement used Model A, but if the legislation passed, the client was given the option to switch to Model B. This allayed the clients' fears, and we were able to get the deal done despite the uncertainty about the regulation under consideration.

How you serve clients during emergencies are important moments of truth. As they say, you can only tell who your real friends are when disaster strikes. If your client has concerns about disasters, sometimes referred to as "force majeure" then outline a reasonable approach that will minimize the impact to the client. There are infinite ways to do this. Just remember to keep it reasonable and keep it win-win. You can't agree to deep-six your whole company to help protect your client from force majeure. That's lose-win.

Having said that, I find that these are wonderful opportunities to show-case your company values and that can be a tremendous trust-building experience for you and the client. You want your client to succeed - regardless of the circumstances. When challenges arise, this is an opportunity to prove our quality.

I had one client that serviced large 3rd-party shipping companies (3PLs). A disaster struck one of their customers, and the majority of their most important staff were unable to come to work for several months. My client used their own team to staff these key positions for two months until the client could get back on their feet. It was not in their agreement to do so, yet it created tremendous goodwill and guaranteed their customer's success during an emergency. Whenever a prospective customer would bring up force majeure, my client would share this story and suggest they speak to the customer they had served. So far, they have closed 100% of the prospects they've had speak with this customer.

This is a perfect example of strategy #2 Offer Empirical Proof. Service experiences like these are worth more than gold. Tell the story far and wide. Institutionalize them in your organization. Make sure every employee hears and knows these stories. They are the very fabric of your company's values. Then make them available to prospective clients in the form of case studies, reference clients, testimonials, and articles.

General Strategy Questions

As we wrap up this chapter here are some key questions and strategies to explore:

- How can we do a better job of delivering the right information to the right person at the right time?

- How can we improve the way we communicate to clients how we personally, and our company stand by our solution and how we will ensure they get the results we are promising?
- How can we do a better job of establishing trust and credibility?
- How can we offer evaluations or rankings from trustworthy 3rd parties?
- How can a guarantee of results be offered in some way?
- How can we offer ROI tools that help the customer see how the return is attainable?
- How can we provide detailed project plans that show clients we have a reliable, repeatable process for achieving success?
- How can we offer them insights and best-practice advice on implementation and ways to leverage their new capabilities?
- How can we adjust the details of our deal in ways that lowers client risk?
- How can we offer reference accounts, case studies and other forms of empirical social proof?

Conclusion

In Part 5 of this book we have broken down and discussed the three reasons customers suffer from indecision along with the risk reduction strategies that help prevent and unstick deals stalled due to Client Indecision. Once clients become convinced of the upside and value of change, they then pivot to concerns around the risks of taking action and making a decision. We as sales professionals need to pivot along with them by accentuating the safety of making a decision. More than anything else, defeating Client Indecision is about showing clients they cannot fail.

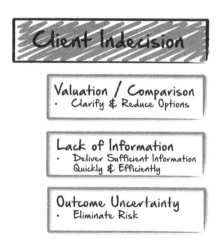

Figure 19-3: Client Indecision Summary

All stakeholders suffer from Outcome Uncertainty. And that means Outcome Uncertainty will be a factor in every sale. To unstick deals or prevent them from sticking in the first place, anticipate the proof or assurances each stakeholder will need to be confident in moving forward. Anything that reduces risk for clients will help address Client Indecision. The more precise your risk-reversal strategies are, the more effective they will be.

The basic strategy against valuation and comparison issues can be summed up in a single word - Simplify. We want to deliver the right information, to the right person, at the right time. Too much information paralyzes clients. Wrong information paralyzes clients.

By becoming proficient at addressing the four categories of client risk you can unstick deals that are stalled due to Client Indecision. And by implementing the strategies that address client risk and indecision right from the beginning, you can prevent deals from sticking due to client Indecision issues.

In the next chapter we will address the strategies for unsticking deals that are stalled because of business case issues.

PART 06

Strategies for Unsticking Deals Caused by Business Case Issues

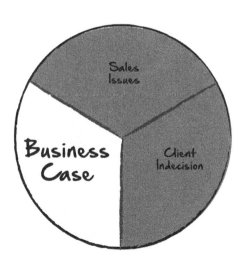

Figure P6-1: Business Case

WHY DEALS STALL DUE TO BUSINESS CASE ISSUES

"Return on Investment" (ROI) in business is predicated on the ability of the company to deliver as promised in product, profit, and its accompanying service."

- JEFFREY GITOMER

The Big Ideas:

- Business case is about priority.
- Clients use Muchness, Soonness and Sureness to answer the question "Is solving this problem the best use of our time and money right now?"
- After eliminating Client Uncertainty (Sureness) business case issues can only be about Muchness or Soonness.

Figure 20-1: Business Case

The third most common root cause of stuck deals is Business Case. Surveys reveal that salespeople and sales leaders rate issues with their business case as the number one or number two cause of the reasons deals stall. While deals do stall to business case issues, in my experience it is far from being the top issue.

As mentioned in Chapter 9, at the core, Business Case is about just one thing – Priority.

That's it.

If you think about Business Case in these terms, not only will it make creating your business case much easier and much more effective, but it will also allow you to position your solution much more effectively against other projects that are competing for the client's attention, time, and money.

Clients have a huge number of areas and possible projects that they can invest their time and money on. Each of these possible projects is different in nature and very difficult for stakeholders to compare. And because they are difficult to compare this very often leads to errors in judgment, also known as cognitive anomalies or biases which cause certain factors to be overvalued when comparing disparate opportunities.

You might be proposing a landscaping solution to a homeowner. That same homeowner may be considering using those same landscaping funds to invest in a franchise, invest in solar for their home or even go on vacation. The CEO of a healthcare organization may be considering investing in new software or IT to improve efficiency, hiring additional staff, or putting a new wing on their hospital. These are all very different opportunities. Yet, in both cases, they are all competing for the same money. How will they make the right choice?

The truth is, until trained, humans are terrible at making these kinds of comparisons. And as a result, they very often fall into cognitive traps such as: Recency, Vividness, Framing, Availability, and other cognitive biases. Outside of Client Indecision which we covered in the previous chapter it is beyond the scope of this book to cover these types of behavioral economics. They are very much worth studying however and may be the topic of a future work.

The key takeaway here is that left to their own devices, customers are bad at making these types of comparisons. Unless we proactively help them make these comparisons, they are likely to get it wrong.

How to Compare Wildly Different Investments

The good news is, by using three simple criteria, there is a simple way to compare any two investments with each other.

Those three criteria are:

- **Muchness** – Muchness is how much benefit or revenue the project will return.
- **Soonness** – Soonness is how soon that return will materialize.
- **Sureness** – Sureness is how certain they are to get the return being promised.

Using these three criteria, wildly different investment opportunities can be compared.

Figure 20-2: Any two investments can be compared using Muchness, Soonness and Sureness.

Some solutions such as luxury, affinity, or any solution that›s main benefit is an emotional payoff can be compared using this same model. It is, however, more difficult to measure the benefit or the «muchness» of these types of products. It can still be done but requires more soul searching on behalf of the customer.

For example: What will deliver the greater emotional payoff, a family trip to the Caribbean that they will remember forever, or the prestige and importance they will feel by owning a Rolex Oyster Perpetual Datejust?

These things are subjective and unique to each individual.

Usually this requires an iterative conversation with the client about the opportunities and facilitating the comparison. Another way of accomplishing this is by asking the customer to rate whatever the benefits are on a scale of 1 to 10. Regardless, selling luxury, affinity and emotional payoff products requires a high degree of empathy and emotional intelligence. But the model of how differing solutions are compared is still the same.

Answering The Key Question

Our business case helps the client answer this question: "Is solving this problem the best use of our time and money right now?"

By providing these three elements in our business case we enable clients to compare dissimilar opportunities.

This brings us to a key point. Effective business cases must include all three elements of: Muchness, Soonness and Sureness.

> Our business case, helps the client answer this question: "Is solving this problem the best use of our time and money right now?"

And the corollary is: When we present business cases that **do not** include all three elements, we actually create uncertainty, risk and indecision.

And that stalls deals.

Nuances

How to create a complete business case for your solution is beyond the scope of this book. However, to save you time and energy, I will mention just a couple of important nuances about communicating your business case.

- Vagueness in answering the three key elements (muchness, soonness and sureness) results in uncertainty, risk, and indecision. Be specific. If you can't be specific, give general ranges as to the degree of value, time frame and certainty they can expect to receive. For example, $500-800k, 30-45 days, etc.
- Claiming too big a return can hurt your credibility. Data from a Harvard Business School study suggests that returns beyond 8-14% are seen with skepticism. If your returns are genuinely larger than this, great. Just expect to be able to defend your claim.

Stakeholders Have Different Business Goals

Business case is about priority, and it is important to remember that every stakeholder has different priorities and goals. That means that priority is both personal and subjective. Remember this as you are working your deal. A business case that is compelling to one stakeholder may not be compelling to another stakeholder because they have different priorities. And if you're up against a competitor, this dynamic can be a very good thing, and a way to outsell your competition.

> When we present business cases that do not include all three elements of Muchness, Soonness and Sureness, we actually create uncertainty, risk and indecision.

We will compare four very different initiatives using Muchness, Soonness and Sureness in Chapter 21.

How to Identify Business Case as the Root Cause

How can we tell if our business case is the reason our deal is stuck? To be candid, a lot of times the client will just tell you. "Your deal stinks." they say. It's a good thing when that happens because we're communicating and it's easy to address. Being transparent encourages this behavior.

It's more challenging when the client has gone silent but won't tell you it's because of your business case. Or when they're afraid to tell you there's a problem with your business case because they think it will insult you or they think you don't have the ability to change it.

When this happens, at least the communication channel is still open, so we're going to use our assessment skills of listening and asking questions. By asking questions and listening to their answers, we'll know exactly where we need to make a correction. It's very straightforward.

The first question we want to answer is: Where does the stakeholder's concern stem from? Is it from the business case or risk?

For example:

"It's been [amount of time, quite a while, etc.] since we started talking about this project and I want to make sure it's a win for everyone, but I feel like we're stuck a little bit."

> "Would you say it's more about the business case and the return, or would you say it's more about some folks having some uncertainty about the overall success of the project?"

"Can you tell me, would you say it's more about the business case and the return, or would you say it's more about some folks having some uncertainty about the overall success of the project?"

And then we're just going to listen. Do not say another word until they've replied.

It doesn't matter how they respond. Either response will ultimately lead us to the stakeholders or issues that need addressing.

If it's uncertainty, (i.e., Sureness) assess the situation further using what you learned in Part 5 and then employ the appropriate play in Chapter 8.

If it turns out to be Business Case, then count yourself lucky. Business Case is generally the easiest issue to address. Since you've already eliminated Uncertainty (Sureness), it can only be one of two things: Muchness or Soonness.

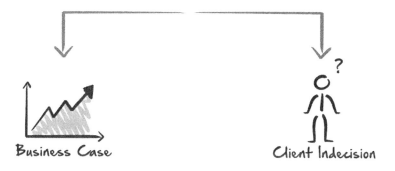

Figure 20-3: Identifying if Business Case is the issue.

The good news is there are lots of things we can do to improve our offer and overall business case. We will cover some of the tactics we can employ to improve business case in Chapter 21.

Deal-in-Hand

This is not a negotiation book but let me introduce you to a concept I have successfully used with my own teams for many years that will allow you to close 99% of the deals you bring to your executive management. It's called "deal-in-hand". Deal-in-Hand is a situation where you have won client preference and only the terms need to be worked out.

> **Deal-in-Hand** — A situation where you have won client preference and only the details of the terms remain.

At some point, after the client has had a chance to evaluate all their options, you're going to ask some variation of this question: "Imagine that the investment for all the options you are looking at is exactly the same. Which one would you prefer at this point?" Tailor it to suit your own style.

One of two things will happen. If they say they prefer you, then congratulations! You have deal-in-hand. The selling part for this stakeholder is over and the only thing left is the deal or the business case.

> "Imagine that the investment for all the options you are looking at is exactly the same. Which one would you prefer at this point?"

If they say anything else, then there is still selling to do, and you will use their answer to springboard into a conversation about why they prefer another solution at this point.

A lot of professionals feel handcuffed or constrained in their ability to negotiate or make deals with clients. In fact, some feel almost powerless because they are only given a very narrow range to change the dynamics of the deal or offer. Usually, this power is a small ability to discount.

I'm about to empower you in a way you're going to find very liberating by sharing two management secrets nobody wants you to know. And using these secrets, if you have deal-in-hand, you'll be able to close 99% of the opportunities you bring to management. (Managers and executives – don't hate me for what I am about to share.)

First, you actually have all the latitude in the world. Your managers and executives just don't trust you enough yet to give you unfettered deal-making power. They are concerned that if you had full deal-making authority that you will lead with price and crazy deal arrangements rather than leading with value. And rightfully so, because most salespeople do **exactly** that, and bring in deals that ultimately become lose-win. (And any arrangement that is not win-win ultimately deteriorates into lose-lose.)

Leveraging deal-in-hand will give you unfettered access to the full deal-making authority that your company can offer. Here's how:

You're going to ask the deal-in-hand question and determine if you have won client preference. The deal-in-hand question neutralizes the price so you can figure that out. If you don't have deal-in-hand, then you have more selling to do to address the client's preference for another solution. Don't work on the offer when the solution is the problem. When the solution is the problem, no offer will work.

> Don't work on the offer when the solution is the problem. When the solution is the problem, no offer will work.

If you do have deal-in-hand, then wonderful. You are the preferred solution. We now have to contend with the Business Case. The offer. Tell them that it is wonderful that you are their preferred solution.

Sometimes clients will jokingly remind you that the investments are NOT equal. Now, in the context of investment, ask them some variation of "What do you think we need to do to make this work?" (By the way, this is just a more direct version of "What do you think is a good next step?" from The Perfect Close.)

Listen to their answers carefully. The client will tell you exactly what in the Business Case or offer needs to change for you to win. Take notes. We're going to bring these to our executives.

Address anything outrageous directly. It doesn't happen often, but if the client suggests that to make it work, the solution would have to be free, then you've missed the boat somewhere. Before I tell you the secrets, let me tell you this:

Do not bring stupid deals to your executives. You will only destroy your credibility and reinforce that they are doing the right thing by limiting your deal-making power. You must establish value before deal-in-hand will work. We will discuss how to improve your business case later in this chapter. Establishing value is the professional part of selling. Anything else is order-taking and is not worth high commissions.

> You must establish value before deal-in-hand will work. Establishing value is the professional part of selling.

When you've established value, clients rarely ask for crazy stuff. In fact, I've often had clients tell me the offer is great just how it is. Isn't that nice.

Usually what follows is some dynamic around your offer or some internal constraint they are dealing with. I've heard things around training, maintenance, terms, the price, and many other things. And I'll give you some deal-making ideas in the next two chapters.

Flinch. Tell them (truthfully) that what they are asking for is pretty special and that you're not sure you can pull that off. Confirm that they are ready and willing to move forward if you can make their request happen. Be transparent and say, "Just to be clear, I'm going to have to go to the CEO for this, so we're only going to get one shot at it. If we can make this happen for you, are you guys ready to move forward?" We are framing this to be a one-question decision for your executive team. If there is a ton of back and forth that needs to happen, you are not ready to take it to the executive. You'll see why in a minute.

Once they agree, tell them you'll go see what you can do without promising anything. You are being their agent and friend.

Take notes and bring the reasonable items to your executive team. Even if it's a stretch. Just be careful not to pass into the realm of the ridiculous.

Here's what you're going to tell executive management. You're going to say I have deal-in-hand. All the selling is done and the only thing holding the client back is this one issue. (Or sometimes it's a couple of issues.) Then you're going to say, if we are willing to do these things then I can bring this deal in tomorrow.

Then you're going to ask the yes/no question: "Are we willing to do these things?"

Very often you really are dealing with your CEO, even though that might be through your manager.

Secret #1 – Your sales manager is almost as handcuffed when it comes to deal-making as you are.

In most cases they cannot approve the concessions either. They are going to send it up the flagpole. That's why it is critical that you explain clearly and exactly what is being asked for and ask the yes/no question. Because your email is going to be reviewed by the CEO and they are not interested in a long conversation to discuss the unknowns of your deal. It should be a clear yes/no decision. You are empowering your manager when you approach things this way.

Secret #2 – (And this is the big one) Executive management has no willpower. Unless your deal is clearly losing money, they will always say yes.

In essence, you're saying to executive management, I can bring you $XX,XXX,XXX,XXX by tomorrow if you say yes. Or you can just say no

> Secret #1 – Your sales manager is facing the same deal-making constraints you are.

> Secret #2 – Executive management has no willpower.

and have nothing. Which do you prefer?

One of two things will happen. You will get a call with clarifying questions from your manager or your CEO. Or, you'll get a reply saying "Yes."

The first time you do this you will generally get a call with clarifying questions. Expect a shakedown on whether your deal will really come in if the concessions are given. Once your management is trained and they can see that the deals really come in as you have said, you will simply get an email back granting approval. You forward this email to anyone else that needs to see the approval for the concessions to be incorporated into the agreement.

Occasionally, the terms will not be able to be met. When that happens, you won't get a "no" response. Rather, you'll end up with a brief call and some form of compromise which is what you report back to the client.

What makes deal-in-hand work is that you have already completed the selling part and now the only thing left is to make the deal work. Since you don't have that authority, it appropriately ends up on the desk of executive management where you have simplified everything down to a single yes/no question. Your executive management wants the deal to happen. Sometimes executive management is under even more pressure than you are. So, if it can be made to happen without being lose-win, they always say yes.

My teams and I have closed hundreds of deals with somewhat exotic concessions using exactly this method. There is really nothing sneaky about it. Your executive management knows exactly what is going on - and they like it. Professionalism on your part makes it easy for them to do their part. You often get fantastic insights as to what you can and can't do directly from your CEO which gives you even more power and options for the next opportunity.

This Deal-in-Hand approach works especially well with the "Something Special" variation of The Perfect Close [1]

Root Cause of Deals Stuck Due to Business Case

Back to Business Case. We already talked about the importance of Muchness, Soonness and Sureness. When we get to this point, we've already addressed sureness. That's reducing risk and showing the certainty of an outcome that we discussed in Chapter 19.

Since we've already eliminated Sales Issues and Client Indecision, and since Client Indecision is about Sureness, if our deal is stalled due to business case issues, it can only be one of two things: Muchness or Soonness. And that is the subject of our next two chapters.

Summary

Business Case is about just one thing – Priority. It answers the question "Is solving this problem the best use of our time and money right now?" Customers can compare completely different initiatives using three criteria: muchness, soonness and sureness. Unfortunately, they rarely do, which leads to poor decision-making. Effective business cases must include all three elements. When we present business cases that do not include all three elements, we <u>create</u> uncertainty, risk, and indecision.

You can identify whether the issue is about Client Uncertainty or Business Case with a simple question: "Would you say it's more about the business case and the return, or would you say it's more about some folks having some uncertainty about the overall success of the project?" The answer to this question leads you to Client Uncertainty or Business Case. And when it is Business Case, there are only two issues to consider: Muchness and Soonness.

And in the next chapter, we will address stalls caused by Muchness and you'll discover the surprising truth that you don't have to win Muchness to win your deal.

CHAPTER 21

UNSTICKING DEALS CAUSED BY MUCHNESS

"An investment is deemed an investment only through its returns."
- Lamine Pearlheart

The Big Ideas:

- When Muchness is the issue, we need to increase the size of the return somehow. There are only two ways to accomplish that: Increase the size of the return or reduce the investment cost.
- There are three ways to increase the return without reducing costs: 1. Increase the scope, 2. Improve the solution efficiency, or 3. Change the purchase model.
- To reduce costs, think in terms of Total Cost of Ownership (TCO).
- There is more to Business Case than just Muchness. The biggest return does not always win. You can create competitive advantage without touching Muchness by developing your Soonness and Sureness.
- Believable claims trump big claims.

Addressing Muchness

When we discover that the issue is muchness, or the size of the return, then the basic strategy is extremely simple. We have to increase the overall return somehow.

> Basic Business Case Strategy - Increase the overall return.

The Basic Formula

The basic formula for muchness is simple.

Muchness = Promised Return - Investment Cost

> Muchness = Promised Return - Investment Cost

Hard & Soft Costs

There is also the concept here of Hard Costs & Soft Costs.

Hard Costs: Operating Expense (OpEX) takeouts e.g., removing people, tools, capital equipment needs, benefits, and other fixed expenses that your solution is guaranteed to reduce. CFOs think in terms of hard costs.

Soft Costs: Time, Risk, Compliance, Engagement, Productivity, etc. These are things that are harder to quantify and represent non-guaranteed savings or unquantifiable outcomes. In these areas it is important to go past the initial metric assumptions and quantify opportunity cost.

As an example, if we save Y people X amount of time, what will they do with that time, and what new outcomes will be created. This is how you turn soft costs that are hard to quantify into quantifiable numbers that a finance person evaluating the business case can understand, believe, and endorse.

When Muchness is the Issue

When Muchness is an issue, we only have two options:
1. Increase the Return or
2. Reduce the Investment Cost

How to Increase the Return

Without touching costs, there are basically three ways to increase the return:
1. Increase the Scope
2. Change the Solution to Increase Efficiency
3. Change the Purchase Model

Increasing the Scope - Perhaps the return can be increased by increasing the scope of the purchase. Maybe the client is just not purchasing enough to get to an economy of scale. If each dollar they spend generates an additional 3-4 dollars out, then an easy way to increase the return is to put more dollars in. For example, if the return promised for a single hospital seems low compared to other initiatives, then maybe the solution is to invest in it for all 12 hospitals of the health system. Then the return will get up there into the interesting zone.

Change the Solution - Often extending the solution beyond the client's initial goals, or incorporating a higher cost, but better approach/technology increases the return efficiency. Many times, clients think in silos, and because of that, they often miss opportunities that are outside the box. Perhaps changing the solution in a way that solves additional problems will increase the return.

For example, I was working with a Radiation Oncology center that was trying to solve a charge capture issue by investing in a new Accounts Receivable system. The real answer, however, was to implement a charge capture system that would capture services at the point of delivery. Even though this was a big operational change for them, once we discussed the return upside, they agreed to modify the solution so that it included the technology that made charge capture possible at the point of service. Not only did this increase the size of the return, it also increased the size of our deal.

Change the Purchase Model - Changing the model by which the client acquires your solution can change the return. There is real potential here for innovation on your part. Sometimes a large up-front capital purchase can reduce long-term costs significantly. Sometimes using a model that leverages a higher percentage of remote training and implementation will increase the return. There are infinite possibilities here if you and your organization are willing to think outside the box. This generally requires close collaboration with the client but also has the potential to increase the return without affecting margins.

The Enabling Solution Argument - As a sidebar, sometimes the investment in your solution can be a catalyst for even greater returns elsewhere. Explore this. Can your solution become an enabling steppingstone that delivers even greater future returns? If so, you can claim some of the return from these other initiatives that you have enabled. There are many examples of this including: networks, storage solutions and productivity suites. They enable greater returns elsewhere which increases our return.

How to Reduce Costs

The other way to improve Muchness is to reduce investment costs. I only want you to use this approach as a last resort. (See my comments further below) Many salespeople see cost as a one-trick pony - the initial investment. This is naive. Costs are much more nuanced. To keep things simple, I want you to think of things in terms of Total Cost of Ownership or TCO.

Total Cost of Ownership is calculated as:

Total Cost of Ownership = Initial Expense + Ongoing Expense + Maintenance Expense

Total Cost of Ownership = Initial Expense + Ongoing Expense + Maintenance Expense

These are broad categories. For example, a per-transaction cost is an Ongoing Expense. So is fuel or electricity for operating equipment. Many things fall into this category. Ongoing maintenance for software or equipment is an example of Maintenance Expense.

Some kinds of Ongoing Expense are hidden and not directly related to your offer. Things like insurance and taxes are often left out of TCO calculations. If your solution reduces any hidden ongoing expense be sure to call it out and draw attention to it, because it improves your business case.

Changing the method and model by which your solution is purchased can often save the client a great deal of money on financing and taxes. Taxes on capital purchases are typically higher than services. So offering your solution as a Saas solution instead of a capital purchase can lower costs for the client. Similarly, financing can be a major expense in many types of sales. Carrying the paperwork yourself or offering your solution as a "rent to own" can give you control over financing costs and allow you to lower the cost component of your business case.

Many solutions contain a variable cost that scales with usage. Sometimes playing with these models and creating tiers where per-unit variable costs are lowered as volume rises can create a compelling reason to bring you more business while reducing their costs. If the per-unit hard cost to you is low (or perhaps even zero) then you may be able to develop an all-you-can-eat model that again, lowers costs and encourages your clients to utilize you more heavily.

Implementing Muchness Plays

If your deal is stuck due to Muchness, then all of the elements we've just discussed will involve Unsticking Play #2 - Introduce New Information where you are introducing new paradigm-shifting information to the client that we learned about in Chapter 8. As a reminder, when introducing new information your information should be:

1. **New** - Something they haven't seen or heard yet.
2. **Paradigm Shifting** - It should be relevant and shift their paradigm in the direction we want.
3. **Compelling** - The new information should be believable and impactful.

If your deal is stuck due to Muchness (i.e., insufficient return) then I recommend that you lead with a message similar to the following:

Formula: [Name], because of [recent trigger event] we have a new purchasing model that we didn't have before that could reduce your investment by [amount or percentage]. It's very exciting and you should see it. When would be a good time to review it together?

Example: "Hey Jeff, because of our recent partnership with ABC Partners we have a new purchasing model that we didn't have before that could reduce your investment on this by almost 30%. It's very exciting and you should see it. When would be a good time to review it together?"

There are infinite possibilities here. The recent trigger event on your side is important because it addresses the client's question, "Well, why didn't you offer me this before?" The answer is that we didn't have it before. This is what makes the information "New".

This is not a copywriting course, but when mentioning the savings in general, when the percentages you are saving the customer are small it is better to use the actual value of the savings rather than the percentage. For example, saving $361,000 sounds more compelling than 2% even when 2% might be more than $361,000. We are talking about addressing muchness here, but you can use this same formula to introduce a new feature or element of your solution. Just replace the money part with your new function or component.

Don't try to solve the wrong problem by changing your offer. Remember what I said earlier about working on your offer when your solution is the problem. When the solution is the problem, no offer will work. This would be like the customer saying, "I'm not sure your solution is going to do what I need it to." and you replying, "Ya, but it's half price!" Do you see how ridiculous this is? Amazingly, I see this all the time.

If you try to use Business Case to solve a problem with your solution it will be seen as desperate low-balling and you will lose credibility and make your problem worse, not better. We are covering Business Case last because you want to **use** it last.

There's More to the Story Then Muchness – What to do when you can't win Muchness

Sometimes you can't win Muchness. The good news is that while our Muchness may not be as big as other possible projects, our Soonness and Sureness can still make our investment an easy no-brainer. For example, as a competing project, building a whole new hospital will generate a lot of money. But it isn't gonna happen soon. And there's a lot that can go wrong. So the risk is very high. In contrast, our solution may deliver a return faster and much more reliably. So while we can't win Muchness, we can argue that bang for their buck, our solution is superior. In fact, the return from our solution could help fund the other initiative if that's what they want to do with the return.

This is an extremely important strategy so we're going to expand on it. While this concept is valid for all types of sales, if your sales do not involve diverse competition outside your product category, I encourage you to skip to the next section.

Eye Opening Example

To illustrate this point, we are going to compare four very different investment initiatives that a hospital CEO might be considering. You will see all four compared in terms of Muchness, Soonness and Sureness. As you review these, I want you to think like a CEO or CFO. You are trying to get the biggest possible return in the shortest amount of time at the least amount of risk. Which of these initiatives would you prioritize first?

Initiative	Muchness	Soonness	Sureness
Hiring New AR Staff	- $1M for 10 new AR staff - 3% improvement on $100M = - **$3M Revenue** - **3X Return**	- **3-9 Mths**	- **No guarantee** - Risks: market availability of staff, timely training, low/no turnover
Upgraded ICU	- $4M for ICU upgrade - 30% rev improvement on $10M = - **$3M Revenue** - **1.3X Return**	- **20-24 Mths**	- **No guarantee** - Risks: Sufficient utilization, availability of staff, timely construction
Investing in New Software	- $400k / yr. - 1% on $100M AR = - **$1M Revenue** - **2.5X Return**	- **90-180 Days**	- **Guaranteed** - Risks: Implementation challenges
Outsourcing RCM	- 4% of Net Collections (current cost to collect is also 4% - wash) - $500k implementation cost - 2% improvement on $100M AR = **$2M** - **4X Return**	- **6-12 Mths**	- **No Guarantee** - Risks: Implementation lag, less than 2% return, no CBO to fall back on if critical issue

Figure 21–1: Comparing Business Case for wildly different initiatives.

Here we have four very different hospital initiatives compared using the three criteria we learned about in Chapter 9.

First, we have a simple initiative to hire additional Accounts Receivable staff to get a 3% improvement on a $100M Accounts Receivable. We can see that the initiative is predicted to generate $3M in revenue which is a 3X return. And we expect that in 3-9 months. And since we're doing this internally, we have no guarantee of a return. We're simply up to our own devices. And, we have to consider risks around the market availability of the staff we need, that the appropriate training can take place successfully in a timely fashion and that we don't end up with any unexpected turnover while this is happening.

Next, we have an initiative to upgrade our Intensive Care Unit (ICU). It's going to cost us $4M to do that and we're predicting that it will generate an additional $3M in revenue for us, which is a 1.3X return. Because we have to build, and get our ICU utilized, we expect that it will take 20-24 months to fully realize our return. And again, because we're doing this internally, there is no guarantee of a return. Our risks are that our ICU upgrade will be completed on time, that we're able to staff it and actually get it fully utilized.

Next, we have a software initiative that improves accounts receivable (AR). The investment is $400k a year and the predicted return is a 1% improvement on a $100M AR which is $1M for a 2.5X Return. We expect to realize that return in 90 to 180 days. The vendor is willing to guarantee the results and not invoice us until we have gotten a complete return, so the return is guaranteed, and the risk is zero. Our only risks for this initiative are just implementation challenges.

Lastly, we have an initiative where we are completely outsourcing revenue cycle which comes at a cost of 4% of Net Collections. But our current cost to collect is also 4%, so the cost there is a wash, but the vendor has an up-front cost to implement of $500k. The expected improvement is 2% on a $100M AR for a total of $2M which is a 4X return on the implementation costs. The implementation is 6-12 months, and our risks are around implementation lag, and maybe not getting the 2% return promised. There is also the risk of not having a CBO anymore if something goes wrong.

You are trying to get the biggest possible return in the shortest amount of time at the least amount of risk.

Notice that despite how different these initiatives are, we can now compare them using Muchness, Soonness and Sureness.

Take a moment and analyze these. Rank these in the order you would choose to initiate these projects.

Which initiative would you start with first? Which one would you initiate last?

Write your answers down.

If you are like most people, you ranked these initiatives in the following order in terms of desirability and priority.

1. Investing in New Software
2. Outsourcing RCM
3. Hiring New Staff
4. Upgraded ICU

Sometimes people rank 2 and 3 differently, but Investing in New Software always comes out on top, and Upgrading the ICU always comes out on the bottom.

But wait, how can that be? Investing in New Software had the lowest return in terms of actual revenue. It didn't have the most "muchness". And Upgrading the ICU ties with Hiring New AR Staff for the highest return. Why then, does the ICU always get ranked last? And why do both rank lower than the software?

It's simple. There's more to the equation than Muchness.

> There's more to the equation than Muchness.

The Investing in New Software initiative had a good return (but not the best). It had the fastest return (Soonness) of all four. And it completely destroys the other three initiatives in terms of Sureness because not only are results guaranteed, but there is no up-front expense until the project produces a return.

This is exactly how CEOs, Executive Directors and CFOs think.

Business Case Ah–ha

For many, this is a huge insight. Two-thirds of the sales professionals I have surveyed have never thought about their solution in this way. You may have a competitive advantage in Soonness or Sureness you didn't realize you had. More importantly, without even touching Muchness, you can literally **create** competitive advantage by developing your Soonness and Sureness.

> Without even touching Muchness, you can create competitive advantage by developing Soonness and Sureness.

Your Biggest Deal Ever

Let's say you're working the largest opportunity of your life and your deal stalls out. And after weeks and weeks of effort you're finally able to talk to your client, and they confess that they like your solution, but it just doesn't deliver the size of the return they are looking for.

What would most salespeople do?

I can tell you unequivocally what they would do. Because I've witnessed it many times. They drop the price. Many sales managers and executives would do the same.

Is it possible to improve the business case return by dropping the price? Absolutely. And sometimes we do. But hopefully the previous exercise has demonstrated to you that you may not need to discount. And when you are competing with wildly different initiatives, it's quite likely that you will never win the Muchness comparison. That's because building a new manufacturing plant has greater revenue potential than implementing software. That's just the way it is. But building a new manufacturing plant comes with far greater risks and takes much longer to deliver a return.

> Without training, executives tend to evaluate initiatives in silos.

Here's the rub. Without training from somewhere, most executives will not compare initiatives this way. Rather, what the data shows is that they tend to see each initiative in its own space - a silo if you will - because they are dissimilar. This leads to errors in judgment and bad decision-making.

This is why your client needs you, and how you can become a trusted advisor to them. Teach clients to use Muchness, Soonness and Sureness to evaluate dissimilar initiatives. By teaching clients how to evaluate business opportunities this way, you help them make better business decisions. And that makes working with you inherently valuable.

The best way to introduce this to clients is simply to share how you learned it and how valuable you found it to be. Do not be arrogant, and do not tell them what they are doing is wrong. Remember the way of gentleness. You are simply sharing something that has helped you and others. If this seems abstract, let me offer some sample dialogue that will get you started.

> Teach clients to use Muchness, Soonness and Sureness to evaluate dissimilar initiatives.

Professional - "Are you guys looking at any other key initiatives this year?"

Client - "Yes. We're looking at big project A, big project B and we're really excited about big project C."

Professional - "Wow. That's a lot of projects. How are you going to go about prioritizing them?"

Client - "Well, we want to do all of them. But they're all big projects."

Professional - "I learned a very cool way to compare these types of projects from Dave Bigguy, the Executive Director at Famous Organization. He does over twenty of these projects every year."

Client - "Twenty projects a year. Wow. Ya, I'd love to hear how he does that."

Professional - "Well, he basically compares each initiative using three criteria: Muchness, Soonness and Sureness." [Professional explains what those are.] "In fact, I recently helped another client do one of these for some initiatives they were looking at. Would you like me to send it to you? I'm sure he wouldn't mind."

Client - "Yes. This sounds pretty straightforward, but I think seeing something might help."

See how this works?

And all you are doing is facilitating better decision-making. Your clients will love you for it.

Be Balanced in Your Claims for Muchness

Certainly, we want to claim as big a return as possible for clients. However, claiming too big a return can hurt your credibility and cause stakeholders to question your numbers. Let me share a fascinating story that illustrates this point perfectly.

To this day you can purchase Popular Mechanics and find direct response ads in the back of the magazine. Direct response advertisers are extremely scientific about ads. Ads are continuously tweaked and tested to improve results. The ad that has the highest conversion is referred to as the "control" and all future tests are compared against the control to evaluate performance.

In the 1970s, a now famous experiment was conducted that revealed an important insight regarding the claims we make in sales messaging. The experiment was a two-word change to the advertisement's headline.

The control headline read: Fix Any Part of Any Car ... Fast.

The new test headline read: Fix Almost Any Part of Almost Any Car ... Fast.

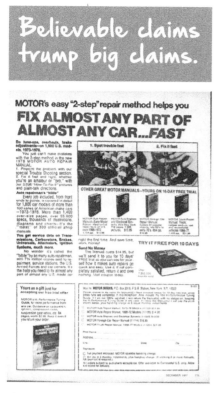

Believable claims trump big claims.

Figure 21–2: Popular Mechanics ad from 1978.

Amazingly, the addition of two instances of the word "Almost" sky-rocketed response by 900%.

This is very counterintuitive. One would think that the addition of the word "Almost" was actually weakening the value proposition, not strengthening it. Why then, did response increase so dramatically?

Analysts concluded that for this audience, the control headline just wasn't as believable as the new headline. And when it comes to customer response, believable trumps big.

There are many lessons here, but the one I want to highlight is simply that the biggest claim or return doesn't always win. Overplaying the size of your return hurts more than it helps.

Discounting, and Increasing Muchness

I've given you some strategies for increasing Muchness. Are these the only strategies for increasing muchness? No. There are many strategies depending on the specific solution you offer. Is discounting one of the ways you can increase muchness? Yes. But I hate this strategy and I recommend you use it only as a last resort. You are far better off adding additional value than lowering costs. In many cases, if you are leveraging guarantees properly, the investment to the client almost becomes irrelevant.

If you find yourself in a situation where you must use discounting to improve your business case, here are some things to consider.

Value is more than the numbers in your business case.

Different elements of your solution have different margins and different perceptions of value to stakeholders. Focus on areas that have the highest perception of value to stakeholders. Ideally, what you are looking for are things that are high value to them and low cost to you.

Value is more than the numbers in your business case. Remember that two-thirds of customer concerns are fears that they will not execute properly. This means clients typically value training and implementation assurances far beyond their list price. When possible, consider increasing the amount of these services rather than discounting them.

A strategy I used very successfully as an individual contributor, was to offer very high amounts of training for clients and then tell the client that if there were any training hours left over after implementation that they could save it for later or we could credit it to their maintenance dollar for dollar. There was literally no risk in purchasing extra training. My training hours (and revenue) were often more than double my competition and yet we were winning every time. Clients were often very vocal about the fact that they suspected other vendors were offering inadequate training to make the price look more attractive.

Be careful about reducing scope to improve your business case. A certain level of resources is required to achieve the promised result. As in the example of my competitors above, you don't want to scope your solution down so much that the client fears you can't deliver the results. Scoping down the offer is a legitimate way to improve Business Case. But scoping down too far can create uncertainty and indecision and stall your deal further.

Bonus Play - Faces of Impact

This bonus play comes from David Weiss and will help make the impact of the client's situation more important and real to stakeholders. He calls it the Faces of Impact Play and I think it is especially useful when the impact of a given challenge is difficult to monetize.

One area people get stuck in is the area of priority and getting stakeholders to recognize the magnitude of the problems that should be taking priority. Perhaps they don't believe in the magnitude of the problem, or that other problems are more important. In this situation you want to create a wave of support and make the problem unignorable.

Faces of Impact Play – Have conversations with end users, influencers, coaches, and as many people as you can find with the problem you are trying to solve. In your presentation, create multiple slides with images to document your learnings. You can break these down by department, functional level, or just a large group; the goal is to categorize them in a way that makes sense. Now put the people you engaged with faces on those slides with the 1–2 problems, quotes, sound bites, etc., that you learn from your conversations.

This deck grows as you progress in the deal and is reviewed often to solidify the "why change" message. It is hard to overlook the words and faces of the actual people that are affected by the problem. The faces make the challenges real and much more impactful to those more removed from the issue. These are real people with real challenges working to do their best.

The Faced of Impact Play raises the impact of their challenges and makes the problems and issues real to stakeholder.

From David Weiss', book The Sales Tactician's Playbook.

Summary

When Muchness is the issue, we need to increase the size of the return somehow and there are only two ways to accomplish that: Increase the size of the return or reduce the investment cost. There are three creative ways to increase your total return without reducing costs: 1. Increase the scope, 2. Improve the solution efficiency, or 3. Change the purchase model.

When considering adjusting the cost side of the formula before adjusting price consider things in terms of Total Cost of Ownership (TCO). This will lead you to many frequently ignored areas of cost reduction that you can use to improve your business case.

There is far more to Business Case than just Muchness. The solution with the biggest return does not always win the sale. You can create competitive advantage without touching Muchness by developing the Soonness and Sureness attributes of your business case.

And finally, be cautious about making overly big claims about the return on your business case. Believable claims trump big claims. Also be careful about scoping your solution down to reduce costs. Scoping down too far can create new uncertainty and indecision about your effectiveness to solve and stall your deal.

In the next chapter, we will address strategies to address Soonness which includes some surprising insights that are also useful when selling during a crisis.

CHAPTER 22

UNSTICKING DEALS CAUSED BY SOONNESS

"Payback period is the time it takes to recover the cost of an investment. Shorter paybacks are more attractive investments, while longer payback periods are less desirable."

- JACK PHILLIPS

The Big Ideas:

- During emergencies, clients seek solutions that pay off quickly.
- Long payoff periods can cause deals to stall.

Addressing Soonness

Soonness is the amount of time it takes for an initiative or investment to produce a return. And in the context of delivering a compelling business case, time to return or Soonness doesn't get the attention it deserves. This is very much because of human nature. So, before we discuss strategies and tactics around improving Soonness. Let's look at the Covey productivity quadrant.

> **Soonness** – The amount of time it takes for an initiative or investment to produce a return.

The Covey Time Management Matrix

The Covey Time Management Matrix is a matrix with two axes: 1. Urgency, and 2. Importance. In this model we have importance on the left and along the top we have urgency.

In quadrant 1 we have things that are Urgent & Important. And in quadrant 2 we have things that are Not Urgent but are Important. In Quadrant 3 we have things that are Urgent but Not Important. And in quadrant 4 we have things that are Not Urgent or Important.

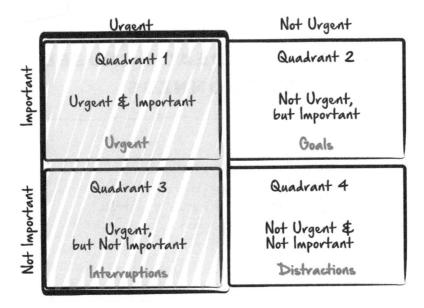

Figure 22-1: The Covey Time Management Matrix

Organizations tend to get stuck in quadrants 1 and 3 where they are always putting out fires. They are already overloaded and with limited resources and time, so it is hard to stay focused on the things that are the most important in the long run. This is especially true during a crisis and a wide range of emergencies. Fires are more urgent (not more important) and take time, resources, attention, and priority. So often, prospects can only focus on what's right in front of them—right then.

During emergencies, clients seek solutions that pay off quickly.

Here are the sales implications of this insight. If we propose an initiative with a 3–5-year payoff during an emergency or a time of uncertainty, it will get relegated to quadrant 2 and will be ignored in favor of faster payout initiatives. This means it's important to get our initiative into Quadrant 1. And there are a few ways we can do that:

> **During emergencies, clients seek solutions that pay off quickly.**

1. **We can sell the urgency of the project.** We can illuminate the bad things or traps that will befall the client if they don't adopt our initiative.

2. **We can elevate the importance of the project.** What makes this initiative strategic for the client? Why is it a bigger deal than they currently realize?

3. **Shorten the payoff period.** During a crisis, organizations are looking for very fast returns. Along the order of 1-6 months and probably no longer than 12 months.

> Business cases with long payoff periods can actually cause deals to stick.

The point I'm trying to make here is that business cases with long payoff periods can actually **cause** deals to stick. Because they end up getting prioritized lower. People don't consider incremental growth initiatives when their house is on fire.

Be careful about using options one and two above. If you've identified that Business Case is truly the root cause of your stuck deal, then leverage them. But remember what you learned in Part 5, if the root cause of the stall is actually Client Indecision, using these two strategies may make your problem worse because you are increasing the risk of doing nothing when the client is suffering from Omission Bias (the risk of doing something). I'm not saying not to use these strategies. I'm saying use them when it is appropriate.

One way to do this is by leveraging Opportunity Cost. Opportunity cost is not part of the Total Cost of Ownership formula. Opportunity is the cost of NOT doing something. While you cannot use it to reduce costs directly and improve your TCO, you can use it to establish what the cost of inaction is for the client. This has been covered wonderfully in Michael Nick's book **ROI Selling**, which I recommend. To leverage opportunity cost to create urgency or elevate importance, you simply calculate the cost of inaction. You then use this as a frame or reason to act. You'll be able to say things like, "Wow. It seems not addressing this might be costing you as much as $XX,XXX a day. Could that be right?" You've basically monetized the cost of inaction.

Again, playing this card will not help you if the client is suffering from Client Indecision, in fact it may actually increase their fear of making a wrong decision. So, use it wisely and selectively.

Shortening The Payoff Period

The strategies available to you to improve Soonness tend to be unique to the specific solution you are selling. With that said, here are some questions and

How can the speed of the return be reduced?

useful ideas that will spark your thinking on possible ways you might shorten your payoff period.

The overall question is this: How can the speed of the return be reduced? In my experience, when organizations get serious about speeding implementation and ROI, they end up finding dozens of ways they can speed-up the time to return.

Questions and Ideas for Improving Soonness:

- How can we involve partners, existing clients, or the prospect themselves to speed the return? (This includes 3rd party tools and resources.)
- How can we guarantee a return within a specific timeframe? What is the soonest amount of time we **can** guarantee a return?
- How can we adopt a model where the initial return comes sooner knowing that we will make greater margin on the back end? How can we change our pricing model such that the return or break even point comes more quickly?
- How can we implement **part** of the solution in such a way that some portion of the return comes sooner?
- How can we roll out the project in a way that makes other initiatives possible sooner? (Even though the current project is not complete.)
- How can we adopt a more innovative (training, implementation, deployment, delivery, etc.) that delivers the return more quickly?
- How can we front-load resources where we are using more resources at the beginning of the project and less at the end so that returns come more quickly?
- How can we remove dependencies in the (training, implementation, deployment, delivery, etc.) so that more things can be done in parallel?
- How can we better prioritize the elements in our (training, implementation, deployment, delivery, etc.) so that the return comes more quickly?
- How can we leverage an A-Team of professionals to more quickly hit the more challenging milestones and leave more mundane responsibilities to the B-Team?
- Sometimes the client is the constraint. How can we take on more responsibility and remove client responsibility as a constraint?
- How can we preconfigure the solution in some way that speeds (training, implementation, deployment, delivery, etc.)?

These are different than the other types questions we've explored because we're working to spark and jumpstart your thinking. Communicate the value that your delivery team has in making the sale and then do this exercise with them. Your acknowledgement of them makes them feel appreciated and they always help.

> "The best time to plant a tree is 20 years ago. The next best time to plant a tree is today."

There is a Chinese proverb that says, "The best time to plant a tree is 20 years ago. The next best time to plant a tree is today."

This is a time-tested message and an important truth you can share with clients as you discuss Soonness with them.

Thinking Outside the Box

I was once working with a large multispecialty clinic in the rocky mountain area that was growing rapidly. The prospective client had done their due diligence and we were their vendor of choice, but the client had an aggressive schedule of new locations opening. And each new location would delay the contract 3-4 months. "We wish we had chosen sooner." They told me. "We need to hire and train the staff for each new location, and that is a huge lift. Things won't settle down until next spring." That was nine months away.

We brainstormed through various possible ways they could alter their rollout to make system adoption possible, but because of their aggressive rollout schedule there just weren't any resources available to apply to the system implementation until after the rollouts. And because the system implementation had its own 3–4-month implementation schedule, it always conflicted in some way, and opening the clinics was the top priority. We were at an impasse.

I returned to my company, and we explored different ways we might implement the client that would avoid the nine-month delay. My team ultimately proposed an idea where our team would implement and operate one of the new clinics while we trained their staff side-by-side. Our team would be their team. It required a lot of resources initially, but lessened the resources needed later so that the implementation costs were nearly the same as before. More importantly for us, however, is that we could get started immediately and all future locations would have the benefit of having the new system.

I brought our director of implementations with me, and we suggested the idea to the client. They were ecstatic. Not only did they want to move forward right away, but they were also happy to pay the small increase in the implementation cost. We closed our deal two weeks later and successfully implemented the client.

This is an example of a very legitimate reason that a deal (very nearly) got stalled. We could have easily just used play #4 Patience from Chapter 8 and waited until the following spring to get our deal. And I'm sure you can see that we almost fell victim to the urgency trap from the Covey Time Management Matrix.

Instead, we collectively applied some innovation to our implementation process and created a win-win arrangement for both us and the client. Solving the Soonness problem closed our sale.

Even better, however, is that the particular solution we used to address Soonness greatly improved our relationship with the client. Being together as co-members of their staff and team brought everyone closer together and made everyone feel like family. It aligned us with the client (which they recognized) and forged a phenomenal relationship which exists to this day.

Summary

There is always a crisis of some kind happening. Organizations can easily fall into traps where they are always putting out fires. They get stuck focusing on what is urgent at the expense of what is important. This is especially true during emergencies. In times of crisis, clients seek solutions that pay off quickly. And when the payoff of our solution falls beyond that expected horizon, it can actually cause deals to stall.

We can get our solution in quadrant 1 (both important and urgent) by: 1. Selling the urgency of the project, 2. Elevating the importance of the project, or 3. Shortening the payoff period.

Innovation and creative thinking about the delivery of your solution can not only improve your Soonness but also increase the overall value of your solution.

In the next chapter, we will look at your business case as a whole and reveal the surprising truth about what is truly the most valuable thing about your business case. (And it's not what you think it is...)

CHAPTER 23

IMPLEMENTING YOUR BUSINESS CASE

"Your business case includes ROI calculations that prove to your customer the financial logic of investing in your solution."
- FRANK GERIC

The Big Ideas:

- Weave Muchness, Soonness and Sureness into your client communication.
- The real value in developing your business case is developing it with your customer.
- Collaborating on your business case addresses elements of Client Indecision as well as Business Case.

Reviewing Your Business Case as a Whole

Remember the key insight that you learned in Chapter 9. At its core, Business Case is about just one thing – Priority. Your business case answers the question: "Is solving this problem the best use of our time & money right now?"

To answer that question for clients, you must include all three elements of Muchness, Soonness and Sureness in your business case. When we present business cases that **do not** include all three elements of Muchness, Soonness and Sureness, we actually create uncertainty, risk and indecision. Or said another way, incomplete business cases can cause you to stall your own deals. Highlight all three elements in your business case and weave these into all your communications.

Weaving, Muchness, Soonness and Sureness into Your Communications

Weaving your business case elements into your conversation is easy and has the additional benefit of attracting executive buyers. You tend to get delegated

> You tend to get delegated to the stakeholders you sound most like.

to the stakeholders you sound most like. So if you spend a lot of time talking about technical things you'll get delegated to technical stakeholders.

Because business case messaging is what executive buyers respond to most, as you incorporate business case messaging into your communications you'll tend to get delegated to executive stakeholders. Your messaging will literally get you access to the stakeholders you want.

In your early conversations you will not have enough specific information to make definitive statements about Muchness, Soonness and Sureness. Instead, you will use softer language and ranges to communicate the value of your business case. This is important because customers will push back on any definitive statements about value until you've collected sufficient information that qualifies you to make such statements.

Here are some examples of early-stage messaging that will not cause pushback:

Muchness

- For most organizations your size we typically see a return between $X and $Y.
- We usually see cost reductions between X% and Y%.
- Most clients double their [important result or metric].

Soonness

- In most cases we can produce that return somewhere between 90 and 120 days.
- We typically hit [important milestone] about the sixth month mark.
- It takes about X to Y months to get a full payback.

Sureness

- We don't invoice until we've hit [milestone] so there's no risk for you guys.
- Since we only make money on the upside there's basically no cost until we've produced a return.
- We guarantee that you will [achieve result or milestone] as part of our service level guarantee so there's no risk to you.

Combined

- Most organizations your size see a return between $X and $Y, and that comes somewhere between 4 to 6 months. And the nice thing is that we don't invoice until we've hit [milestone] so there's no risk for you guys.
- We typically see cost reductions between X% and Y% in 3 to 5 months. And since we only make money on the upside there's basically no cost until we've produced a return.
- Most clients double their [important metric] in X to Y months. And since we guarantee that you will [achieve result or milestone] as part of our service level guarantee, there's really no risk.

Notice the following in these examples:

- **Soft Language** – We always share typical results and leave room for this client to be the exception to the rule. This language includes things like: "for most organizations", "we typically see", "usually", "most clients", "in most cases", etc. This allows us to communicate the dimensions of our business case without triggering pushbacks.
- **Ranges** – We never offer a single number. It's always a range that the client can see themselves fitting into. If you know your model well and enough about the client, you can use actual hard dollars in the range. This is the strongest. If not, then you can use percentages instead. Then the client can always see themselves fitting into the range. We do this for both Muchness as well as Soonness. Give yourself flexibility in the time it takes to produce a return.
- **Guarantees** – Sureness is mostly about your guarantees, so you'll want to use your strongest risk-reducing lever in these statements.

After hearing statements like these it is very natural for clients to ask how you are able to produce the return or what makes the return take longer or shorter. Or how your guarantee works. This is excellent and exactly what you want. It pulls them into the business case conversation. In many cases these provocative business case statements will cause the client to ask specifically what the return would be for them. Your answer will be, "Well, why don't we figure that out?" And now your deal advances to the Defining Problem stage that you learned about in Chapter 4.

You'll also find that speaking in these terms will get you much more respect and differentiate you from your competitors. This is because you are speaking 100% in terms of producing results. Ordinary salespeople tend to talk too much about the details of their solution. Communicating in these terms

> There is a world of difference between talking about results versus your solution. One is about them, the other is about you.

sends a very strong message to stakeholders that you are all about delivering results. And that is exactly what they want. Your solution is simply a means to produce those results. For the record, there is a time to talk about the details of your solution, but in general, your client will take you there when they are ready. To your client, there is a world of difference between talking about results versus your solution. One is about them, the other is about you.

Be Transparent – The Value of Collaborating on ROI

I recommend collaborating closely with your client when calculating your business case and return on investment. Use a transparent methodology or calculator with your client to project returns.

Let me share a secret with you. Many professionals are confused by where the value is in ROI calculators. Most people mistakenly believe that the value in the business case and ROI calculator is to create the expected return the client will receive. That is not true. The return value that the calculation creates is only a secondary benefit. The real and primary value of calculating business case and return on investment is doing it **with** your customer.

> The real and primary value of calculating business case and return on investment is doing it with your customer.

[The real and primary value of calculating business case and return on investment is doing it **with** your customer.]

This is because as you collaborate with your client on the Business Case and ROI they begin to see HOW it is possible that they will receive the return. They see the mechanism of action. And they begin to believe and see how it is obtainable. As we saw earlier, believability trumps big claims.

Don't believe me? Just create a business case or ROI without collaborating with your client and email it to them. Did it work? I already know the answer, because I've seen it hundreds of times. It doesn't work.

I recall a time when I was standing in a buffet line with one of my sales team when he received a call. I could hear both sides of the conversation. My rep says, "Did you get the return on investment I created for you?" I hear the client say, "Yes". My rep says, "Was it the biggest return of all the proposals you received?" I hear the client say, "Yes." I was completely shocked and embarrassed when I heard my rep say this, "Well then you HAVE to buy us. We have the biggest return." I literally covered my eyes while shaking my head. "No, no, no!" I thought. He doesn't HAVE to do anything. When you create your business case in a vacuum, clients will see the results as nothing more than a claim. They will not believe it. And then I heard the client say this: "Well that's why I was calling. I have some serious questions about some of the assumptions you've made here." Ouch.

> When you create your business case in a vacuum, clients will see the results as nothing more than a claim.

Do not create your business case in a vacuum. And do not just email your business case and expect the client to figure it out. It never works.

A magical thing happens when you collaborate with your client on the business case and return. They start to see the path to success and how your solution will deliver the results you're promising. This addresses all three elements of Client Indecision and all three elements of Business Case.

Collaborate with the client. Use their data and their assumptions. Play with it together and take as long as you need. This is when the client receives the ah-ha moment that you can produce the business result that creates their personal win.

Unsticking After Committing the Business Case Sin

When you create your business case in a vacuum and simply send it without any review, if the prospect looks at your numbers and sees holes, or has major questions, you may not get a response at all. You'll have stalled your own deal.

You already committed the cardinal sin you say? How do I unstick my deal now?

Well, know that you just took a big credibility hit. This doesn't happen when you collaborate with clients using their input and their figures. You also get immediate feedback when something looks off. This is why we always review proposals and business cases with clients personally.

> We always review proposals and business cases with clients personally.

Again, you're going to get back on their radar using one of the five key plays from Chapter 8. Acknowledge that you have spotted some potential mistakes. Apologize and declare your intentions to build a more refined and specific business case after some conversation.

Another way to come at this is to introduce new information. (Play #2) You have some new options that weren't available when you created your business case, and you'd like to discuss these, since it could make a big difference for them. Get your meeting, then revise the business case while collaborating with the client.

How to Collaborate on Business Case Right From the Beginning

There is a way to informally collaborate with the client right from the beginning. This is tremendously powerful and will help you qualify every opportunity (even complex ones) during your first discovery call. It will create a basic high-level business case for you around Muchness in just minutes. Amazingly, you can even do this for industries that you know very little about. At the end of the process, you and the client will both know if the problem or goal is worth addressing.

I learned these questions from my mentor Mahan Khalsa. He calls them the 5 Golden Questions. Here is an abbreviated approach to using the five questions.

Question 1 – How do you measure it?

Once you get into a conversation around the stakeholder's desired outcomes you are going to ask some variation of, "How do you measure this now?" You are looking for measurable performance indicators. These are usually manifested in terms of time and money. Most industries have standard metrics. It will help you to know these, but it is not necessary since the client is giving you the metrics.

Question 2 – What is it now?

Once you know how they are measuring results in the area they seek to improve, we need to get a baseline. So we ask some variation of, "What is it now?" This needs to be measurable but it doesn't need to be precise. Clients will not have the exact figures off the top of their head. Don't let them get hung up on that. Just have them guess. We only need to be directionally correct.

Question 3 – What do you want it to be?

Now that we know what our baseline is, we need to know the target. So, we're simply going to ask, "What do you want it to be?" Clients will sometimes want you to suggest what is possible and it is ok to suggest benchmarks that are typically attainable, but it's critical that you use **their number**, whatever it is. Clients always believe their own numbers.

Question 4 – What is the value of the difference?

Now you get to be a consultant, facilitator, and trusted advisor, because you are going to help the client monetize the value of the improvement. Every business is different and often there are additional metrics that are needed to calculate the value of the difference. Simply facilitate and walk the client through calculating the value of the delta.

This is the first ah-ha moment for the client because they will have monetized their problem. It's also a landmark moment for you, because in the absence of value everything looks like a cost. If the value of the difference is $4M, then investing $1M is going to be a no-brainer.

Question 5 – What is the value over time?

Now we calculate the value over time. Usually, 3-5 years is reasonable.

At this point you're simply going to say something like, "Wow, it seems like solving this problem is worth $12M over the next 3 years. That seems like a lot. Could that be right?" My personal experience is that 9 out of 10 times the client will say, "If anything that's low." And that's because they were being conservative with their estimates.

And all of this can be done on the back of an envelope.

The 5 Golden Questions

1. How do you measure it?
2. What is it now?
3. What do you want it to be?
4. What is the value of the difference?
5. What is the value over time?

Figure 23-1: The 5 Golden Questions

This approach is pure genius and I count it among the most valuable things I know. You can get a fuller treatment of the 5 Golden Questions in Mahan Khalsa's landmark book **Let's Get Real or Let's Not Play** which I highly recommend.

What you're really doing here is facilitating the client's understanding of the size of their own problem. If you begin your sales process with this microcosm of Business Case, you will be coming from a position of value and strength right from the beginning and that will continue to be the frame for your entire sales process. This is the beginning of your business case.

Eliminate Price Concerns Forever

You can virtually eliminate pricing pressures if you follow this one simple rule:

Establish value before presenting price.

> You can virtually eliminate pricing pressures if you follow this one simple rule: Establish value before presenting price.

When you establish the return your solution delivers before you present the investment price, the price becomes a detail. This is because the return always exceeds the price. (If it doesn't then you don't really have a business.)

The trap ordinary salespeople fall into is thinking that sending the proposal or offering the price, all by itself, is advancing the sale. It isn't. That is a myth that stalls deals. Do not fall for it. Customers are always curious about the price. Even disinterested prospects will be curious about the price, and they will be happy to let you waste your precious time creating a proposal to satisfy their curiosity.

Let me offer two tips that will save you a great deal of time and virtually eliminate pricing pressures:

1. Never volunteer a proposal. Make the customer ask you for it.
2. Never offer a proposal until you have established value first.

Making the customer ask you for a proposal tells you important information about where that customer is in their buyer's journey. When you suggest a proposal, you lose that opportunity. Be patient. They will ask. You will still get curious parties that ask but this will eliminate a huge percentage of unqualified requests.

When the customer does ask for the price, use that opportunity to engage in a deeper level of discovery that collects the business case information you need. Agree to create the proposal but say that you will need additional information to accomplish that, and then gather the details you need for your business case.

Just in case this is a new concept for you let me offer some possible dialogue.

Client – "This is all very interesting. Could you put together a proposal for us?"

Professional – "Absolutely. I'd be happy to. There's just a few pieces of information I'll need first."

Client – "Sure, what do you need?"

Professional – "We'll need some Aged Trial Balance details and some reports around what your current denials look like. I have a document that outlines exactly what we need. I'll send that to you. And if you need some help, just let me know and I can help you through it or I even have some people that can pull it for you."

We are creating a minor hurtle here that the client has to clear in order to get the pricing. This eliminates virtually 100% of trivial requests and greatly qualifies the quality of your opportunity.

Now, I used a hairy example here on purpose. Many sales don't require this level of detail. The principle is still the same. The proposal request entitles you to a deeper level of information that you are going to use to create your business case. With that information you are going to use what you learned in Chapter 7 to present and review your business case and proposal with the client personally.

A Personal Experience

As of the time of this writing I was engaged with an ophthalmic organization with clinics and surgery centers throughout the western United States. They are acquiring other clinics and surgery centers and were looking for someone to work the remaining accounts receivable for these acquired clinics.

For the record, this is generally difficult, unprofitable work that we would likely not take on. However, when they asked the price for the work, I followed the formula you see above and let them know I would need some information to do that. It took some time because there were many systems, but we got all the information we needed which greatly qualified the client.

During the analysis, we uncovered many opportunities for improvement that went beyond the AR wind-down they were requesting. (This always happens by the way. We always find improvement opportunities.) We monetized those and presented them to the client as a series of improvement opportunities along with figures and returns for the AR wind-down.

> When you establish the return your solution delivers before you present the investment price, the price becomes a detail.

The improvement opportunities were so much greater than the wind-down AR project that the client quickly lost interest in favor of the other improvement possibilities. We ultimately settled on three major projects, all valued in the millions.

The return for each opportunity was 4 to 5 times the investment for each. So when it came to finally closing the contract, we got zero pushback on price. In fact, it's possible that we left money on the table. But the goal is not to extract maximum dollars from the client. It's to create a win-win arrangement that lasts forever. And our arrangement accomplished that. We got no price pressure precisely because we established value before presenting price.

Imagine if we had just thrown out some wind-down AR pricing without following this process. Neither we nor the client would have uncovered the greater opportunities and a new relationship worth millions of dollars to each of us would have been lost.

Business Case Affects Personal Wins

As we wrap up this section on Business Case I want to remind you what we learned in Chapter 11. Personal wins are conditions that appeal to a stakeholder's self-interest. They are the reason stakeholders buy. And Business Results create personal wins. A strong business case that addresses the areas stakeholders are vested in will make stakeholder management much easier.

Summary

In Part 6 of this book, we have discussed the three elements of Business Case: Muchness, Soonness and Sureness. And because Sureness is addressed by our Client Indecision strategies, when we've identified that Business Case is the issue, there are only two levers to consider for unsticking deals: Muchness and Soonness. When Muchness is the issue, we need to increase the size of the return somehow. And there are only two ways to accomplish that: Increase the size of the return or reduce the investment cost.

Without touching costs, there are basically three ways to increase the return: 1. Increase the scope, 2. Improve the solution efficiency, or 3. Change the purchase model. To reduce the cost side of the formula we think in terms of Total Cost of Ownership (TCO) and use the three elements of TCO to reduce the client's overall costs.

There is more to Business Case than just Muchness. The biggest return does not always win. You can create competitive advantage without even touching Muchness by developing your Soonness and Sureness. And when it comes to making claims, believable claims trump big claims.

During emergencies, clients seek solutions that pay off quickly. This means that long payoff periods can actually cause deals to stall. Ask yourself how you can speed up the return for this client.

Communicating the elements of your business case right from the beginning in both casual and formal exchanges differentiates you against your competition, points you towards executive stakeholders, and prevents deals from sticking due to Business Case issues.

At the end of the day, Business Case is about just one thing – Priority. Our business case helps the client answer the question: "Is solving this problem the best use of our time and money right now?" Using Muchness, Soonness and Sureness helps clients compare different solutions and initiatives.

The real value in developing your business case is developing it with your customer. When we create our business case in a vacuum, clients will see the result as nothing more than a claim. On the other hand, when we collaborate with clients on Business Case a magical thing happens and clients start to see the path to success, and how your solution will deliver the results you're promising. This ends up addressing elements of both Client Indecision as well as Business Case.

It is possible (and valuable) to establish your business case right from the beginning by leveraging the 5 Golden Questions during your discovery process. This will help both you and your client understand the scope and value of their challenge.

I've given you some amazing insights and actionable strategies that have served me greatly. If you apply what you've learned here in your daily practice, not only will you be able to unstick the deals that have stalled due to Business Case, you'll also be able to craft business cases that are incredibly compelling to clients. It will destroy your competition and preemptively keep your deals from sticking in the first place.

You now know everything you need to unstick deals caused by business case issues. In the next chapter we will pull together everything you've learned into one simple, easy-to-use framework.

CHAPTER 24

PUTTING IT ALL TOGETHER

"Execution is a process. Don't confuse activity with results."
- LOU GERSTNER

The Big Idea: Unstick your deal using three simple steps.

Let's pull everything you've learned into three simple steps. Use this section as a checklist next time you have a stuck deal.

1. Identify the root cause of your stuck opportunity.
2. Brainstorm which strategy to employ.
3. Decide and execute your plays.

1. Identify Root Cause
2. Brainstorm Strategies
3. Decide & Execute Plays

Figure 24-1: Stuck Deal Checklist

Identifying Root Cause

When identifying root causes, start with Sales Issues, then look at Client Indecision, then look at Business Case issues. In that order.

Use the assessment details in Parts 4, 5, and 6, and the downloadable assessment tool available for free at http://unstickingdeals.com.

Brainstorming Strategies

There's more than one way to solve a problem. Once you know the root cause of your stuck opportunity, brainstorm with your manager and peers to identify which strategy or strategies to employ. There might be several complementary strategies available to you.

I personally find this process fun and very satisfying. You are problem-solving in its purest form. You are taking a set of circumstances and designing interventions that change the outcome. Most people find this very empowering.

Interventions Made Easy

Once you've identified your root cause, the interventions you choose are straightforward. Here they are summarized without commentary.

Sales Issues

Bad Targeting
1. Is this still worth pursuing?
2. Evaluate current challenges based on remaining root causes.
3. Target better next time.

Wrong/Incomplete Stakeholders
- Identify, gain access, and interview all stakeholders to identify personal wins.
- Explain or incorporate stakeholder personal wins into your solution.

Champion Management
- Identify, develop, and engage new champions and coaches.

Relationship
- Adjust your style to address chemistry issues.
- Change your engagement team to address chemistry issues.

Competition
- Position yourself against the competition in terms of Muchness, Soonness and Sureness.

Client Indecision

- Pivot to overcoming indecision.

Validation / Comparison
- Simplify comparisons of your own solutions and against the competition.

Lack of Information
- Get the right information to the right stakeholders.

Outcome Uncertainty
- Eliminate risk in any form.

Business Case

Muchness
- Increase the overall return.

Soonness
- Increase the speed of the return.

Category	Issue	Intervention
Sales Issues	Bad Targeting	• Is this still worth pursuing? • Evaluate current challenges based on remaining root causes. • Target better next time.
	Wrong/Incomplete Stakeholders	• Identify, gain access, and interview all stakeholders to identify personal wins. • Explain or incorporate stakeholder personal wins into your solution.
	No/Weak Champion or Coach	• Identify, develop, and engage new champions and coaches.
	Relationship	• Adjust your style to address chemistry issues. • Change your engagement team to address chemistry issues.
	Competition	• Position yourself against the competition in terms of muchness, soonness and sureness.
Client Indecision	(Generally)	• Pivot to overcoming indecision.
	Validation / Comparison	• Simplify comparisons of your own solutions and against the competition.
	Lack of Information	• Get the right information to the right stakeholders.
	Outcome Uncertainty	• Eliminate risk in any form.
Business Case	Muchness	• Increase the overall return.
	Soonness	• Increase the speed of the return.

Figure 24-2: Interventions Made Easy

Choosing Your Plays

Choosing plays is easy. If we're still communicating with the client, then we're just going to inquire where our deal is getting stuck and make the appropriate adjustments.

The remainder of the time you'll almost always be using plays 2 and 3 where we're delivering new information and using some form of unique messaging to do that.

Occasionally the right thing to do will be to be patient and wait for better timing or a trigger event or send a disengage message to protect your precious time and force the customer to reevaluate how badly they want their desired outcomes.

Note to Managers

Over time you will become very proficient at identifying root causes and suggesting plays. However, that's not what your team finds most valuable.

When sales professionals are surveyed about their managers, the number one complaint they have is: "My manager adds no value to me or my sales process." Don't let this be you.

Here are the areas you can add the most value:

- **Facilitate Self-Discovery of Root Causes** – Don't hand them a fish. Teach them to fish. Help them become proficient at identifying their own root causes. Then the prevention techniques will kick in.
- **Brainstorm Strategies** – This is what surveys show your sales team values the most. Talk through many possible options so they can become familiar with the possibilities. Then let them decide. Do not decide for them.
- **Develop the Assets they Need** – Introducing new information (Play #2) will always uncover gaps in your supporting materials over time. Create these for your team. It is a high-leverage activity on your part.

Conclusion

Who would have thought we could simplify everything down to two and a half pages? But there it is. And now you know all the science and technique behind it too.

Stuck deals are a fact of life. Even the best of the best have deals that stall out from time to time. You now have all the strategies, tools, and plays to unstick them when they happen. If you proactively apply what you've learned here, stalled deals will happen a whole lot less often for you. And by extension, it will shorten your sales cycles and accelerate your commissions.

There's just one last thought I'd like to leave you with.

Selling is Serving

It can be frustrating when deals get stuck. And it's easy to get caught up in what might look like irrationality or injustice. During these times always remember that selling is an act of service.

We, as professionals, don't get paid for the actions we take. We only get paid based on the actions our clients take and the results we produce for them. The action we facilitate for our clients improves their condition as well as our own in a virtuous win-win cycle.

Understand that what you've learned in this book is much more than just unsticking your sale. This is leadership. People have so few mentors and leaders in their lives that when you arrive in the scene with a path that leads them to the improvement they want, and you take them through the steps they need to take to achieve it – big or small, challenging or easy – they will thank you.

Embrace your role as a leader and change agent. Prospects meet with you because they want to improve in some way. They want your guidance and leadership. Through your knowledge, skills, and facilitation you become the catalyst that empowers them to reach their goals.

That is a noble calling.

Whenever we are taking on something new or challenging, we all love having a coach helping us move forward at our own pace. Clients engage us precisely because they want help making positive change. They are expecting us to be that coach. If they could do it on their own, they wouldn't be engaging us.

Truly understand your clients. Guide them through each of the little commitments it takes to achieve their goals. It's about more than unsticking deals and advancing the sale - it's leadership.

And most professionals can do a significantly better job of coaching and serving clients than they are doing today. So that is my challenge to you. Be a better coach. Be a better facilitator and problem-solver. Be a better teacher and leader. So you can serve your clients better.

I genuinely hope the insights in this book help you as much as they have helped me and my own teams. It has made a big difference for me and brought me much joy. I urge you to internalize and master the principles and techniques within these pages. Doing so will make you happier and more successful. And I look forward to hearing about your success.

—James Muir

HOW TO IDENTIFY YOUR IDEAL CUSTOMER

The single biggest thing you can do to improve sales is to only sell to ideal customers. That's what the data shows. And the reason for this is because with the wrong prospect all our efforts fall on deaf ears. It's garbage in - garbage out. You're better off finding an ideal prospect than continuing to waste time on non-ideal customers. And I know that's a tough message. Because most salespeople find communicating with an engaged prospect more fun than prospecting.

The highest leverage of your time is to focus on ideal, high-probability prospects to begin with.

Getting this one principle right – all by itself – can make you massively successful. And I'll give you a dramatic example below. The reason for this is because focusing on ideal, high-probability prospects is the highest leverage strategy you can employ. All other strategies are downstream from this one. They are all dependent on it.

Niche Markets are More Effective

Narrow your target market as far as possible. Narrow targets allow you to craft stronger value propositions and messaging. It allows you to position your company as a specialist for that target market and make it easier for prospective buyers to find you and for you to find them.

This is counter-intuitive. Most professionals and organizations define their target markets far too broadly. This not only ends up making their messaging weak, but it also wastes massive amounts of sales time forcing sales to engage and follow-up on non-ideal customers. Don't do it. Start with a narrowly defined market. Once you dominate it you can always expand to other markets.

What Does an Ideal Customer Look Like?

A description of the perfect company or customer for your business is often referred to as an ideal customer profile or (ICP). A complete ICP will have six elements:

1. Demographics
2. Psychographics
3. Key Stakeholders
4. Challenges/Issues/Problems
5. Goals/Objectives/Strategic Initiatives
6. Triggering Events

Demographics

Demographics are measurable things you can find in databases. They include things like: Industry, Size, Location, etc. Here is a list of demographic elements to jumpstart your thinking:

Industry - Typically measured by NAICS code. (North American Industry Classification System)

Size - This includes things like: Revenues, Number of Employees, Plants, Locations, etc.

Company Type - Corporation, Small Biz, Private/Public, Government, Centralized, Decentralized, etc.

Physical Location - City, State, Country, Global, Headquarters Location, etc.

Distribution Channels - Retail, Direct Sales, Distribution, Catalog, On-line, etc.

Customers Model - Business-to-Business, Business-to-Consumer, Business-to-Channel, etc.

Development Stage - Start-up, Rapid Growth, Mature, Declining, etc.

Technology - Applications, Hardware, Networking, Manufacturing Systems, etc. Also how deployed these technologies are.

Revenue Potential - What is the estimated revenue potential of this potential customer? There are lots of possible formulas here based on whether you are B2C or B2B. For example, if our solution generates an average of 4% of Net Revenue, then Net Revenue time 4% = Revenue Potential. ($55M * 4% = $2.2M)

Expansion Potential - What products or solutions is this potential customer likely to acquire after investing in the first solution? What are those products or solutions? What percent make additional investments? What is the typical size of those investments?

Growth Potential - Can this customer help us gain access to other customers in or outside their organization? Is there a network effect?

Volume Drivers - What volumes does this customer have?

Specific Problem or Issue - Does this customer have a known issue, problem, or requirement that needs addressing?

Negative Criteria - Is there something this customer doesn't have that qualifies them to be a potential client?

Psychographics

Psychographics are the attitudes and culture of the customer or organization. Psychographics tend to be harder to obtain than demographics. They usually require surveys, in-person meetings, or the reading of reports. Some of these are organizational and some are unique to each stakeholder. Here is a list of psychographic elements to jumpstart your thinking:

Vision / Values - What are the vision and values of the customer?

Goals / Objectives - What goals and objectives does the customer have?

Priorities - What are this customer's priorities right now?

Reputation - Does this customer view themselves as an innovator, a low-cost provider, specialist, etc.?

Willingness to Address Challenges - What is the customer's willingness to address challenges or achieve goals?

Means - Does this customer have the means to address problems or initiate growth?

Leadership Style - What is this customer's leadership style? Autocratic, Individualistic, Consensus-driven, etc.

Change Response - How does this customer tend to respond to change?

Strategy / Methodology - What is this customer's approach to solving problems?

Technology Adoption - Is the customer an early adopter, in the mainstream or a laggard when it comes to adopting technology?

Situation Perspective - How does this customer see their situation? Growing, Stagnant, In trouble, Downward Spiral, Rebirth, etc.

Climate Perspective - How does this customer see the current business climate? Gold Rush, Opportunistic, Pessimistic, Cautious, etc.

Catalyst for Action - Does this customer have a strong catalyst for action?

Challenges - What challenges is this customer experiencing right now?

Fears - What are this customer's biggest fears and concerns?

Pressure - What pressure is this customer experiencing from customers, supervisors, executive management, shareholders, etc.?

Reference / Testimonial - Would this client be willing to act as a reference or provide a testimonial?

Key Stakeholders

Key stakeholders are the individuals that will need to be interacted with to gain access and complete the sale of your opportunity. During targeting exercises, it is best to think of these in terms of personas. Personas are fictional personalities based on a stakeholder's role or title. They include common attributes that make it easier to understand and craft messaging for each stakeholder role. Creating detailed personas is beyond the scope of this book. You will find some great resources in the Recommended Reading section of this book.

For developing your Ideal Customer Profile, the number one thing here is simply to identify all of the key stakeholder titles and roles that are typically involved in making decisions around your solution.

Here is a list of considerations when it comes to evaluating stakeholders to jumpstart your thinking:

Title - What is the stakeholder's title?

Authority - What influence does this role or title have over your solution offering?

Tenure - How long has this stakeholder been in this role?

Personality - Is there a common personality type for this stakeholder role or title?

Common Concerns - What are the common concerns for this title or role?

Belief System - What are the common belief systems and values for this title or role?

Associations - What associations do they typically belong to?

Information Sources - What websites, podcasts, magazines, newsletters, TV programs, radio programs, personalities, does this title or role typically subscribe to?

The psychographic elements: Leadership Style, Change Response, Strategy / Methodology, Technology Adoption, Situation Perspective, Climate Perspective, Catalyst for Action, Feels Challenges, Fears, Pressure, Reference / Testimonial all apply here. Be sure to consider them when creating your personas.

Challenges/Issues/Problems

Challenges, issues and problems are all terms that describe the conditions that a customer might have that make it right for them to consider your solution. You help them address these things. The problems you solve determine who you sell to. Or said another way - problems are markets.

To know your most ideal targets, you need to do a problem inventory. A Problem Inventory is a collection of problems you solve for clients. You must know what specific problems your prospect has and the value you bring before you can craft messages that will trigger them to engage.

Once you've identified the problems you solve, the big question is: Who has the problems you solve? And who has those problems in the biggest way? - That's our target market.

B2C problems are as varied as the sands of the seashore but all consumer goals and problems tend to fall into seven categories:

- Financial Independence
- Business & Career
- Health & Fitness
- Family & Relationships
- Productivity
- Simplifying Life
- Spiritual

Here is a list of common B2B problems to jumpstart your thinking:

- Decreased Profitability
- Increased Competition and Pricing Pressures
- Competitive Differentiation
- Inefficiency / Poor Productivity
- Declining Market Share
- Workforce Turnover / Finding Good Employees
- Challenges Implementing Key Initiatives
- Implementing / Complying with New Regulations
- High Costs
- Weak Sales / Stagnant Growth
- Industry Trends Threatening Market Position
- New Customer Requirements
- Poor Internal / External Communications
- Merging / Integrating Companies

Goals/Objectives/Strategic Initiatives

The specific goals, objectives, and strategic initiatives clients are focusing on often qualify them to be ideal customers when your offering can positively affect these areas.

Once again, individual consumer goals are diverse and varied but tend to fall into the seven categories mentioned above:

- Financial Independence
- Business & Career
- Health & Fitness
- Family & Relationships
- Productivity
- Simplifying Life
- Spiritual

Here is a list of common B2B goals and objectives to jumpstart your thinking:

- Growth - Revenue, Sales, Market Share, etc.
- Enter New Markets
- Improve Operational Efficiency
- Reduce Costs
- Improve Profitability and Margins
- Improve Cash Flow
- Improve Quality
- Increase Shareholder Value
- Improve Marketing and Brand Recognition
- Improve Sales Effectiveness
- Expansion - Opening New Locations, Plants, Facilities, etc.
- Launch New Products or Services
- Improve Workforce Productivity
- Improve Customer Service
- Employee Attraction and Retention
- Change Management
- Improve Customer Loyalty
- Outsourcing
- Improve Supply Chain
- Stay Ahead of Competition
- Acquire a Business or Competitor
- Adopt / Update Technology or Equipment
- Create Strategic Partnerships

Triggering Events

Trigger events are changes in a customer situation that create opportunities for your solution offering. Before the trigger event the client may show little interest, but after the trigger event the client becomes very active and intentional in solving the problem.

B2C trigger events are wide and varied. Here are just a few examples of B2C trigger events.

- Having Children
- Moving
- Starting a New Job
- Starting/Ending of Relationships
- Getting a New Pet
- Starting School/University
- Season Changes
- Holidays
- Fresh Starts – beginning of the week, month, year, season.
- Special Events (eg. wedding, birthday, anniversary)
- Death of a Loved One
- Broken Car, Appliance, etc.
- Feeling Insecure
- New Friends
- New legislation or policy changes relevant to individuals

B2B trigger events tend to be a much more consistent list. They can be broken down into Internal and External triggers. Here are some examples of B2B trigger events to jumpstart your thinking:

Internal Trigger Events
- Rapid Growth
- Cash Flow Problems
- Poor Quarterly Earnings or Annual Results
- Change of Ownership or Management
- New Location
- New Business Relationships (partners, affiliates, etc.)
- Mergers and Acquisitions
- Downsizing
- Restructurings
- Key Personnel Turnover

External Trigger Events
- Legislative Changes (new laws and regulations)
- New Competitors
- New Technologies
- Economic Conditions
- Cost / Availability of Borrowing Money
- National / International Emergencies

Trigger events speak to the timing of the need for your offering. When you see these events, you'll know it is a good time to engage and that they are very likely to be receptive. Using trigger events to trap the conditions that make them ideal customers can create massive improvements in your conversion rates.

Creating Your Ideal Customer Profile (ICP)

Don't be daunted by the lists above. They are only meant to stimulate your thinking. The process of actually identifying your Ideal Customer Profile is actually very straightforward. There are just three steps:

1. List your best customers.
2. Identify their defining attributes.
3. Identify the commonalities between them.

That's it.

The above criteria just gives you a starting place for looking at your customer's defining attributes.

Once you've identified what the common attributes are of your best customers, you now have a template for the criteria for your ideal customers.

Identifying Your Best Customers

Most likely you've already done some targeting. However, your target market may be too broad because you are still trying to keep multiple options open. Remember, narrower is better.

Most folks know immediately who their best clients are. However, just in case, here are some questions you can ask yourself to help you identify which of your current customers are "best" for the purpose of defining your ICP template. As you do this, consider all of the factors we listed above. Be as specific as you can.

- What businesses or market segments have you been most successful with in the past?

- What types of companies have presented challenges or struggles that you want to avoid in the future?
- What types of customers have been the most profitable and enjoyable?
- What conditions triggered your best clients to seek you for solutions?

Using a matrix to evaluate each customer will make it easy to be systematic and identify the common patterns of your best clients.

Problem Inventory

Conduct a problem inventory as described in the Challenges/Issues/Problems section above. The problems we solve determine who we sell to. Problems are markets. Here are some easy steps to help you conduct your problem inventory.

1. Brainstorm all the problems you solve for clients.
2. Describe and calculate the impact of that problem.
   - Monetize where possible.
   - Collect stories that illustrate/describe the problem. (these are important)
3. Indicate which personas or stakeholders own this problem.
4. Describe the emotions each persona feels as they experience this problem.
5. Discuss any a-ha moments or insights.

Be exhaustive. This is especially important if you are a startup with fewer established clients.

Once we've inventoried the problems we solve, now we ask: Who has these problems? And who has those problems in the biggest way? - That's our target market.

Professional Credibility

Often professionals are still exploring their service offerings. You need to decide this as soon as possible. If you're not sure which offering is or which customers might benefit most from what you do, I offer the following questions to stimulate your thinking about your ideal target market.

1. What specific expertise do you have? What are you really good at? What do you do so effortlessly, that you don't even realize it's a big deal?
2. When you worked in a company, what problems did you solve for your employer? What were the ramifications and impact of solving these problems?

3. How would you describe the demographics, psychographics and enabling conditions of the last organization in which you made an impact?

When you are a consultant or independent professional, you'll have the highest credibility with companies that are similar to your past employers. It will be much easier to build a business focusing in that area as opposed to starting fresh in an environment where you have not demonstrated any success.

An Often-Missed Element to Consider for Identifying Ideal Target Customers

There is an important element for identifying ideal customers that is often missed. Leverage.

Leverage is the existing proof you have that you can solve the problems and affect positive change for your target market. It's about having proof.

What researchers have discovered is that of all the elements that improve response - proof is the most important element. Focusing on proof improves response more than any other element in messaging.

In the context of targeting, and identifying our ideal customer profile (ICP), we don't want to go into battle without a sword. It's important that we target an area where we actually HAVE some proof to use.

So when we're defining our target market, pick areas where you have strong proof. Because you're going to need it. Focusing on areas where you already have the greatest proof will deliver huge time savings for you.

That begs the question: "What constitutes proof?"

And we have already covered this earlier in the book, but for the sake of review, here are the top two things:

- Recognizable, referenceable clients. Which includes things like: testimonials, case studies, and market share or large numbers of clients.
- Objective, 3rd Party Endorsements. That includes things like: awards, studies, and reviews.

The reason these are the strongest form of proof is because they come from 3rd parties.

Anyone can make a promise. Anyone can claim they solve a problem. And clients know that. And they also know that proof from 3rd parties is the hardest to fabricate. So they weigh it most heavily.

If you are a startup, don't lose heart if you don't have this type of proof yet. There are other kinds of proof you can use. But your company should start working in these areas right away because the data shows they are the strongest.

The key take-away here is: As you work to identify your ideal targets, take into account the six Ideal Customer Profile elements discussed and the leverage you have at your disposal in terms of clients, testimonials, case studies, and 3rd party endorsements.

This will get you focused on working with the highest probability opportunities. And in doing so you will get a much higher return on your time and energy.

This one strategy – ALL BY ITSELF - can make a massive difference for you. It is a super-high-leverage strategy. Let me give you an example.

Example of Targeting Success

Hill-Rom makes beds and furniture in the healthcare space. In a now famous case study reported in Harvard Business Review, just by changing the accounts their sales team focused on - nothing else - they added 70 million dollars in revenue. In fact, it:

- It increased product margin by 6.7%
- It increased their operating income by 51%
- They actually lowered their costs by 1%
- And improved their customer satisfaction by 6%.

They didn't do anything else but change who their sales teams targeted and focused on. Targeting the right customer makes a huge difference. They're more profitable, easier to sell, and happier. That's what I want for you.

Summary

Because all other strategies are downstream from targeting. The single biggest thing you can do to improve sales is to define your ideal customer profile and only sell to ideal customers.

It also represents the foundation of your marketing plan. You will use it to:

- Craft all your sales and marketing messages.
- Clarify and focus your value proposition.
- Develop your website and marketing collateral.
- Determine where to focus your time and energy prospecting and generating leads.
- Determine where to invest your marketing spend in terms of advertising, public relations, speaking engagements, events, promotions, articles and all forms of messaging.
- Determine which referral partners are the best match.
- And much more.

It is also the foundation of your sales plan. You will use it to:

- Identify high-probability prospective accounts that are most likely to become customers.
- Plan and execute successful sales outreach that continue advancing to the next step.
- Identify trigger events that reveal when prospects are most likely to be receptive.

Ideal target markets evolve. If you haven't reviewed your Ideal Customer Profile in some time, I encourage you to review it at least annually so you are capturing all of the opportunity afforded to you.

I hope this short discussion gives you the ammunition you need to define and refine your Ideal Customer Profile. It has made a big difference for both me and my clients.

Happy selling!

MAPPING INFORMATIONAL NEEDS

Exit Criteria

We discussed Exit Criteria briefly in Chapter 4 and 18. Exit Criteria are the things that the stakeholder needs to see, hear, feel, understand, and believe before they can move to the next stage of their buyer's journey. Exit criteria can be hard or soft.

If our stakeholder is in the Evaluate Solutions stage, then a "hard" exit criteria might be: Database must support ANSI SQL. Either we meet this, or we don't.

An example of "soft" exit criteria might be: Believe that the technology solution is complimentary with their existing IT infrastructure. There is wiggle room there and a question of degree to consider.

When we don't meet the exit criteria for a given stakeholder it dramatically reduces our chances of winning over the stakeholder.

Depending on circumstances it may or may not be beneficial for you to crystallize soft exit criteria into hard criteria. For example, if our exit criteria is "Believe support is excellent." and we offer a response time of 30 minutes or less, it may prove differentiating to ask, "What response time do you consider excellent?" That will drive to criteria that may differentiate you.

On the other hand, you may be able to address the exit criteria in other ways. For example, maybe your response time is below average, but your first call resolution rate is 99%. In that case it's better to leave the exit criteria as a general goal.

When mapping informational needs, we want to identify specifically what our stakeholder or persona need to see, hear, feel, understand and believe to move to the next stage.

This has been covered wonderfully in Mike Kunkle's **The Building Blocks of Sales Enablement.**

What follows is a high-level example of common informational assets that help clients move from one stage to the next.

Figure AP2-1: Buyer's Journey Informational Strategies.

Using this framework, collaborate with your leadership and marketing department to identify and create the informational assets and messaging you need for your ideal customers. (see Appendix 1)

Unaware Stage

Unaware Stage	
Primary Question	Unaware of challenges or any potential gain/upside
Information Needs / Messaging Strategies	• Create awareness • Identify industry challenges & risks • Offer insight on the gap between where they are & where they could/should be.
Exit Criteria	Willingness to Explore a Problem, New Goal they'd like to Attain, Trigger Event Occurs

Figure AP2-2: Information Needs for the Unawareness Stage

Awareness Stage

Aware Stage	
Primary Question	Do I have a problem?
Information Needs / Messaging Strategies	• Compare to other issues, challenges & initiatives • Measurement Criteria & Metrics • Problem ROI / Business Case • Offer Impact Assessment Tools
Exit Criteria	Problem Measurement, Determination of Consequences / Positive Impact

Figure AP2-3: Information Needs for the Awareness Stage

Defining Problem Stage

Define Problem Stage	
Primary Question	How big is my problem?
Information Needs / Messaging Strategies	• Help quantify the potential impact of current problems and/or upside with a given opportunity. • Comparison of Methods of Solving / Attaining • "How to Solve" articles • "Trainwreck" disaster stories
Exit Criteria	Explores Options to Solve, Invests in Uncovering Requirements, Determination of Who's Involved Internally

Figure AP2-4: Information Needs for the Defining Problem Stage

Consider Options Stage

Consider Options Stage	
Primary Question	How can I solve my problem?
Information Needs / Messaging Strategies	• Help them understand which options are best matched to their desired results. • Offer comparisons of alternative solution methods & "How to solve" articles. • Vendor comparisons, • Industry rankings / reports • Product summaries • Reference accounts
Exit Criteria	Demonstrations, Contacting References, Investing in Comparisons, Watching Online Videos, Attending Trade Shows, Requesting Statements of Work, Say "Narrowing Options"

Figure AP2-5: Information Needs for the Consider Options Stage

Evaluate Solutions Stage

Evaluate Solutions Stage	
Primary Question	Which solution is best?
Information Needs / Messaging Strategies	• Alert them to pitfalls. • Suggest ways to reduce risks associated with moving forward. • Vendor Comparisons / Industry Rankings / Reports • Demonstrations • Reference Accounts & Case studies • Business case / ROI Tools • Project Plans • Proposals
Exit Criteria	Seeks Proposals, Reviews/Develops Business Case, Seeks/Creates ROI, Evaluates Risk, Contacts References, Requests Statement of Work

Figure AP2-6: Information Needs for the Evaluate Solutions Stage

Justify Decision Stage

Justify Decision Stage	
Primary Question	Is this really worth doing?
Information Needs / Messaging Strategies	• Business case / ROI tools. Project Plans. Case studies. Reference accounts. Guarantees. • Agreement or sample agreement • Discuss terms / finance options • Summarize / discuss non-financial terms • Final proposal
Exit Criteria	Seeks copy of agreement, Asks about terms / finance options, Asks for contract changes, Requests final proposal

Figure AP2-7: Information Needs for the Justify Decision Stage

Final Selection Stage

Final Selection Stage	
Primary Question	What are the terms? What is the best deal I can get?
Messaging Strategies	• Advise them on the most beneficial business model or terms. • Share consensus & executive approval strategies. • Final Proposal / Agreement • Discuss Terms / Finance Options • Discuss non-financial terms
Exit Criteria	Seeks project plan, Requests contact with implementation team, Contacts references

Figure AP2-8: Information Needs for the Final Selection Stage

Committed Stage

Committed Stage	
Primary Question	How can we begin?
Messaging Strategies	• Offer best practice advice. • Recommend ways to leverage their new capabilities & take their game to the next logical step. • Schedule implementation meetings • Project Plan
Exit Criteria	Seeks project plan, Requests contact with implementation team, Contacts references

Figure AP2-9: Information Needs for the Committed Stage

Help Others By Leaving a Review!

I sincerely hope you have enjoyed and benefited from this book. I am on a mission to take the dysfunction out of sales and teach sales and service professionals how being genuinely authentic creates the highest levels of success and happiness.

Please help others to learn more about how they can improve their approach to selling. The best way is simply to share it with your friends and colleagues. But there is another way we can reach even more people. If you write a simple review on Amazon, you can help hundreds or perhaps even thousands of other readers to make a buying decision that will improve their lives. Like you, they work hard for every penny they spend on books. With your information and encouragement, you can help them focus on the right things and take action right away.

In your review, share anything you think will be useful to others. Here are a few suggestions to help:

- Why did you decide to read this book?

- What did you like most about this book?

- What makes this book different from others you have read?

- Did it give you practical ways to apply the info it provides? If so, share what you are going to be doing differently because you read it.

- What kinds of readers do you think would benefit most from reading this book?

The best time to write a review is immediately after you've read the book while everything is still fresh in your mind. Please head over to Amazon.com and write a quick review right now.

Thank you so much!

RECOMMENDED READING

I read a lot of books, and I am frequently asked to recommend sales books. Here are some of my favorites in the areas of sales and sales management.

Sales

A Mind for Sales: Daily Habits and Practical Strategies for Sales Success - Mark Hunter

Achieve Sales Excellence: The 7 Customer Rules for Becoming the New Sales Professional - Howard Stevens, Theodore Kinni

Always Be Qualifying: MEDDIC and MEDDPICC – Darius Lahoutifard

Amp Up Your Sales: Powerful Strategies That Move Customers to Make Fast, Favorable Decisions - Andy Paul

Be Bold and Win the Sale: Get Out of Your Comfort Zone and Boost Your Performance - Jeff Shore

Bottom-Line Selling: The Sales Professional's Guide to Improving Customer Profits - Jack Malcolm

Building a StoryBrand: Clarify Your Message So Customers Will Listen - Donald Miller

Buyer First: Grow Your Business with Collaborative Selling - Carole Mahoney

Buyer Personas: How to Gain Insight into your Customer's Expectations, Align your Marketing Strategies, and Win More Business - Adele Revella

Buyer-Centered Selling: How Modern Sellers Engage & Collaborate with Buyers – Thomas Williams and Thomas Saine

Combo Prospecting: The Powerful One-Two Punch That Fills Your Pipeline and Wins Sales - Tony J. Hughes

Consultative Selling: The Hanan Formula for High-Margin Sales at High Levels - Mack Hanan

DISCOVER Questions Get You Connected: For Professional Sellers - Deb Calvert

Do It! Selling: 77 Instant-Action Ideas to Land Better Clients, Bigger Deals, and Higher Fees - David Newman

Eat Their Lunch: Winning Customers Away from Your Competition - Anthony Iannarino

Emotional Intelligence for Sales Success: Connect with Customers and Get Results - Colleen Stanley

Escaping the Price-Driven Sale: How World Class Sellers Create Extraordinary Profit - Tom Snyder, Kevin Kearns

Fanatical Prospecting: The Ultimate Guide to Opening Sales Conversations and Filling the Pipeline by Leveraging Social Selling, Telephone, Email, Text, and Cold Calling - Jeb Blount

Get the Meeting!: An Illustrative Contact Marketing Playbook – Stu Heinecke

Go for No! Yes is the Destination, No is How You Get There - Richard Fenton, Andrea Waltz

Go-Givers Sell More - Bob Burg

High-Profit Prospecting: Powerful Strategies to Find the Best Leads and Drive Breakthrough Sales Results - Mark Hunter

High-Profit Selling: Win the Sale Without Compromising on Price - Mark Hunter

How I Raised Myself from Failure to Success in Selling - Frank Bettger

How to Get a Meeting with Anyone: The Untapped Selling Power of Contact Marketing - Stu Heinecke

How to Get a Meeting with Anyone: The Untapped Selling Power of Contact Marketing – Stu Heinecke

How to Win Friends and Influence People - Dale Carnegie

Hybrid Selling: How salespeople can use a complete approach to drive opportunities in the new world of sales – Fred Copestake

Influence: Science and Practice - Robert B. Cialdini

Insight Selling: How to sell value & differentiate your product with Insight Scenarios - Michael Harris

Insight Selling: Surprising Research on What Sales Winners Do Differently - Mike Schultz, John E. Doerr

Integrity Selling for the 21st Century: How to Sell the Way People Want to Buy - Ron Willingham

Jeffrey Gitomer's Little Red Book of Selling: 12.5 Principles for Sales Greatness: How to Make Sales FOREVER - Jeffrey Gitomer

Lead, Sell, or Get Out of the Way: The 7 Traits of Great Sellers - Ron Karr

Let's Get Real or Let's Not Play: Transforming the Buyer/Seller Relationship - Mahan Khalsa

Love Is the Killer App: How to Win Business and Influence Friends - Tim Sanders

Mastering the Complex Sale - Jeff Thull

MEDDICC: The ultimate guide to staying one step ahead in the complex sale – Andy Whyte

New Sales. Simplified. The Essential Handbook for Prospecting and New Business Development - Mike Weinberg

Nice Girls DO Get the Sale: Relationship Building That Gets Results - Elinor Stutz

Objections: The Ultimate Guide for Mastering the Art and Science of Getting Past No - Jeb Blount

Perfect Selling - Linda Richardson

Perpetual Hunger: Sales Prospecting Lessons & Strategy - Patrick Tinney

POWERFUL SALES SCRIPTS SELL THE MEETING: Reach Buyers, Hear Yes, When B2B Cold Calling to Set Discovery Calls: A Business Development Process to Craft Lead Generation Phone Scripts with Buyers - Scott Channell

Predictable Revenue: Turn Your Business Into a Sales Machine with the $100 Million Best Practices of Salesforce.com - Aaron Ross

Questions that Sell: The Powerful Process for Discovering What Your Customer Really Wants - Paul Cherry

Quit Whining and Start Selling! A Step-by-Step Guide to a Hall of Fame Career in Sales - Kelly S. Riggs

Rainmaking Conversations: Influence, Persuade, and Sell in Any Situation - Mike Schultz, John E. Doerr

Really Care for Them: How Everyone Can Use the Power of Caring to Earn Trust, Grow Sales, and Increase Income. No Matter What You Sell or Who You Sell It To – Mareo McCracken

Rethink The Way You Sell: The Five Forgotten Fundamentals of Prospecting - Jeff Bajorek

ROI Selling: Increasing Revenue, Profit, and Customer Loyalty through the 360 Sales Cycle - Michael Nick

Sales Chaos: Using Agility Selling to Think and Sell Differently - Tim Ohai

Sales Differentiation: 19 Powerful Strategies to Win More Deals at the Prices You Want - Lee Salz

Sales EQ: How Ultra High Performers Leverage Sales-Specific Emotional Intelligence to Close the Complex Deal - Jeb Blount

Sales Secrets: The World's Top Salespeople Share Their Secrets to Success - Brandon Bornancin

Sales Truth: Debunk the Myths. Apply Powerful Principles. Win More New Sales. - Mike Weinberg

Sell Different!: All New Sales Differentiation Strategies to Outsmart, Outmaneuver, and Outsell the Competition - Lee Salz

Sell It Like a Mango: A New Seller's Guide to Closing More Deals - Donald C. Kelly

Sell More with Science: The Mindsets, Traits, and Behaviors That Create Sales Success - David Hoffeld

Sell The Meeting: Set Discovery Calls & Sales Appointments To Close New Accounts: A Lead Generation Process With Phone Script Samples For B2B Appointment Setting & Cold Calling - Scott Channell

Sell Without Selling Out: A Guide to Success on Your Own Terms - Andy Paul

Selling Against the Goal: How Corporate Sales Professionals Generate the Leads They Need - Kendra Lee

Selling from The Heart: How Your Authentic Self Sells You! - Larry Levine

Selling to Big Companies - Jill Konrath

Selling to the C-Suite: What Every Executive Wants You to Know About Successfully Selling to the Top - Stephen J. Bistritz, Nicholas A.C. Read

Selling With Dignity – Harry Spaight

Seven Stories Every Salesperson Must Tell - Mike Adams

SHIFT and DISRUPT: Stop Selling Widgets. Start Selling Wisdom. – Bernadette McClelland

Shift! Harness the Trigger Events That Turn Prospects Into Customers - Craig Elias, Tibor Shanto

Smart Calling: Eliminate the Fear, Failure, and Rejection from Cold Calling - Art Sobczak

SNAP Selling: Speed Up Sales and Win More Business with Today's Frazzled Customers - Jill Konrath

SPIN Selling - Neil Rackham

Stop Selling and Start Leading: How to Make Extraordinary Sales Happen - Deb Calvert, James Kouzes, Barry Posner

Strategic Sales Presentations - Jack Malcolm

The 7 Habits of Highly Effective People: Powerful Lessons in Personal Change - Stephen R. Covey

The Art of Commercial Conversations: When It's Your Turn to Make A Difference - Bernadette McClelland

The Challenger Customer: Selling to the Hidden Influencer Who Can Multiply Your Results - Brent Adamson, Matthew Dixon, Pat Spenner, Nick Toman

The Challenger Sale: Taking Control of the Customer Conversation - Matthew Dixon, Brent Adamson

The Fanatical Prospecting Playbook: Open the Sale, Fill Your Pipeline, and Crush Your Number - Jeb Blount

The Go-Giver, Expanded Edition: A Little Story About a Powerful Business Idea - Bob Burg, John David Mann

The Greatest Salesman in the World - Og Mandino

The JOLT Effect: How High Performers Overcome Customer Indecision - Matthew Dixon

The Key to the C-Suite: What You Need to Know to Sell Successfully to Top Executives – Michael Nick

The Lost Art of Closing: Winning the Ten Commitments That Drive Sales - Anthony Iannarino

The Miracle Morning for Salespeople: The Fastest Way to Take Your SELF and Your SALES to the Next Level - Hal Elrod

The New Model of Selling: Selling to an Unsellable Generation - Jerry Acuff

The New Strategic Selling: The Unique Sales System Proven Successful by the World's Best Companies - Robert B. Miller, Stephen E. Heiman, Tad Tuleja

The No. 1 Best Seller: A Unique Insight Into the Mind, Strategy and Processes of a Top Salesman - Lee Bartlett

The Only Sales Guide You'll Ever Need - Anthony Iannarino

The Psychology of Selling: Increase Your Sales Faster and Easier Than You Ever Thought Possible - Brian Tracy

The Sales Tactician's Playbook – David Weiss

The Science of Selling: Proven Strategies to Make Your Pitch, Influence Decisions, and Close the Deal - David Hoffeld

The Seller's Challenge: How Top Sellers Master 10 Deal Killing Obstacles in B2B Sales – Thomas Williams and Thomas Saine

The SPIN Selling Fieldbook: Practical Tools, Methods, Exercises, and Resources - Neil Rackham

The Trusted Advisor - Charles H. Green

The Velocity Mindset: How Leaders Eliminate Resistance, Gain Buy-in, and Achieve Better Results—Faster - Ron Karr

Think and Grow Rich - Napoleon Hill

Think Like Your Customer: A Winning Strategy to Maximize Sales by Understanding and Influencing How and Why Your Customers Buy - Bill Stinnet

To Sell Is Human: The Surprising Truth About Moving Others - Daniel H. Pink

Trust-Based Selling: Using Customer Focus and Collaboration to Build Long-Term Relationships - Charles H. Green

Unleash the Power of Storytelling: Win Hearts, Change Minds, Get Results – Rob Biesenbach

Unlimited Selling Power: How to Master Hypnotic Skills - Donald Moine

Unlocking Yes: Sales Negotiation Lessons & Strategy - Patrick Tinney

Virtual Selling: A Quick-Start Guide to Leveraging Video, Technology, and Virtual Communication Channels to Engage Remote Buyers and Close Deals Fast - Jeb Blount

Virtual Selling: How to Build Relationships, Differentiate, and Win Sales Remotely – Mike Schultz

Whale Hunting: How to Land Big Sales and Transform Your Company - Tom Searcy, Barbara Weaver Smith

Whatever It Takes: Master the Habits to Transform Your Business, Relationships, and Life - Brandon Bornancin

When They Say No: The Definitive Guide for Handling Rejection in Sales – Richard Fenton and Andrea Waltz

Management

Coaching Salespeople Into Sales Champions: A Tactical Playbook for Managers and Executives - Keith Rosen

Cracking the Sales Management Code: The Secrets to Measuring and Managing Sales Performance - Jason Jordan, Michelle Vazzana

Elite Sales Strategies: A Guide to Being One-Up, Creating Value, and Becoming Truly Consultative - Anthony Iannarino

Leading Growth: The Proven Formula for Consistently Increasing Revenue - Anthony Iannarino

Predictable Revenue: Turn Your Business Into A Sales Machine With the $100 Million Best Practices of Salesforce.com - Aaron Ross

Sales Management Simplified: The Straight Truth About Getting Exceptional Results from Your Sales Team - Mike Weinberg

Sales Manager Survival Guide: Lessons from Sales' Front Lines - David Brock

The Building Blocks of Sales Enablement – Mike Kunkle

The First-Time Manager: Sales (First-Time Manager Series) – Mike Weinberg

The Sales Acceleration Formula: Using Data, Technology, and Inbound Selling to Go from $0 to $100 Million - Mark Roberge

The Sales Development Playbook: Build Repeatable Pipeline and Accelerate Growth with Inside Sales - Trish Bertuzzi

The Sales Manager's Guide to Greatness: 10 Essential Strategies for Leading Your Team to the Top - Kevin F. Davis

The Ultimate Sales Machine: Turbocharge Your Business with Relentless Focus on 12 Key Strategies - Chet Holmes

ACKNOWLEDGEMENTS

This work would have never happened without the support, teaching, and encouragement provided by so many individuals. It would be impossible to acknowledge them all—especially all of the thought leaders and authors that have influenced my thinking over the years.

I want to say thanks to those who have been so helpful to me in the completion of this book. I am a lucky person to have so many individuals willing to help me both personally and professionally.

To my wife and the love of my life Marin Muir for all your encouragement and patience during the early mornings and late nights while writing and creating material for clients.

To my best friend Jeff Mildon for your inspiration and example—I want to be like you.

To Kelly Skeen for your undying support and encouragement. I am your padawan.

To Anthony Iannarino for your tremendous thought leadership and for writing the forward to this book.

To Warwick Brown, Lee Bartlett, Lahat Tzvi, Mike Kunkle, Simon Hares, Deb Calvert, Josh Eck, Fred Copestake, Jeff Bajorek and Harry Spaight for your tremendous feedback on the initial writing of this work. Your input and feedback have made this a completely different and better work. #Gratitude.

To David Weiss for his wonderful contributions to the sales plays contained within and for his contributions to my thoughts on MEDDICC & MEDDPICC, coaches and champions and hard and soft costs.

To Nathan Simmons for his natural editing talents. You have made this book much more readable and accessible.

To Jeb Blount, Mark Hunter, Matt Dixon, Mahan Khalsa, Victor Antonio, Mike Weinberg, Dave Brock, Tom Williams, Lee Salz, Andy Paul, Donald C Kelly, Ron Karr, Skip Miller, Tony Durso, Patrick Tinney, Meridith Elliott Powell, Joe Micallef, Bernadette McClelland, Paul Watts, Julie Hansen and the many other inspiring thought leaders mentioned in this book. You all elevate our craft. Thank you.

To Amy Sebero and the entire Streamline Health team that triggered this tremendous effort.

Thank you, Luigi Prestinenzi, Mareo McCracken, Kelly Riggs, William Bartlett, Patrick Tinney, Carole Mahoney, Skip Willcox, David Strange, Tim McKeough, Larry Levine, Jenni Butz, Dan Sixsmith, Riccardo Carducci, Jackie Coult, Dan Pfister, Joon Chang, Tony Martello, Tobia La Marca, Bret Barrie, Kathy Veldboom, Douglas Burdett, Marcus Cauchi, Patrick Boucousis, Patti Peets, Steven Rosen, Nicole Holland, Diane Helbig, Michael Mason, Hanna Hasl-Kelchner, Danita Bye, James Vincent, Mario M Martinez Jr. and many, many others for your tremendous ongoing support. Without your support this would not have been possible.

REFERENCES

Introduction

1. 40-60% of all sales are lost to no-decision. The JOLT Effect - Penguin Random House; (September 22, 2022), p.7.
2. Research conducted by Sales Benchmark Index, 58% of qualified deals end in no decision. http://www.salesbenchmarkindex.com/
3. Research from Customer Centric Selling estimates that 60% - 80% of deals are lost to no-decision. http://www.customercentric.com/news-and-resources/articles/failing-to-close
4. Don Linder, the founder of Major Client Selling reports that 40% of deals are lost to no-decision. http://www.majorclients.com/articles/200707lostabigsale.html
5. Research conducted by Wayne M. Thomas, author of The Sales Manager's Success Manual, AMACOM, suggests that 55% of deals are lost to no-decision.

Chapter 2

1. Eat That Frog! - Brian Tracy Berrett-Koehler Publishers; 3rd edition (April 17, 2017) p.13
2. Many studies from various industries including:
   - Healthcare - https://www.magonlinelibrary.com/doi/abs/10.12968/nrec.2014.16.5.269
   - Transportation - https://www.sciencedirect.com/science/article/abs/pii/S095741742300698X
   - Clinical Trials - https://trialsjournal.biomedcentral.com/articles/10.1186/s13063-018-2769-2

Chapter 5

1. Gong.io - DOES IT MAKE SENSE TO SAY "DOES THAT MAKE SENSE?" ON A SALES CALL? https://www.gong.io/resources/labs/does-that-make-sense-sales-closing-question/
2. The Perfect Close – James Muir, Best Practice International, 2006 p.65-67.

Chapter 10

1. Steven Tulman - 5 Things You NEED to Pre-Qualify a Lead - https://www.linkedin.com/pulse/20140307031026-36714090-4-things-you-need-to-know-when-qualifying-leads-b-a-n-t-how-to-convert-leads-into-buying-customers-part-3-the-qualifying-stage/

Chapter 11

1. According to Gartner the average number of stakeholders in complex sales ranges from 6 to 10 and can often go much higher. https://www.gartner.com/en/topics/successful-tech-buying-process

Chapter 15

1. Inferior Products and Profitable Deception - Paul Heidhues, Botond Kőszegi, Takeshi Murooka, The Review of Economic Studies, Volume 84, Issue 1, January 2017, Pages 323–356.
2. The Perfect Close – James Muir, Best Practice International, 2006 p.107-114.

Chapter 16

1. The JOLT Effect - Penguin Random House; (September 22, 2022), p.18-19
2. Approximately 87% of sales opportunities suffer from moderate to high levels of indecision. The JOLT Effect - Penguin Random House; (September 22, 2022), p.22
3. See references 1-5 Introduction.
4. Approximately 56% of losses are caused by client indecision as opposed to preference for the status quo. The JOLT Effect - Penguin Random House; (September 22, 2022), p.21-22
5. The JOLT Effect - Penguin Random House; (September 22, 2022), p.41-47
6. The JOLT Effect - Penguin Random House; (September 22, 2022), p.xvii-xviii.

Chapter 17

1. Predictably Irrational - Dr. Dan Ariely, Harper May 19, 2009, p.1-7.
2. Product Offering: Use the Power of Packaging and Pricing - Zoltan Vardy, https://zoltanvardy.com/2022/06/07/product-offering-use-the-power-of-packaging-and-pricing/

Chapter 18

1. Frontiers in Psychology, 28 April 2021 Section, Personality and Social Psychology, Volume 12 - 2021 | Not Too Much and Not Too Little: Information Processing for a Good Purchase Decision by Claudia Vogrincic-Haselbacher, Joachim I. Krueger, Brigitta Lurger, Isabelle Dinslaken, Julian Anslinger, Florian Caks, Arnd Florack, Hilmar Brohmer, Ursula Athenstaedt - https://doi.org/10.3389/fpsyg.2021.642641
2. Buyer-Centered Selling: How Modern Sellers Engage & Collaborate with Buyers Paperback – Thomas Williams and Thomas Saine, Strategic Dynamics August 2, 2019, p.28-46

Chapter 19

1. The Perfect Close – James Muir, Best Practice International, 2006 p.34-36
2. Framing Trust: Trust as a Heuristic – Roy J Lewicki and Max M Brinsfield, In Donohue, W. A., Rogan, R. G., & Kaufman, S. Framing Matters: Perspectives on Negotiation Research and Practice in Communication. New York: Peter Lang Publishing. 2011.
3. The Perfect Close – James Muir, Best Practice International, 2006 p.109-112.
4. The Perfect Close – James Muir, Best Practice International, 2006 p.27-44.
5. The Perfect Close – James Muir, Best Practice International, 2006 p.223-227.
6. The Perfect Close – James Muir, Best Practice International, 2006 p119-120.
7. The Perfect Close – James Muir, Best Practice International, 2006 p114-140.
8. Internal survey by Best Practice International, 2023

ABOUT THE AUTHOR

James Muir is the founder and CEO of Best Practice International and the author of the #1 book on closing sales - The Perfect Close.

James is a 30-year veteran of sales having served in every role from individual contributor to Executive VP. His mission - to make the complex simple.

James has extensive background in healthcare where he has sold-to and spoken-for the largest names in technology and healthcare including HCA, Tenet, Catholic Healthcare, Banner, Dell, IBM and others.

Those interested in learning more about messaging, prospecting, discovery, closing, complex sales management and other sales topics can reach him at PureMuir.com.

EMAIL
JMuir @ PureMuir.com

WEBSITE
https://puremuir.com/

LINKEDIN
https://www.linkedin.com/in/puremuir/

Made in the USA
Middletown, DE
11 April 2024